The Jay Treaty Debate, Public Opinion, and the Evolution of Early American Political Culture

A VOLUME IN THE SERIES

Political Development of the American Nation: Studies in Politics and History

edited by
Sidney M. Milkis and Jerome M. Mileur

The Jay Treaty Debate, Public Opinion, and the Evolution of Early American Political Culture

Todd Estes

UNIVERSITY OF MASSACHUSETTS PRESS
Amherst

Printed in the United States of America
First paperback printing 2008

LC 2005018481
ISBN 978-1-55849-515-9

Designed by Sally Nichols
Set in Sabon
Printed and bound by Thomson-Shore, Inc.

Library of Congress Cataloging-in-Publication Data

Estes, Todd, 1963–
The Jay Treaty debate, public opinion, and the evolution of early American political culture / Todd Estes.
p. cm. — (Political development of the American nation)
Includes bibliographical references and index.
ISBN 1-55849-515-0 (cloth : alk. paper)
1. Political culture—United States—History. 2. Great Britain. Treaties, etc. United States, 1794 Nov. 19—Public opinion. 3. United States—Foreign relations—Great Britain—Public opinion. 4. Great Britain—Foreign relations—United States—Public opinion. 5. Public opinion—United States. I. Title. II. Series.
JK1717.J393 2006
306.2'0973'09033—dc22

2005018481

British Library Cataloguing in Publication data are available.

For Kathy
and for the memory
of my father

Contents

Acknowledgments

The debts I have accumulated can never be adequately acknowledged, much less repaid. But I trust that every scholar knows exactly what I mean, and I am proud to be part of a community of scholars where such debts are never called in.

I have been blessed with many great teachers (beginning with my parents). I doubt, however, that I have had a better one than Chet Hedgecoth, not a historian but a profound influence ever since junior high school. At the University of Tennessee, my thanks especially go to such gifted teachers and mentors as the late Milton Klein (who died just as I was preparing to send the book to press), Jonathan G. Utley, John Bohstedt, Michael McDonald, and Paul Pinckney. The greatest influence exerted on me was that of William Bruce Wheeler. It is a testimony to his skills and ability to inspire that, when I took Bruce's class in Jeffersonian America as an impressionable twenty-year-old college junior, I knew two things immediately: that I wanted to be a college professor, and that I wanted to specialize in the early republic. Bruce Wheeler's teaching, his example, and his enthusiasm inspired me tremendously. He, more than any other single person, is the reason I decided to become a professional historian.

As a graduate student at the University of Kentucky I came under the tutelage of another great group of scholars and teachers. Thanks go to George Herring, Daniel Blake Smith, Tom Cogswell, Mark Summers, and David Hamilton in particular for their instruction, guidance, support, and friendship. I went to Kentucky in the first place to work with Lance Banning. Lance is as fine a scholar as there is, but he may be, through instruction as well as example, even better as a graduate mentor. Lance was the ideal dissertation director—sympathetic and encouraging, yet demanding. He seemed to know with unerring timing when to be patient and allow me to think things through and when to prod me for more chapters. Since the completion of my dissertation he continues to provide invaluable advice, most of which I have followed. I am proud and grateful to have worked with Lance, just as I am now pleased to call him a friend.

At Oakland University, I wish in particular to acknowledge the practical and moral support of department chairs Ron Finucane and Carl Osthaus. My colleagues Karen Miller, Bruce Zellers, Dan Clark, Sara Chapman, and Roy Kotynek either read portions of or discussed the book in its various stages and indulged me in long, valuable conversations about political culture. Several colleagues I haven't named provided help, guidance, and encouragement along the way. To all of them, my deepest thanks for making the Department of History a good place to work.

I also wish to acknowledge the timely and generous financial support provided by the Oakland University Research Office and by the Dean of the College of Arts and Sciences.

I have also benefited enormously from the help of many friends in the profession, some of whom have served as commentators of my work on conference panels and/or have read parts of my work. In particular I thank Susan Branson, Andrew R. L. Cayton, Joanne Freeman, Philip Gould, Matthew Rainbow Hale, Donald Hickey, Owen Ireland, Albrecht Koschnik, Cathy Matson, Paul Douglas Newman, Jeff Pasley, William Pencak, Herbert Sloan, Mark A. Smith, David Waldstreicher, and Alfred Young. I'm particularly grateful to Joanne Freeman, not only for being (with Mark Smith) a charter member of the Fisher Ames Society and coauthor of "The Ames-iad," but mostly for her friendship and for the fun (and funny) times that always ensue whenever we attend the same conferences. And I am grateful to audiences at the regular meetings of the American Historical Association, Organization of American Historians, Society of Historians of the Early American Republic, New England Historical Association, Newberry Library Seminar in Early American History, and other venues at which aspects of this work were presented and discussed.

Other friends, some academics, many not, have helped me along the way, too—sometimes by discussing my work, often (happily) by discussing things completely unrelated. I especially thank Rosalind Remer and Jim Green, Steve Ealy, Kathie and Marv Ninneman, Roger Tilden, Don and Elsie Overy, Arline Gaudet, and my brother, Lane Estes, who was always ready to talk basketball and music. Two physicians—Michael Duffy and Stephen Priest—managed my Crohn's Disease treatment with great technical competence as well as extraordinary compassion.

Portions of this work have appeared, in different forms, in *Journal of the Early Republic, The Historian, Virginia Magazine of History and Biography,* and *Historical Journal of Massachusetts.* I thank those journals for permission to reprint those works here. At the University of Massachusetts Press I have found a wonderful and professional group of people who have taken great care in working this manuscript into a book. Special thanks go to my editor, Clark Dougan, who has been unfailingly kind, considerate, helpful, and reassuring at every step along the way. He is a model of what editors should be. Special thanks also go to Carol Betsch, managing editor at the Press, who skillfully steered the manuscript to publication, and to Ed Vesneske, Jr., my copy editor, whose careful work improved the book considerably. Sidney Milkis, co-editor of the Political Development of the American Nation series for the Press, first grasped the potential in this work and provided encouragement and advice. Finally, my outside readers—Ralph Ketcham, Thomas Slaughter, and John L. Brooke—gave the manuscript a thorough reading and made numerous suggestions for improving the final product. I thank everyone connected with the University of Massachusetts Press for making the publishing experience pleasant as well as rewarding.

My parents and I have always been very close. My mother used to read to me daily when I was a child; now she reads everything I write (and collects it with pride). It is from her and Dad that I got very early my love of books and music and most of the things that really matter to me. My father, an academic himself, provided a role model for me in countless ways. I hope I've lived up to his example. Sadly, he never lived to see the completion of this book nor the many other things I have longed to share with him in the years he has been gone. Not a week passes that I don't think of him and miss him terribly. This book is partly dedicated to his memory.

I trust that my children, Elizabeth Claire Alison Estes and Brian Patrick Pfeiffer Estes, know how much they mean to me. Their young lives provide the rich and full context and counterweight to my university life and make coming home a joy—on most days! But even when they are trying their father's patience, they are delightful companions and wonderful reminders of what is truly important.

Finally, my wife, Kathleen Pfeiffer, is many things—a first-rate scholar and professor herself, a loving and dedicated mother to our children, and a true partner and companion in all things. Kathy has lived with this book—and with the constant presence of this book and my research in our marriage—for far too long. She has made innumerable sacrifices with grace, compassion, and love and kept our life running so that I could attend, yet again, to The Book. She has been through so many drafts of articles and manuscripts that I've lost count. I do know that she has improved everything she has read, saving me from errors and pushing me to get things just right. Often she can see what I need to do before I can. More important, she has given me some enormously happy years with the promise of a lifetime more still to come. I hope she feels her love has been reciprocated. Kathy, you know the rest. In recognition of all that she does and all that she means to me, I dedicate this book to her with love and gratitude.

Introduction

The Fourth of July 1795 was a joyous occasion in Rutland, Vermont, a frontier town on the periphery of the young nation. Townspeople were up at dawn to prepare for the elaborate meals, festivities, and customary toasts which would be sandwiched in among the regular duties of the day. The citizens of Rutland had, from their local newspaper of July 6, only the faintest hint of the trouble then stirring elsewhere in the country. After a detailed and self-congratulatory account of the communal Independence Day rituals, the paper passed along notes from a Philadelphia correspondent who wrote of the news then making the rounds, of a treaty between the United States and Great Britain, negotiated by John Jay. The newspaper acknowledged that their facts were few; however, they also noted (almost as an aside, in an issue filled with glad tidings and celebration) that "We have information, that the Senate of the United States have confirmed the Treaty with Great Britain. Particulars probably in our next."[1]

The citizens of Rutland had little idea of the firestorm the "particulars" had ignited in other American towns with more news of the Jay negotiations. Crowds in Philadelphia, Boston, and New York gathered for their own celebrations of the Fourth denounced the treaty and lashed out at Jay, the Federalist administration, and the Senate, whose secret debates and ratification of the measure had only recently been revealed. The Jay Treaty and the furor it touched off are traditional highlights of the political and diplomatic history of the 1790s, marking both a crucial foreign policy development and a cementing of domestic partisan political divisions. But beyond its significance to party formation or diplomacy, the treaty debate provides a template for studying the methods and practices of politics and the interrelationship of political conflict, print culture, party development, crowd actions—in short, the political culture of the new nation. From this angle, the debate appears every bit the crucial touchstone for party and diplomatic development that other scholars have identified, but it also emerges as more. It was a major step along the way in the evolutionary work in progress which was 1790s politics.

The debate did not signal a perfectly aligned end of one stage and beginning of another. Few situations do. Some of the tactics and techniques used in the debate were not new, but their scale and deployment and effect on public opinion were. In a curious way, the "winning" side on the treaty question "lost" the broader war, ironically owing in part to the bold new political world of democratic or popular politics which they helped usher in. The "losing" side was chastened but soon regrouped, shrewdly recognizing that the political tectonic plates were realigning—and that the realignment would shortly benefit them in ways neither they nor their opponents could fully realize at the time. Thus, the Jay Treaty debate is replete with irony and unintended consequences, with winners who lost and losers who won, leaving a portrait not as neat and tidy as some might like but one which squares with the historian's understanding of the complicated nature of the past. It is precisely the complexity, the ambiguity, the untidiness, the irony, and the counterintuitive nature of the debate that are most fascinating. And one can see a definite shift in the political landscape during and after—in no small part *because* of the treaty debate.

Wildly unpopular, provoking great outrage in the streets on the part of some citizens when it became public, the treaty was nonetheless ratified by the Senate, signed by President Washington, and finally funded by the House of Representatives (though only after dramatic efforts by both sides). A brief overview of the year-long debate will provide a context for the discussion that follows. With his appointment as special minister to Great Britain in 1794, John Jay's charge was to resolve a number of outstanding commercial issues between the two nations, and he spent the better part of the year in intermittent negotiations in London. The treaty made its way back across the Atlantic and was debated in secret by the U.S. Senate, which, in June 1795, voted 20–10 (exactly the two-thirds majority necessary) to ratify the measure and sent it to President George Washington.

The secrecy was broken, however, by Virginia senator Stevens T. Mason, who opposed the treaty and leaked his copy to publisher Benjamin Franklin Bache. By July 1 copies of the document were making their way throughout the country after months of speculation about its contents. Publication touched off waves of protest and petitions aimed at persuading Washington not to sign the treaty. Opponents charged that the treaty yielded too much to Great Britain and gained far too little for the United States, would harm relations with France, failed to address several substantive issues of controversy, had been negotiated and debated in too much secrecy, and would serve to link the United States closely and subserviently with England. The initial hostility waned a bit as supporters mounted a counterattack in the newspapers, and on August 14 Washington put his signature on the document. This led to an abatement of, though not an end to, the controversy. Because the treaty contained provisions for establishing commissions to mediate disputes and those commissions required funding, the House of Representatives still had to deal with the issue. Washington, seeking to let the countercurrent on the treaty run its course, delayed in submitting the business to the House until March 1, 1796. That touched off a fierce two-month battle—fought in the papers, the streets, and in Congress—complete with speeches, petitions, and various forms of popular politics, before the House followed the Senate in narrowly voting to put the Jay Treaty into effect on April 30, 1796.

The contest over the treaty holds the promise of resonant insights into political culture, ideas about the roles of citizens and the people's representatives, the concept of public opinion, and the democratization of early America. This new approach yields an interesting and fruitful way to understand the efforts of Federalists and Republicans to address and mobilize the public in support of their positions. And in discovering and appreciating what Federalists in particular did in behalf of the treaty, we gain a more nuanced understanding of the debate itself, one which seriously challenges our facile assumptions about how Federalists acted, as well as insight into more problematic questions of deference, the nature of public opinion, and the public sphere in the 1790s.

As Federalists (who overwhelmingly favored the treaty) and Republicans (who nearly all opposed it) battled in the summer of 1795 and again in the spring of the following year, they were, unbeknownst to themselves, at a turning point. For the Jay Treaty debate can be seen as the last vestige of an older, more deferential political culture championed by Federalists, even as the debate itself (and the tactics used by both sides) helped to hasten the acceptance of a more open, democratic culture espoused by the Republicans. In short, the Federalists won in the short term but found themselves losing the long-term struggle for control of the nation's political culture.

Any understanding of this broader evolution, much less of the treaty debate itself, depends on a grasp of 1790s politics. Thus, a brief overview is necessary of the broader social and political forces at work during the decade, along with high points of the treaty debate. Party conflict, although unforeseen and decried by the drafters of the Constitution, emerged quickly in the 1790s, largely in reaction to Alexander Hamilton's ambitious plans for centralizing authority in the executive branch, creating a strong centralized system of banking and finance, and encouraging manufacturing and industrialization. Hamilton immediately encountered criticism from those such as James Madison and Thomas Jefferson who favored a decentralizing approach and advocated a future as an agrarian nation. Quickly, nascent parties grew up around these leading individuals. By the mid-1790s clear ideological divisions had emerged between what were labeled, variously, as "parties," "interests," or "factions," and were generally recognized by the names "Federalists" and "Republicans." Each of a variety of issues—the national bank, the Neutrality Proclamation, the Citizen Genet affair, the Democratic Societies, the Whiskey Rebellion, and the Jay Treaty—along with a series of congressional debates and votes furthered the development of this party activity, which was, in turn, publicized and further politicized through the proliferation of newspapers, most of which had a clear partisan identity. Thus, by the time of the treaty debate in 1795–96, the nation was clearly divided into two distinct political and ideological camps which, if lacking the full structure and operational bureaucracy of modern parties (or even those of the mid-nineteenth century), certainly *functioned* as parties do and provided the nation with arguably its most intense level of political combat ever. For the sake of clarity I use the terms "Federalist" and "Republican" to denote the opposing sides of the argument, even while recognizing that the parties were still in the midst of formation and were far from complete structures.[2]

But the treaty debate fits into a broader context socially as well as politically. American life in the years after the Revolution was powerfully and permanently transformed. Old habits in work, social relations, family ties, politics, religion, and economics were giving way to new models and practices. Seemingly every aspect of older American life and culture was being touched not only by new practices, but by new ways of thinking. Everywhere men and women threw off familiar, longstanding modes of thinking and began to see their world in a new light.[3] The results were breathtaking. Drawing on Revolutionary ideas of egalitarianism and democracy, Americans reordered their thinking on politics and government as well. They challenged older notions of deference, refused to recognize a "better sort," and demanded not only a voice in government but actual power for themselves.

This process created a serious challenge, one which would assert itself repeatedly in the political life of the early republic. The ubiquitous spread of democracy threatened the order and stability of both government and society. It challenged authority and institutions. It made governing every sort of body—whether a family, a church, a community, a state, or a nation—increasingly difficult. Because this democratization struck directly at authority and order, government and political culture now faced obstacles they had not previously seen. The great challenge for the political order in the post-Revolutionary era was to reconcile—to balance—rising democracy, with all its concomitant impulses, with the order and stability necessary to make any government function effectively and meet its responsibilities.

This task proved far more daunting than first appeared. It required leaders and citizens to think anew about the relationship between liberty and order, democracy and authority, popular will and public interest. It forced Americans to decide what—if any—restrictions should be placed on popular participation in government and the responsiveness of government to popular sentiment. It refocused attention, not on the source of government authority, but on the degree to which that source (popular or public opinion) could be accommodated without undermining order and stability. In short, it made Americans debate the proper role of individuals and institutions—of citizens and constituted authorities—in a democratic society. Necessarily, the nation's first political party system was shaped, transformed, and ultimately overwhelmed by the democratization of politics. The Federalists, who had first crack at governing, were eventually destroyed when the antidemocratic attitudes of some of their leaders ran counter to public opinion and long-run historical development. The Republicans, who came into being as a party on democratic currents largely in reaction to Federalist obstinance, were badly divided as their leaders (and supporters) failed to agree on the extent to which a democratic government should honor the wishes of a democratic electorate.

The process was not quite this simple, however. None of this political positioning was foreordained, nothing was entirely predictable. If Federalists generally favored order over liberty, they were by no means antidemocratic in all they believed and did while in power. Indeed, the Jay Treaty debate provides a sterling example of the Federalists acting counterintuitively. Conversely, if Republicans valued liberty over order, there were a good many party members who believed that order and stability were vitally important if a lasting government were to be established. Some Republicans who stood second to none in their devotion to liberty and democracy nonetheless believed that there were limits to how far their government and their party could safely go in responding to the direct wishes of public opinion without jeopardizing the republic's stability. This dilemma—faced by both parties, mastered by neither—forms the essential backdrop to the treaty debate. It was not fully resolved during the debate over the treaty, of course; some might argue that it has never been satisfactorily resolved, or even that it defies resolution. But the contest of 1795–96 represented a landmark in the development not just of political parties but of the conduct and content of political culture. What took place during the nearly year-long period had important short-term ramifications and equally significant if not immediately grasped implications for the evolution of politics and political culture.

At its most basic level the debate over the Jay Treaty was a contest to shape public opinion. That contest forms the center of this book, just as the concept of public opinion came to be central to early national political culture. Defining "public opinion" was problematic in an age well before polling, focus groups, and market research, and it was an amorphous term in the political debates of the 1790s. What was the public? Were there multiple publics? Could they all be reached in the same way? How could public opinion be determined and measured? Did petitions represent public opinion? Town meetings? Did (or could) specific, self-identified groups of citizens—merchants, laborers, farmers—constitute (and claim to speak for) public opinion or only a portion of it? Did the weight of some groups offset or overwhelm the weight of others? All of these questions confront historians of early America, and all of these issues were at the heart of the Jay Treaty debate, rendering problematic any clear-cut definition or standard.[4]

Both Federalists and Republicans claimed that public opinion supported them and that they were acting on that opinion. Each side dismissed expressions of support for the other side as illegitimate, as representing a pernicious faction of "Jacobins" or, alternatively, "aristocrats," and immediately questioned the authenticity and authority of any rival manifestation of public opinion. Well before the idea of a loyal or legitimate opposition was an accepted commonplace, parties in the 1790s—not quite comfortable with their own identity as parties—vigorously attacked the notion of divided public opinion.[5]

Any objective measure of public opinion is impossible to gain for the 1790s; public opinion was whatever either party said it was, and each party set out to measure or influence public opinion by mobilizing its own supporters, hoping that by energizing the base, they might persuade those citizens yet undecided. To do so involved often elaborate and multifaceted campaigns designed to influence, shape, or "seed" public opinion and then "collect" this mediated and refined public opinion expressed in the form of petitions, resolutions, resolves of town meetings, and the like. As Joanne B. Freeman writes, the process involved "the proper seeding of public opinion and the reaping of the desired response . . . . To national politicians, public opinion represented the response to strategic conversations orchestrated by political leaders."[6] Thus, both sides attempted to influence public opinion, such as it was, with pamphlets, newspapers, and essays, and then in turn "collected" that opinion in petitions and resolutions which were then printed for further distribution and held up as expressions of public opinion. Each side also found ways to discount the other's arguments as well as to question the legitimacy of the other side's base of support.[7]

As early as 1791, James Madison addressed this subject when he penned an essay for Philip Freneau's *National Gazette* on "Public Opinion," anticipating issues which arose later in that decade. Madison began: "Public opinion sets bounds to every government, and is the real sovereign in every free one. As there are cases where the public opinion must be obeyed by the government; so there are cases, where not being fixed, it may be influenced by the government." Thus Madison presciently summarized the contests of the next several years for control of public opinion. But he also noted the difficulties of accurately measuring or gathering public opinion. "The larger a country, the less easy for its real opinion to be ascertained, and the less difficult to be counterfeited; when ascertained or presumed, the more respectable it is in the eyes of individuals. This is favorable to the authority of government. For the same reason, the more extensive a country, the more insignificant is each individual to his own eyes. This may be unfavorable to liberty."

He closed the essay by observing that anything which promotes a broad mixing of ideas ("a general intercourse of sentiments"), such as "good roads, domestic commerce, a free press, and particularly a *circulation of newspapers through the entire body of the people,* and *Representatives going from, and returning among every part of them,* is equivalent to a contraction of territorial limits, and is favorable to liberty, where these may be too extensive [original emphasis]."[8] Colleen A. Sheehan, in a broader discussion of Madison's "Notes on Government" essays of 1791–92, contends that public opinion was a key component to Madison's republicanism generally. She also observes that for Madison public opinion did not consist merely in expressions of popular opinion nor in the statements disseminated by governmental leaders. Rather, it emerged from the interplay between the public and leaders, in the course of which opinions were shaped, modified, and refined. This was a two-way street, and, in a healthy republic, according to Madison, public opinion would take time to emerge, furthered along the way by newspapers, good roads, commerce, and communications between congressmen and their constituents. In Sheehan's words, such "general intercommunication of ideas among the people and guidance by their political leaders" would ultimately produce "an enlarged and refined opinion." It was this refinement and the processes by which it occurred that were critical to Madison.[9]

Beyond linking the treaty debate to these larger questions of democratization and the role of public opinion, this book has several other major objectives. First, it broadens existing literature on the treaty by examining not the diplomatic negotiations or the debates in the halls of Congress, but the public debate over the measure, and the considerable efforts on both sides to shape the views the public held and to mobilize citizens for or against the treaty. It is the first full-scale examination of the public debate and the first book devoted to the Jay Treaty since Jerald A. Combs's excellent 1970 study.

A second contribution is to revise our understanding of Federalism in the 1790s. Most of the outstanding studies of the Federalist party focus on the years after 1801 when they were, in Linda Kerber's phrase, "Federalists in dissent." An outstanding body of work has documented the mindsets and political activities of the party as they lost power and then influence in their struggle against the Jeffersonians.[10] But, as I argue below, the Federalists in the treaty debate engaged in popular politics willingly—and were far more effective—even earlier than some of these studies suggest. Specifically, David Hackett Fischer's *The Revolution of American Conservatism* contends that a group of younger Federalists led the party into the practice of democratic politics in response to the Jeffersonians after 1801. I argue—without disputing Fischer's argument for the Jeffersonian years—that Federalist involvement in popular politics dates to at least the early 1790s, and can reasonably be seen as an extension of the 1787–88 campaign to win ratification of the United States Constitution. Thus, the practices Fischer finds Federalists engaged in after 1801 actually predated the ascendancy of the Jeffersonian Republicans. The Federalists played popular politics very successfully well before their dissenting years, as Owen Ireland and other scholars have also shown.[11]

My contention—baldly stated—is that while Federalists were often ideologically elitist, they were also operationally democratic. That is, many of them retained their belief in rule by the better sort while at the same time practicing a popular politics of regular appeals to the people to rally them to their side. But, having said that, let me acknowledge that this is perhaps too bold a formulation. Federalists were never quite as elitist as they were accused of being, nor were they as truly democratic as they sometimes thought themselves to be. Still, Federalists, not at all hypocritically, maintained their older, intellectual commitment to deferential politics even as they practiced a more democratic politics. For a time, in the shifting and evolving world of 1790s politics, this amalgam worked.

I am not arguing that Federalists were not elitists. Nor am I suggesting that they were always comfortable with the efforts required to compete in the emerging political culture. Nor am I denying what Federalism became later. Furthermore, I do not dispute that popular politics—as it developed over time—was embraced more fully and practiced more skillfully by Republicans. However, it took some time for popular political culture (as well as for political parties) to develop, especially given the anti-party climate of the early republic. My contention is that those evolutions were in progress in the mid-1790s but not yet fully realized. Thus, popular politics was still emerging and developing in a fluid political environment. The grounds, terms, and context of popular politics at the time of the Jay Treaty debate were such that popular politics had yet to reach its highest levels. It was at a point where Federalists, despite mis-givings and objections, could still enter the arena—as it existed for a brief moment of transition between deference and democratization—and succeed brilliantly, largely on their terms. However, as what Simon P. Newman calls the "regularization of popular politics" became more widespread, the Federalists' difficulties grew apace.[12]

A third contribution of this work is to the emerging historiography of political culture in the early republic. By examining the nuts and bolts of the treaty debate—how crowds and meetings were organized, what treaty proponents and opponents did, what they wrote and said, how they were responded to—we can better understand what political culture was and how it worked. This work seeks to complement a recent spate of scholarship on early national political culture. Simon Newman has directed attention to parades and crowd activity. David Waldstreicher has examined rituals and festivals as political events and linked those partisan events to a rising but contested sense of American nationalism. Joanne Freeman has explored the implications of honor culture in the early republic and suggested that relations between a handful of key leaders necessarily had huge political implications in an era in which the rules of politics were as yet not fully defined and in which parties were still in their infancy. Jeffrey Pasley has argued for the importance of newspaper politics in the early republic and traced the political activities of papers and their editors and printers. Each, in short, provides important new insights into the broader political world of the 1790s.[13] My book draws on all of these outstanding recent works and uses them as a backdrop against which to examine and measure the impact of a single, momentous, long-running political event—the Jay Treaty debate—and to see what further insights may be gained by applying the multiple perspectives provided by this recent scholarship to such a specific and seminal event.[14]

Another facet of this book examines the treaty debate in light of the broader study of the public sphere in Europe and America. The public sphere, a concept identified with the philosopher Jurgen Habermas, is commonly described as consisting of civil associations, frequently convened in taverns, coffeehouses, clubs, and the like, for the purpose of providing a forum for the thoughtful (or rational-critical) discussion of public matters. Discourse and print culture were critical to the existence and expansion of the public sphere. Over time, in this historical narrative, the public sphere widened and became more democratized. Most scholars now argue that, as this development unfolded, the public sphere became more fractured and contested; the inclusion of different voices and perspectives led to struggles for control of an expanding, democratizing, but still somewhat smallish public sphere. The exact nature of the public sphere is a point of scholarly contention and the very concept and nature of the public sphere may not, ultimately, help us to fundamentally change our understanding of the early republic.[15] Still, the use of the concept as an analytical tool for making sense of United States politics and social structure in the 1790s has yielded some important work.[16]

However, though I have drawn on the scholarship of the public sphere, this book is decidedly a work of history, not political theory. To the extent that the concept of the public sphere can be useful to my ends I have borrowed some of its insights, including such valuable ones as notions of the contested nature of public discourse and the importance of shaping public opinion. But I try to adopt them selectively, where useful, rather than being driven by any theoretical construct. In short, this study seeks to bring the newer interest in popular political culture and the public sphere down from the realm of theory and apply it to an important, specific episode.

It is important, however, to recognize some of the limitations in scope and composition of the public sphere in the 1790s. While expanding during the decade, it was still a small space, still inhabited mostly by elites—a small group consisting mostly of men with a few women. Thus, "the spaces in which politics would happen" (in David Waldstreicher's phrase) were limited, even tiny, if expanding.[17] Perhaps a better way to explain my approach is to say simply that I try to understand the Jay Treaty debate in the fullest possible context of the time, while noting that the political world in which the debate took place—with its newspapers, public gatherings, private correspondence, party formation and behavior, and governmental institutions—was in the midst of sweeping, dramatic changes which remade the early national political universe and forced participants to understand and relate to it in new ways.

The debate over the Jay Treaty provides telling evidence of the contested nature of the political culture, politics, and public sphere of the time. Very much a dialectical exchange, the debates between Federalists and Republicans over the treaty provide a glimpse into the content of the public sphere in the early United States, however debatable its scope. It is certainly true that democratization was opening up the public sphere to more and different people and groups than before. But still, as Andrew R. L. Cayton has recently observed, "the public sphere may well have been the province of a relatively small group of men and an even smaller group of 'respectable' women who shared similar values and interests."[18] In evaluating the Jay Treaty debate, determining the exact size of this public becomes less compelling than understanding the contest for influence over that small but expanding and democratizing space.

Thus, to return to an earlier topic, the Federalists' efforts to shape public opinion involved mobilizing a much more constricted political nation than would exist in later years. Still, this public was acknowledged and recognized by both sides, targeted for influence by both, and comprised the fundamental battleground of politics in the 1790s. In other words, the public sphere may not have been very large, and the contest for measuring public opinion may have been largely a matter of each side tapping its base of supporters and getting them involved, rather than incorporating a more modern understanding of persuading the undecided masses, but Federalists plunged into the campaign to influence public opinion fully, directly, and—as we shall see—effectively. Federalists played the game of popular politics as it was played in the 1790s.[19]

Finally, a few words about what this book is not. It is not an examination of the diplomatic mission of John Jay or a detailed narrative of his negotiations with the British. Nor does it consider—except insofar as it became part of the public debate on the treaty—the geopolitical dimensions of the treaty. For such accounts, scholars have two masterworks by Samuel Flagg Bemis and Jerald A. Combs to rely on, which lay out clearly and copiously the context and details of the diplomatic mission and its full import.[20] Combs, in fact, provides an excellent account of the foreign policy questions within the broader political debates of the decade. Thus, there is no need to duplicate these efforts. There also exists a voluminous literature on the creation of the party system in the 1790s. Much of it sees the Jay Treaty debate as a crucial dividing issue, which solidified party lines inside Congress and out and indeed proved, for many citizens, to be the issue that ultimately moved them firmly into one camp or the other.[21] I agree completely with those who see the treaty fight as determinative in the formation of parties; because this point is so well demonstrated, I see no reason to belabor it here. This work will address party formation only as a factor incidental to the debate itself. Nor will this study, since it is primarily concerned with the public debate on the treaty, comment upon or consider extensively the congressional debate on the measure, a subject covered by Combs and a variety of other scholars in great detail. My examination of the role of the House of Representatives will focus chiefly on the impact on the congressional vote of petitions and editorials expressing public opinion, not the speeches and maneuverings inside the House.[22] Finally, this book will not explore the Randolph affair, with its highly charged allegations of improper dealings between Attorney General Edmund Randolph and the French foreign minister purportedly designed to sabotage U.S. efforts at diplomacy with the British. That story, too, has its historians, and the affair itself adds little to my account.[23]

The book is organized into seven chapters. The first explores the complicated three-way relationship between the United States, England, and France in the early republic and establishes the diplomatic context for the treaty debate. Chapter 2 sets the political context by examining the battle for control of popular politics in the early 1790s by both Federalists and Republicans. Chapter 3 lays out the first phase of the treaty debate by examining what happened in the summer and fall of 1795. After two intervening chapters that explore the nature of the rhetoric used in the debate (chapter 4) and the role of petitioning and instructions to Congress and their connection to public opinion (chapter 5), the chronological narrative resumes in chapter 6 with an analysis of the second phase of the debate in the spring of 1796. A final chapter considers post-debate assessments made by participants and observers and offers my own conclusions on the debate and what it reveals about 1790s political culture.

1 | England, France, and the Foreign Context of American Politics

This book focuses on analyzing events from July 1795 through May 1796 relating to the debate over the Jay Treaty, but little sense can be made of the import of those events without a firm grasp of the broader foreign policy context of the young nation in the 1790s. The interconnected, often tangled, relationships among the United States, Great Britain, and France intertwined the fates of all three countries. Against this broader context of foreign relations we can then investigate the specific issues which Jay's 1794 mission to Great Britain was designed to address. The outstanding matters Jay went to England to attempt to resolve bear close examination as well, because one of issues in the subsequent debate—both contemporaneously and later among scholars—was whether or not Jay negotiated a good settlement and whether he might have gotten a better one. Once the details on the specific matters Jay attempted to settle are in place, we can then examine the treaty itself. By then, the ramifications and implications of what the treaty did—and did not—accomplish will become fully apparent, and the reactions of those who supported or condemned the measure will fit into a larger pattern.

In many ways, the diplomatic roots of the Jay Treaty date to the American Revolution, for just as the 1790s attempted to resolve many of the riddles of the Revolutionary legacy, so, too, did the diplomatic efforts of the decade attempt to tie up loose ends regarding U.S.-British relations. The peace that came in 1783 was always rather shaky, and in the aftermath both sides had occasion for regret and recriminations about the terms.

The British reacted hostilely to the Americans in the postwar years. Many in England believed that the terms of the treaty were too lenient, and the Shelburne government which had negotiated it was overturned. The new government adopted a decidedly hostile, aggressive approach to the Americans. Fearing Indian reprisals against British citizens in Canada, it refused to turn over the western forts to the U.S. Angered that forts along the Great Lakes which were key to the fur trade were in American territory, it refused to negotiate a trade treaty with the Confederation government. The British refused to pay compensation to Americans whose slaves were carried off in the Revolution. They sent no foreign minister to the United States and barely acknowledged the presence of U.S. minister John Adams, prompting his angry withdrawal after three years. The British justified these actions by pointing to American violations of the treaty: there had been no compensation of loyalists for property and possessions seized, and no enforcement of private debt collection for sums owed to British merchants.[1]

Matters were further complicated by relations with Spain and France, both of which had a large stake in what happened in North America and in what transpired between the United States and Britain. France was generally benevolent toward the U.S. but enforced tougher trade restrictions than the Americans had expected of their Revolutionary ally. Spain, with considerable territorial holdings in Louisiana and Florida, found itself pressured by an American population surging south and west, and aimed to shut off U.S. access to the Mississippi for navigation. The Spanish argued that their borders reached as far north as the Ohio River, and they regularly intrigued to lure Americans migrating west across the Appalachians into secession from the U.S. by promising access to the Mississippi once they became citizens of Spain. The hard line taken by the Spanish and the British (and even, to a lesser extent, by the French) reminded Americans of their comparative weakness and vulnerability in the world arena—even as many lamented what they saw as the weakness of the Confederation government and the unraveling of domestic order and liberty.[2]

With its new government established in 1789, the U.S. hoped to address these obstacles more effectively. Almost at the outset of the new administration came the start of the French Revolution, an event initially cheered by nearly all Americans. But as that movement grew more violent after 1793, many Americans, chiefly Federalists, feared the potential impact of the French Revolution and worried that a U.S.-French alliance would not only place the still vulnerable United States in a dangerous position, but antagonize an already recalcitrant Great Britain and lead to war. The specific attitudes of national political leaders will be discussed in the pages that follow. As for the nation itself, Jerald Combs has nicely summarized the somewhat paradoxical position many Americans found themselves in by the early 1790s: "The vast majority of Americans still sympathized with France and its revolution; but they also wanted political isolation from Europe, the commercial benefits of foreign trade, and above all, peace." Thus, the U.S. had to steer a difficult and perilous course as it dealt with Europe during the 1790s.[3]

The Washington administration had to confront this problem head on in the months after April of 1793, when news arrived of the French declaration of war against England and Holland. Immediately, two possible paths were proposed. Alexander Hamilton, secretary of the treasury, urged a policy of complete neutrality and renunciation of the French alliance of 1778, arguing that the French government with which that treaty had been negotiated was long since out of power, replaced by a radically different kind of government. Neutrality plus renunciation of the old alliance would reassure Great Britain of American impartiality in the European conflict and perhaps avoid a breach in trade with the young nation's most important trading partner. Thomas Jefferson thought quite differently. The secretary of state argued that the U.S. should not declare itself neutral but should instead triangulate with the two warring nations and use the moment to threaten the British. The United States, Jefferson thought, should maintain the French alliance. He believed that the British did not want and could not sustain two wars, and that they would eventually come to the U.S. seeking neutrality, at which point Americans could demand—from a position of strength—that the British evacuate the western posts, open up the West Indian trade to American ships, and respect America's neutral rights in regard to shipping.[4]

The president, seeking to keep both secretaries mollified, compromised. He issued a Proclamation of Neutrality (though, in deference to Jefferson, he did not call it that), but he did not renounce the French alliance. He recognized the new French government and its minister, Edmond Genet. Washington believed that his proclamation made sufficiently clear to both the British and the French that the United States would honor the alliance with France but not to the extent that it might harm the prospects for peace. This was a dicey approach, and not one the administration was likely to get away with cleanly. In fact, the recognition of Genet opened the way for a difficult summer and fall during which the two nascent parties battled with each other over the perfidious or merely embarrassing (depending on one's perspective) activities of Citizen Genet, who tried to rouse the American populace against its government's stated policy of neutrality. By the time the year 1793 closed, the American public as well as its leaders were badly divided, both in their sympathies toward the European powers and over the proper course for the U.S. to follow in dealing with them.[5]

The ways in which many partisans viewed the country's foreign relations generally, and the Jay Treaty specifically, largely echoed the views expressed by the leaders of the emerging parties. Thus, it is not unwarranted or reductive to examine the views of Hamilton, Washington, Jefferson, and Madison in depth, because their private views were echoed by others and framed the context for the public debate. In fact, allowing for an exception or two, we can speak with some confidence of a "Federalist" foreign policy outlook that was fiercely contested by a "Republican" one, even as those parties themselves and their labels were in their infancy.

The Federalist's attitudes toward England and France were dictated by their understanding of what might be called realpolitik. Federalists were drawn to Britain partly because of a natural affinity for the British, partly through a shrewd calculation about the benefits of British shipping and commerce to American economic interests. As Hamilton once famously exclaimed to British minister George Beckwith, "We think in English." This sentiment, joined with the realization that peace with England meant not only gains for American commerce but also more time to build up American manufacturing and institutions, contributed mightily to the way Federalists saw the world in the 1790s. Already attached to Great Britain and skeptical of revolution and war, Federalists were alarmed at the increasingly violent direction of the French Revolution and by the European war which was its offshoot. When Republicans spoke of intervening on the side of the French, Federalists considered that a double error: war of any kind would destroy the U.S. by exposing its military and economic vulnerabilities; war with Great Britain specifically was not only undesirable but foolish. Thus, Federalists were willing to tolerate a wide range of British slights in the greater interests of preserving peace and protecting American trade. If such ends demanded a peace on British terms—a "mere English neutrality," as Jefferson later denounced it—then Federalists considered that a necessary if regrettable policy for a young nation not yet strong enough to dictate to European powers. This was a cornerstone of Federalist thought in the 1790s.[6]

This sympathy to Great Britain coupled with a fervent desire for peace led Federalists to shape policies accordingly. Hamilton and the Federalists sought time to build America into the great nation they wanted it to be by developing and protecting its credit, implementing a central banking system, developing domestic manufacturing, and strengthening the nation's military. Such ventures would in time allow the U.S. to compete from a position of strength and lessen the need for America to tolerate unfavorable or unfair treatment at the hands of any nation—but time to allow for development was nearly as crucial to Federalist ends as any specific programs. All these ventures—funding, manufacturing, credit, military improvements—required both the passage of time and the maintenance of peace. If building the kind of system Federalists desired and staying out of war meant accepting British depredations in the short run, they saw that as a necessary but temporary condition. All Federalist dealings with Great Britain up to and including the Jay Treaty negotiations proceeded from these assumptions, sympathies, and calculations.

The Republican perspective was quite different. Republicans were ideologically predisposed to view England warily if not with outright hostility. All of the Revolutionary-era fears of aristocracy, corruption, and a loss of virtue were joined in the 1790s by mounting fears that the new administration was mounting a counterrevolution, trying to construct a British system of government and political economy which would make the United States into an urban, commercial, manufacturing, and industrial republic, jeopardizing the agrarian republic of small farmers that Republicans celebrated. Republicans believed that too much reliance on trade with Britain would submerge the republican experiment under the pernicious influence of luxury goods and push the nation down the slippery slope to debauchery and corruption. Too heavy a reliance on English trade would not only undermine American virtue, it would hinder the growth of America's own self-sufficiency in agriculture. Such self-sufficiency would, in contrast, allow the U.S. to respond to Britain from a position of strength and independence, not weakness and subservience. In short, Republicans feared the Hamiltonian system, seeing in it a surrender of virtue which would soon be followed by a loss of real independence. They saw Federalism and Great Britain as being inextricably linked, and attacked the presence of "foreignness" and "foreigners" (by which they meant Federalists) in American politics.[7]

If England was the archenemy for Republicans, France was the beloved fraternal ally. Jefferson and Madison both identified support for France with support for the cause of liberty and accepted the policy of neutrality only out of political necessity. "I fear that a fair neutrality will prove a disagreeable pill to our friends, tho' necessary to keep us out of the calamities of war," Jefferson wrote to Madison. He thought that a "fair" neutrality would be one which honored existing treaties with France, but he was afraid that it might be interpreted as "a mere English neutrality." As both men considered the proclamation, they became even more critical. Madison launched a three-pronged objection, calling it "in truth a most unfortunate error. It wounds the National honor, by seeming to disregard the stipulated duties to France. It wounds the popular feelings by a seeming indifference to the cause of liberty. And it seems to violate the forms & spirit of the Constitution, by making the executive Magistrate the organ of the disposition the duty & the interest of the Nation in relation to war & peace, subjects appropriated to other departments of the Government." As the summer progressed, Jefferson, too, turned up the rhetoric, denouncing the measure in harsher language, his worst fears about a "mere English neutrality" seemingly confirmed.[8] As the Neutrality Crisis played out, the Republicans had to distance themselves from Genet. They beat a strategic retreat that sidestepped a potential disaster and left them, by the end of 1793, no worse off politically than before the crisis broke, but still determined to find ways to attack the British and stave off Federalist efforts to align the U.S. with England.

In an effort to direct their fire more precisely at Britain, Madison, Jefferson, and congressional Republicans took aim beginning in January 1794, having determined that "pinching their commerce," as Jefferson had called it a few months earlier, was the best means of pressuring England. To that end, Madison introduced resolutions calling for the imposition of discriminatory duties on British shipping, something he had sought unsuccessfully since 1789. Madison's proposal in many ways followed the line of Jefferson's mammoth "Report on the Privileges and Restrictions on the Commerce of the United States with Foreign Countries," delivered just two weeks before he retired as secretary of state in December 1793. Madison's plan would increase duties on various manufactured goods, most of which were British. It would increase tonnage duties on the ships of nations with which the U.S. had no commercial treaties (read: Great Britain) and reduce duties on those nations with which the U.S. did have treaties (read: France). Other provisions would impose reciprocity if other nations refused either goods manufactured in the U.S. or carried on American ships. The intent was to take a shot at the British and match them at their own game. Although Madison's resolutions were driven by recent developments, they clearly spelled out and sought to implement a Republican approach to Britain that had been years in the making. Soon, though, as news of the latest British outrages against U.S. shipping arrived, these proposals seemed too mild and thus rapidly became irrelevant in the face of the tensions which led to Jay's mission.[9]

While Madison, Jefferson, and the most prominent Republicans articulated their thoughts on Great Britain, less prominent Republican partisans did likewise, giving historians a broader sense of American attitudes towards the British. William Manning, a Massachusetts farmer and laborer who espoused a common man's political philosophy, spelled out his thoughts on politics in *The Key of Liberty*. Manning's book was written in response to the Jay Treaty debate, but, while only a small part of *The Key* deals with the treaty, the whole work is suffused with the larger political reverberations of the time. No friend to monarchy, Great Britain, or the Federalists, Manning denounced the treaty as "the worst instrument that ever was signed in America." He also noted that when "the monster first came into view, it was reprobated from one end of the continent to the other." Manning turned much of his fire on the way the treaty was negotiated, hinting at dark deeds by John Jay, and charged that the Federalists had both violated the Constitution and its treaty-making powers and had misled and forced the public into compliance by scare tactics. Characterizing the debate as he did most everything else—as a contest between the Few and the Many—Manning accused treaty supporters of raising "the most horrid and frightful falsehoods that ever were invented by the devil to frighten the people." In the end, "the combinations and arts of the Few" prevailed, Manning regretted. "But the plain truth is that the treaty and those that made it are the causes of all our disgrace and difficulty. The treaty was unconstitutionally made, and ought to be forever disowned, and all those that made it banished from the continent." There is little doubt that Manning saw the situation in the same geopolitical terms as Madison and Jefferson. His essay "On Parties" (1798) made that quite clear as he decried the British influence in American politics—something he had done for years—and called for political organization to beat back the Anglican tide. "Therefore, I conclude that it is high time for the Republicans to unite as well as the Royalists."[10]

Even stronger in his antipathy toward Britain was Benjamin Franklin Bache, editor of the Philadelphia Republican newspaper, the *Aurora.* Bache became one of the harshest and most trenchant critics of what he repeatedly called the "British Treaty." Yet while his dismay with the Washington administration reached its peak with the treaty debate, Bache's Anglophobia was on frequent display even before the instrument made its appearance. Before Jay's appointment he declared that the "few among us, who, though sensible of the injuries heaped on us by the British, are not prepared to retaliate, because they have not actually declared war," were, Bache observed wryly, much like a character in a play "who being kicked gave as the reason for not resenting it, that when he turned round to see who had insulted him, he found that the offender did not look angry." He regularly pounded away at the theme of British atrocities, stirring the pot of dissension, as when he declared bluntly, "It is time Americans had done with humbly petitioning the British Court to do them justice." Bache attacked the appointment of Jay to head the mission on the grounds that the New Yorker was an Anglophile, and as the negotiations dragged on through 1794 Bache criticized Jay for wasting time and for a lack of firmness in dealing with the British. As we shall see, Bache played a critical role in the events of summer 1795, when the country was inflamed with the treaty dispute. But well before the Treaty contents were revealed, he was leading the newspaper charge against Great Britain and warning Americans of the duplicity of the British and their allies in the U.S.[11]

Perhaps the figure most closely associated with Jefferson and Madison was their political lieutenant John Beckley, one of the first of what Jeffrey L. Pasley has termed "political professionals." With the most prominent Virginians aware of the campaign but largely sidelined, Beckley assumed leadership, with Bache, of the anti-treaty campaign. Although Beckley was from a very different social rank in Virginia than Madison or Jefferson, he shared their general political persuasion and most certainly their antagonism toward the document, seeing it as the culmination of years of Federalist intrigue and activity. Beckley, himself long since engaged in the anti-treaty efforts, wrote to Madison in September 1795 with a sharply worded assessment of the public's opinion of President Washington. Assuring Madison that public confidence was withdrawing from

Washington, he noted that the president's allies were doing their best to "exalt" his name and "exaggerate" his past service to the nation. "But all in vain," Beckley reported, "the vital blow aimed at the Independence & best Interests of his country, by the impending treaty, mark him an indelible character as the head of a British faction, and gratitude no longer blinds the public mind." This letter, and even moreso the great body of Beckley's newspaper essays, made it clear that Beckley fully supported the Republican position that all things British in American politics and policy carried with them at least a taint if not an outright danger.[12]

Not surprisingly, the war between France and Britain drew the United States ineluctably into its midst. The U.S. had hoped, perhaps naively, that as a declared neutral it might carry on trade with both warring nations, as stipulated by the widely accepted conditions and rights of neutrals. They attempted to do as much, and soon found themselves on a collision course with England. The immediate tensions which culminated in Jay's mission began in December 1793 when news reached the U.S. that the British had negotiated a treaty with Portugal to help the British fight against France. This meant that the Portuguese fleet, instead of patrolling the Straits of Gibraltar and containing the Algerian pirates in the Mediterranean, would be fighting the French and leaving U.S. trading ships suddenly vulnerable to piracy. Many Americans felt betrayed by the British, and President Washington, working with members of Congress, began to lay the groundwork for increasing military preparedness.[13]

But this tension proved to be only a small part of the rupture between the two nations. From this first step things escalated dramatically over the next few months. The British, faced with a desperate fight with the French, were unwilling to allow the United States and France to continue to observe their treaties recognizing the principle that "free ships meant free goods." Quite simply, Britain considered the U.S. trade with France to be too valuable to the French effort and was unwilling to sit back and allow that trade to go on. The British shrewdly recognized that the strength of their navy trumped international law or neutral rights. As the war with France escalated, the British developed narrower and narrower ways of defining neutral rights, knowing that their navy could ultimately enforce their decrees. A British Order in Council of June 8, 1793, ordered English ships to capture any neutral ships carrying corn, flour, or meal into French ports. Neither the materials nor the ships were confiscated; instead, they were led to British ports where the neutral ships were forced to sell their cargoes. Britain racheted up the pressure even further on November 6, 1793, with a far more encompassing order: the British navy was ordered to seize any ships—including neutrals—that carried goods and produce to or from French colonies. France had authorized the United States to trade with a small number of its West Indian ports, and England effectively moved to shut down that trade. Adding insult to injury, England acted preemptively and secretly (as it had long been in the habit of doing toward the U.S.), neglecting to tell the Americans of its policy until after the fact. All told, it seized nearly three hundred unsuspecting American ships. When news of these orders and actions became public in early March 1794, Americans were outraged, and a full-blown crisis was at hand.

Both Federalists and Republicans knew that a diplomatic mission to resolve this Anglo-American crisis would be necessary, but each advocated very different policies in the interim. Congressional Republicans forged ahead with legislation to cut off trade with Great Britain, in the hope that a U.S. envoy would be able to bargain from strength. Federalists argued that such steps would inflame tensions, not reduce them, and ultimately would be futile. Their preferred interim step was to increase military preparedness of both the navy and army. But President Washington saw a glimmer of hope, or at least what looked like a way to achieve Federalist ends short of war. While Britain's actions on the high seas were certainly warlike, neither its public rhetoric nor its diplomatic communications were. It seemed clear that England did not want, or at least did not prefer, war with the United States, so the opportunity for a diplomatic solution presented itself. By March, momentum was building, and a mission to England seemed likely. Less clear was who the diplomat entrusted with this assignment would be.[14]

Washington decided to send John Jay. The president met with Jay on the morning of April 15, 1794, and offered him the envoyship. That afternoon Jay consulted with Hamilton, Rufus King, and others who stressed the seriousness of the situation and urged Jay to accept. He did so the next day. That same day, the president sent Jay's appointment to the Senate, which approved it on April 19. In a matter of days, then, the appointment had been made and approved.[15] Jay accepted the mission more out of a sense of duty than enthusiasm. "I find myself in a dilemma between personal considerations and public ones," he told his wife. Jay granted the importance of the mission and his interest in its results. He also felt "the impulse of duty strongly" and hoped his wife would accede if he decided to answer that call of duty, he wrote on April 15, the day Washington offered him the position. But he made it clear that the appointment was "not of my seeking; on the contrary, I regard it as a measure not to be desired, but to be submitted to." When the Senate approved his nomination, he noted that "No appointment ever operated more unpleasantly upon me." Nonetheless, on May 12, Jay set sail for England.[16]

What exact terms was Jay to seek in his talks with the British? The primary goals were mapped out at a meeting on the evening of April 21 which included Hamilton, Oliver Ellsworth, Rufus King, George Cabot, and Jay. First, they decided that the instructions should be issued by the president alone. Consulting with Congress would only delay matters unnecessarily and might leave Jay burdened with a long wish list of ultimately unobtainable requirements, too many to make a treaty. Instead, they reasoned, Jay should press hard if need be to get indemnification for British seizures of American shipping under the November 6 orders. He should also insist that the unfulfilled portions of the 1783 peace treaty, chiefly regarding the evacuation of the western posts, be executed. He should also seek a more liberal interpretation of neutral rights insofar as they affected American commerce ("Free ships to make free goods" was the phrase from the official instructions) and a document that would grant U.S. ships entry to trade with the West Indies. While indemnification for captures may have been of overriding importance, Jay's instructions contained only two main points which were nonnegotiable: a treaty could not openly conflict with existing agreements with France, and it had to give American ships access to the West Indies. The themes hammered out at this meeting were further developed at a lengthy meeting the next day between Hamilton and Jay, and served as basis for the formal instructions Jay received from Secretary of State Edmund Randolph before departing. While that final list was comprised of nineteen points, easily the most important task Jay was to undertake would be to secure peace between the two nations. Because a state of peace was ultimately preferable to nearly any specific terms or language Jay might negotiate, the American envoy would necessarily have to consider almost all other points expendable or negotiable as against the sine qua non of securing peace and improved relations with Britain.[17]

Priding themselves as realists who saw the world for what it was, Federalist leaders believed, as Jerald Combs wrote, "that they were negotiating from a position of weakness." Consequently they both expected and were willing to give up a good deal to obtain their desired concessions.

Hamilton told Washington that the U.S. must be ever mindful of its true power relative to Great Britain. "Tis as great an error for a nation to overrate as to underrate itself. Presumption is as great a fault as timidity. Tis our error to overrate ourselves and to underrate Great Britain. We forget," he stated cogently, "how little we can annoy[,] how much we may be annoyed." The primary goal for Hamilton and others was to maintain peace. Toward that end Jay's mission was designed, for as Hamilton told the president, "This Country ought not to set itself afloat upon an ocean so fluctuating so dangerous and so uncertain but in a case of absolute necessity."[18] Jay's real mission, it might be said, was to ensure that such an absolute case never became necessary—and he was at liberty to exercise nearly complete discretion in the course of the talks to achieve that end, even if it meant watering down the provisions of the treaty.

Jay departed for England May 12, 1794. The treaty was signed November 19 of that same year. But not all the intervening period was filled with negotiations. Much of Jay's time was occupied with touring, social receptions and events, and simply waiting for his counterpart, Lord Grenville, to meet with him. After nearly four weeks crossing the Atlantic, Jay settled into his accommodations at London's finest, the Royal Hotel, with his son Peter, who accompanied his father as private secretary. On June 18, Jay was introduced to Grenville and they had their first face-to-face meeting. In the nine days that elapsed before the next meeting, Jay was entertained at dinners, theater parties, and weekends at country estates, and his desk was stacked with other invitations and greetings. Jay was ridiculed by the Republican press for these amusements, but Grenville was preoccupied with the pressing business of war with France and, in fairness to Jay, there was little other official work to be done as he waited for his counterpart during the sporadic negotiations.[19]

Jay's early meetings with Grenville were friendly and cordial; most were in private and no formal records were kept. Jay's official secretary John Trumbull commented that he and his British counterpart "had a real holiday for a month." The two principals took to each other and Jay was well-liked and respected by the British from the beginning. The diplomats' preliminary talks hinted at the possibility of reconciliation, and both men seemed hopeful, as Jay's correspondence makes clear. Grenville promised "that no unnecessary delays should retard a full discussion of the points in question"—but the process of negotiation moved in fits and starts, and did not conclude until November because Grenville was frequently called away.

Despite the discontinuity of negotiations, however, several key elements created a framework for the talks. Jay communicated to Randolph that the talks were based on "free conversations, neither of us considering the other as being committed by anything that was said or proposed." The two addressed easily resolved matters first, postponing by design the thornier issues. Jay prepared a series of drafts, which were considered and revised by Grenville and returned to Jay for further consideration. This pattern continued throughout the summer as the negotiators hammered out a workable draft and dug into the more contentious issues.[20]

Despite the charge of critics that he was too compliant and backed down too easily in the face of the British, the reality is that Jay had to negotiate with a comparatively weak hand, one perhaps vitiated even further by an indiscretion of Hamilton's. In a conversation in July, report of which reached Grenville on September 20, Hamilton told George Hammond, the British minister to the U.S., that America would not join a League of Armed Neutrality with other European nations. Hamilton also described Jay's minimum demands in the negotiations. While Samuel Flagg Bemis laid great weight to what he called Hamilton's "amazing revelation," later scholars have concluded that even without knowledge of Hamilton's statement, the British would have known as much anyway, simply from a shrewd assessment of the world situation and of U.S. strengths and weaknesses. Furthermore, if Jay had threatened U.S. membership in such a league as a bargaining ploy, it might have "gain[ed] him not more but substantially less than he actually got." Hamilton's conversation, while injudicious, was likely of little real consequence.[21]

Even if they had been inclined to do so, Jay and the Federalists knew that the United States could not demand the most favorable terms from Britain, nor could they negotiate from an adversarial stance and expect to gain the terms they did seek. That Jay was kept waiting at several points while Grenville first dealt with more urgent business suggests the upper hand the British had in negotiations. Any treaty would be reached in Britain's time—not out of spite, but because, as recent scholarship has noted, settling Anglo-American disputes was simply not as high a priority for the British in 1794 as it was for the United States.[22]

As a result, Jay found the British interested, friendly, generally willing to settle on amicable terms, but also distracted, their attention and priorities clearly focused elsewhere, and already aware that the U.S. would not play what was perhaps its strongest card. Jay's strategy in the negotiations, then, was to wait for the British to respond to his points, to make his case strongly but nonconfrontationally, and to be willing to concede or back away from, rather than insist upon, items the British were reluctant to accede to. The dynamics of the negotiations—the diplomats met when Grenville's schedule and duties allowed it—placed Jay at a disadvantage from the start. Aware of this and also disinclined to press the British lest they walk away, Jay's manner and negotiating strategy both reflected and compounded this state of affairs. He made his case per his instructions, but when it became clear early on that the British would grant the U.S. two critical items—the western posts and compensation for spoliations—he did not push hard on other points. In fact, Jay sought to wrap things up quickly and amicably and to take what he could get, rather than push for more and risk disrupting the talks. As he wrote to Hamilton in mid-September, "If I should be able to conclude the Business on admissible Terms, I shall do it, and risque Consequences; rather than by the Delays of waiting for, and covering myself by opinions & Instructions hazard a Change in the Disposition of this Court." He also assured Hamilton that the British seemed "really desirous of an amicable Settlement of Differences, and of laying a Foundation for Friendship as well as peace between the two Countries." That relationship and maintaining peace were, of course, the ultimate objectives of Jay and the Federalists. With that much seemingly secured, Jay did what he could. However, as he wrote to Edmund Randolph on September 13, on the issue of compensation for slaves carried off during the Revolution and other thorny matters, his approach was "to quit those topics, and to try to agree on such a set of reciprocal concessions as (balancing each other) might afford articles for a treaty, so beneficial to all parties, as to induce them to bury in it, all former questions and disputes." That approach was a summation of Jay's broader negotiating strategy.[23]

Thus convinced by September that the basic outlines of the treaty he desired were attainable—but not if he dallied or persisted in holding out for everything—Jay was, as his biographer notes, "in steady retreat." Given broad latitude by Washington, Hamilton, and Randolph before and during his mission, Jay followed his instincts and declined to press Grenville. When the British minister responded to Jay's September 30 proposed draft by noting that it would take far more time to consider all the terms proposed—and that there were some points which "if insisted upon on your part create as I fear insurmountable obstacles"—Jay acquiesced. Already concerned that British good will and the current propitious moment for dealing might soon pass, he backed away from the sticking points, and the remaining weeks were spent putting the finishing touches on the treaty, which was signed November 19, 1794.[24]

What did Jay's negotiations finally produce? The treaty he sent back to the United States contained twenty-eight articles addressing most (but not all) of the issues the mission was designed to ameliorate. The first article pledged "Peace, and a true and sincere Friendship" between the two nations, and the third stated that citizens of both countries could pass freely across boundary lines of the other and engage in trade. The second article gave Jay one of his principal goals: the pledge that the British would withdraw their troops and garrisons from the western posts, as promised in the Paris peace treaty, the removal to take place on or before June 1, 1796. The fourth, fifth, sixth, and seventh articles established commissions to investigate unresolved and contentious issues, including ascertaining the debts owed to British merchants by U.S. citizens and redressing the losses suffered from the seizure of U.S. ships by the British. The commissioners who adjudicated these matters would be compensated by both nations, which meant that the House of Representatives would have to approve funding. This fact would enter heavily into the thinking of treaty opponents and would provide the great closing drama in the debate during the spring of 1796.[25]

The most problematic feature turned out to be the twelfth article, which was ultimately rejected by the Senate. Addressing the matter of the West Indies trade, the document opened U.S. trade but stipulated that such trade could proceed only in vessels of 70 tons or less, a severely limiting condition. There were other prohibitions and restrictions as well. The fact that the British were willing to allow the United access to the lucrative West Indian trade, but insisted on restricting tonnage, showed both British awareness of the value of West Indian trade and their reluctance to share it in a genuine way. It also showed the relative negotiating power of the British, who could draft such an article in the name of concessions without really conceding much at all. Upset by this and no doubt stung by the imperious and calculated conditions, the U.S. Senate, while approving the treaty as a whole, ultimately rejected this article.[26]

The rest of the treaty represented some not inconsiderable advantages for the U.S. Article 13 cleared American ships for admission to trade in the East Indies, Article 14 granted reciprocal liberty of commerce and navigation between the U.S. and European nations, and Article 15 stated that no higher duties would be paid by ships of one nation in the ports of the other than were paid by all other nations. Several articles dealt with the effects of the ongoing war between Great Britain and France and attempted to clarify what the British could and could not do. Article 17 established that if a ship was found to be carrying contraband items, those items would be taken as a prize, but the ship could sail on. The next article documented the specific items labeled contraband and provided details for executing Article 17. Other articles addressed miscellany: pirates and privateering; assurance that ships of war of each nation would be hospitably received in the ports of the other; provision for the continuation of proper trade between merchants of the two countries should a rupture occur between the nations; and the principle that neither country should begin Acts of Reprisal against the other without statements of proof and evidence. This laundry list of terms concluded with Article 28, which stated that the first ten articles would be permanent and the following seventeen (excepting the twelfth) would be in effect for twelve years. Article 12 (West Indian trade) was to expire two years after the end of the current hostilities between France and Great Britain.

"The negotiation is terminated by a treaty," Jay wrote on November 19, the day the document was signed. To his mind, Jay had done his best, and the treaty he negotiated represented the most that could be obtained from Britain: "In my opinion, we have reason to be satisfied." Jay told a variety of correspondents that it was important to move promptly to ratify the measure, in part because additional concessions from Great Britain "cannot, in my opinion, be attained." The treaty, he wrote to President Washington, "must speak for itself." In a more expansive letter to Alexander Hamilton he exclaimed, "My task is done; whether *finis coronat opus*, the president, senate, and public will decide." Jay believed some parts of the measure would require further explanation to the country. "If satisfactory, care should be taken that the public opinion not be misled respecting it, for this reason the sooner it is ratified and published the better." Jay also cautioned that the "good disposition" of England should be treasured: if "this treaty fails, I despair of another." He wrote to another correspondent that "the building is finished, it cannot be very important to describe the scaffolding, or go into all the details which respected the business." Succinctly, he noted, "My opinion of the treaty is apparent from my having signed it. I have no reason to believe or conjecture that one more favourable to us is attainable."[27]

Had Jay obtained the best treaty he could under the circumstances? Scholars far removed from the stormy passions of the 1790s have long debated that question. Most have, with various qualifications, sided with Jay. He did gain many of the items deemed most crucial: the evacuation of the forts, commissions to settle the matter of spoliations of U.S. ships, limited access to the West Indies, and greater access to the East Indian trade. Most of all, the treaty maintained peace between the two nations. The major shortcoming was Jay's failure to change Britain's position on neutral rights: the U.S. received few substantive concessions on that score, and the treaty essentially failed to alter—indeed, it even tacitly accepted—Britain's violations. However, Great Britain, mired in its war with France, was in no mood to accept any limitations on how it used its navy, and the U.S. was certainly in no position to compel her to. In addition, many southerners found fault with Jay for not gaining compensation for slaves carried off during the Revolutionary War. Jay, a firm opponent of slavery, probably did not try very hard, but even if he had there was a limit to what could have been done. The confusion surrounding how slaves had become separated from their masters and a general dearth of hard evidence would have made this a hard point to resolve. Another issue not addressed in the document was the impressment of American sailors, a direct insult to the country and a real sore spot for many. As Jerald Combs notes, impressment was not mentioned in his instructions and at any rate was not, in 1794, quite the issue that it would become later, since Britain had not yet begun the practice of impressing American sailors on the high seas. So, had Jay really gotten the best treaty he could have? Stanley Elkins and Eric McKitrick answer, "It probably was; it is even likely that no other American could have got anything nearly as good." Jerald Combs, the treaty's most recent scholar, concludes that "Jay seems to have attained most or all of what Grenville and the British cabinet were willing to concede to America's power."[28]

But in a real sense what the treaty actually said became, in the debate ahead, less important than what both sides thought it meant or said it meant. Partly this was because the predispositions of the two sides for or against Great Britain inclined them to see the treaty—any treaty—in a certain light. But also at work was the very human business of rumor, speculation, and leaks, all of which prepared the ground for the treaty's public unveiling. The long cycle of speculation began even as Jay was busy negotiating. The speculation and anticipation, coming as they did on top of the predispositions most had regarding the British, produced by the summer of 1795 a climate in which nearly all Americans judged the document not so much on what it actually did but by how it squared with a series of conflicting expectations people held about it. Reality seemed to matter less than perception—and both perception and reality came in many shades in summer 1795.

Even as Jay concluded negotiations, reports and rumors about the terms of the treaty—what it left out as well as what it included—began to leak and became the source of intense speculation. Republican leaders, officially in the dark about the terms, began to speculate in their correspondence on what the treaty might hold. James Madison in early January 1795 wrote to Thomas Jefferson from Philadelphia that "It is expected here that [Jay] will accomplish much if not all he aims at. It will be scandalous, if we do not under present circumstances, get all that we have a right to demand." One month later, Madison was far more pessimistic, having yet to see a copy of the treaty but privy to the "imperfect scraps of private letters." From such scraps Madison declared his understanding that "the bargain is much less in our favor than might be expected. . . . It is even conjectured that on some points, particularly the Western posts, the arrangements will be inadmissible." Other Republican leaders exchanged similar thoughts. Robert Livingston wrote to Madison from New York and briefed him, disapprovingly, on the sketchy outlines of the treaty which had reached him. "You will at once see that if this is realy the treaty (of which I have no doubt) that Mr. Jay has sacrificed the essential interests of this country."[29]

Just as party leaders were sending private letters to one another, Republican newspapers got into the act. The most prominent early attacks on the still unpublished treaty were spearheaded by Benjamin Franklin Bache, Philadelphia editor of the *Aurora,* and by the anonymous author of the essays titled "Letters of Franklin," which appeared in Philadelphia's *Independent Gazetteer* fourteen times between March and June 1795. Bache had been on the attack from the time of Jay's appointment, accusing Jay of being an Anglophile who could not be an aggressive advocate for the U.S. position. As negotiations dragged on through the summer and fall of 1794, Bache accused Jay of wasting time and lacking firmness in dealing with his British counterparts. On January 31, 1795, Bache published the news that the treaty had been signed. For the next five months he gradually stepped up the assault on Jay, the Federalists, and the undisclosed instrument. The "Franklin" essays, whose authorship remains a mystery, argued that no nation was as passionately despised by the American people as Great Britain and that, if it were up to them, no treaty would be signed, especially if it slighted the French Republic. Knowing that the contents of the treaty were still undisclosed, "Franklin" nonetheless urged readers to assume that the rumors were true and that the terms were as bad as some speculated.[30]

It is helpful to divide the five months from the end of January (when knowledge of the treaty's signing was publicized) to the start of July (when the treaty's text was finally released) into three phases. During the first, the expectation was that the treaty would be favorable, which posed special difficulties for both Republicans and Federalists. James Monroe, on hearing rumors of an extremely favorable negotiation, wrote to James Madison, worried that if anything like that was true, it would put the Republicans in a bind. In some respects, the better the treaty, the worse it would be for the Republicans. On the Federalist side, Fisher Ames anticipated a potential drawback for Federalists, when he shrewdly predicted that Republicans might suggest that the treaty delivered everything as a means of building unrealistic expectations. Jay's success "will kindle war at home. Faction will sound the tocsin against the treaty. I see a little cloud, as big as a man's hand, in Bache's paper, that indicates a storm." Ames predicted what would happen next: "Two things will be attempted. First, before the event is known, to raise the expectation of the public, that we have every thing granted, and nothing given in return; and secondly, that the treaty, when published, has surrendered every thing."[31]

The second phase began in early February, when incomplete but broadly accurate reports of the treaty's contents reached the United States. Republicans began to attack the terms they had heard outlined and accused Jay of selling out American interests because the treaty did not achieve all that some wanted or expected. Madison was cautious, however, telling his father that he was "yet in the dark as to the Treaty. . . . The scraps from private letters afford too imperfect as well as too inauthentic an account of it to justify an opinion on its merits." But Madison continued to gather intelligence and weigh reports. Just a week later he wrote to Jefferson, "It is wrong however to prejudge, but I suspect that Jay has been betrayed by his anxiety to couple us with England, and to avoid returning with his finger in his mouth." Madison concluded that paragraph with a hopeful and significant comment: "It is apparent that those most likely to be in the secret of the affair, do not assume an air of triumph."

On March 7 word got out that the treaty had arrived and was being held in secret and would continue to be so held until the Senate took up debate (also in secrecy) in June. Secrecy itself, as much or more than the possible contents of the treaty, became the dominant issue in this third phase, which lasted until the end of June. Republicans, especially Bache's paper, pounded away at Federalists for refusing to publicly reveal the document's contents and implied that secrecy was used as a cover to hide dark dealings.[32]

President Washington held the instrument for three months as the administration debated the matter internally before submitting it to the Senate, which debated it in secret during June, finally voting on June 24 to ratify by the bare required two-thirds majority (20–10). Having kept the treaty secret for so long, the administration finally decided to release it, but before they could publish it in a paper of their choice, they were scooped by Bache, who obtained a copy of the document from Virginia senator Stevens T. Mason. Bache published an abstract of the measure's contents June 29 and then printed the full text on July 1—the day scheduled by Federalists for publication.[33] This publication, coming after months of intense speculation, rumor, charge, and countercharge, and building on the tensions such exchanges raised, touched off the fiercest protests yet seen in the new nation and marked the beginning of the Jay Treaty debate, a contest that, as this chapter has argued, had its origins well before July 1795.

Once the public was involved, what the treaty actually said and did became rather less important than what the opponents and proponents actually *believed* it said and did. Those beliefs were heavily colored by the predilections Americans held about the triangular nature of U.S. diplomacy in the 1790s and the need to play off both France and England.

2 | Federalists, Republicans, and Popular Politics in the Early 1790s

In many important ways, the debate over the Jay Treaty was an extension of a conflict long since underway. Federalists and Republicans—though not always organized or named as such—had already struggled over a great many issues, dating from the battle for ratification of the Constitution down to the outbreak of the Jay treaty clamor in 1795. From earlier campaigns a consistent pattern of activity emerged which was repeated and embellished in the Jay Treaty struggle. In the clashes over the Neutrality Proclamation and the Citizen Genet affair of 1793, as well as the Whiskey Rebellion and the Democratic Societies controversy in 1794, Federalists and Republicans engaged in the politics of public opinion, taking their cases before the public through the use of newspapers, public meetings, and organized rallies in an effort to press their case and win converts to their side.

This chapter will explore two seminal political conflicts which preceded and provided a crucial context for the treaty debate. In both cases, the two sides articulated thoughts and took actions which foreshadowed what they would do in the later conflict. Many of the same approaches which Federalists used to great advantage in 1793 and 1794 they turned to again during the treaty debate. In each instance, Federalists proved able to blunt criticism of their positions by reframing the debate in ways which decisively favored their stances. In other words, in appealing to the public, Federalists persuaded some citizens and calmed others by articulating themes and positions which stood them in good stead throughout Washington's presidency. Federalist success in these earlier struggles provides a vital context for understanding the battle over the treaty. Likewise, Republicans used many of the same arguments and tactics during the three contests. In some ways their critique of administration policies and tactics was entirely consistent and stemmed from the same ideological sources. This chapter will explore the connections between the neutrality and Genet crisis, the Whiskey Rebellion/Democratic Societies issue, and the Jay Treaty debates by examining the way each side engaged the public and endeavored to shape public opinion in early 1790s political culture.

One of the caveats offered in the Introduction bears repeating here. The state of political development was obviously not static in the 1790s. Political parties did not exist initially; they were decried and denied, even as partisans were organizing and acting in ways conducive to the formation of parties. Because party development was an evolutionary process, neither Federalists nor their opponents were as well established or organized in 1793 as they were three years later. Neither side was as far along the road toward party competition (or even toward recognizing that parties were developing) in the early 1790s as would be the case in the early nineteenth century. Certainly, at the time of the ratification contest, the term "Federalist" had a very different meaning (and could in fact be applied to James Madison) than it came to hold by 1796. So, in this chapter as elsewhere in the book, when I speak of Federalists and Republicans, I do so while recognizing that the parties were embryonic, still developing, and only slowly being recognized and accepted by some. My use of such terms is a shorthand to describe what were, by the time of the treaty debate, clearly developing political interests, factions, or proto-parties, however one wishes to define them. It is not meant to suggest that fully formed parties had already cohered early in that decade. Nor is it meant to deny or misrepresent the gradual process of party development which took place in the course of, and was greatly exacerbated by, each of the conflicts of the decade.[1]

France's declaration of war on Great Britain, Holland, and Spain in 1793 put the United States in a difficult position. While the U.S. was generally warmly sympathetic to its ally from the American Revolution, reality dictated that the country was in no position to fight a war. Strong sentiment existed in some ranks for the nation to join the conflict on the side of France, but it was offset by countervailing pressures arising from the cultural and economic connections to England. With Alexander Hamilton firmly against engaging in any conflict, least of all one with Great Britain, the Washington administration issued, on April 22, 1793, a proclamation of neutrality (although that word was never used). Earlier the same month, French minister Edmond Genet arrived in the United States. Genet was feted widely and received as a hero by American citizens who still wished the French government and people well. But Genet soon wildly overstepped the bounds of propriety as he set about commissioning U.S. ships and recruiting American citizens to engage the British. The resulting furor placed the crisis at the forefront of national politics for the next several months and ushered in the first of the precursors to the Jay Treaty debate.[2]

As the crisis unfolded that spring and summer, Federalist newspapers took two simultaneous tacks, both of which demonstrated how party leaders would engage the public during the entire Washington administration. They blended expressions of faith in the people (and praise for their good judgment) with harsh denunciations of administration critics. The two sentiments were sometimes blended. Taking direct aim at critics of the Neutrality Proclamation, John Fenno's *Gazette of the United States* asserted that "the great body of the people" supported neutrality, and that "a contrary suggestion implies the evidence of the most monstrous absurdity." Fenno attacked those "perpetually at work to excite sedition and opposition to peace and government" and called it no surprise that they should be "the *only* persons who cry out against every measure taken to preserve the peace and neutrality" of the nation. If the country were to be saved from war it would be because the people had faith in the wisdom of their government. Fenno closed by blasting opponents for raising the "infernally wicked sentiment . . . that the *people* and the *government* have different interests."[3]

Administration supporters emphasized this theme and its dangers. Calling it a "spirit of absurdity," one writer asked in mock-Biblical verse how it was possible that "the people shall say one thing, and those who dub themselves the organs of the people shall say another." Those who pretended to speak for the people did not listen to the people's direct voice or that of the people's representatives, but, rather, to "the lying oracles of the secret skulking prophets of the false gods, whom neither the people nor their fathers worshipped." Despite the professed sentiments of the public for neutrality, the people's voice was "reviled and ridiculed by their pretended friends." In a similar vein, "Nestor" decried the clamor against the proclamation and the administration, when it was demonstrably clear, he thought, that public opinion favored the president's policy. Such a paradox could be explained by the fact that "much noise may be made by a few individuals, [and] that a single factious citizen or a stranger who is no citizen" could "raise much dust" by writing under various pseudonyms to give the appearance of "a host of combatants" (not to mention the other "pestilential measures" of "foreigners"). During this crisis (and certainly later, in the Jay Treaty debate) Federalists accused opponents of being few in number but nonetheless capable of making lots of noise through newspapers, town meetings, and "irregular" assemblies. Federalists were confident in summer 1793, as they would be two summers later, that the commotion against administration policy was orchestrated by only a few instigators, while the main body of the American people constituted a silent majority of sorts in support of its president.[4]

Much of the Federalists' fire was concentrated on those who attacked Washington, directly or indirectly, and on those who countenanced such attacks. As with the warnings about the "absurdity" of the people and the government being of different minds, some friends of the government connected attacks on Washington, the administration, and neutrality with the spirit of faction and party (a take which foreshadowed the Federalist response to the Democratic Societies and the Whiskey Rebellion, discussed below). One correspondent, lamenting that Washington had met a "volley of the most unmerited abuse," regretted that the "men of virtue, and friends to the government . . . did not more generally declare their sentiments. . . . Every man ought to bear testimony against any political connection with any country of Europe." Further, it was crucial to "arrest that enthusiasm, which if indulged will necessarily divide our country into factions." As others had done, this writer remarked that it rested with "the good men to restrain the passions of the few who are turbulent."[5] Here, too, note the lament that Federalists had not been more active in taking their case to the people and publicly announcing their support for the administration in response to critics in the public papers.

Echoing this view, "Wilcocks" denounced "foreigners" who attacked the government, believing that in doing so they "fan the fire of party spirit." Even so, he was willing to tolerate such free speaking as long as administration supporters weighed in with their opinions. He, for one, announced his intention to do the same. "I am determined to maintain and exercise the same privilege; and will always in the most public manner assert, that a foreigner of any rank whatever, who intermeddles with our internal dissentions, or who shall dare to insult the first magistrate . . . is a dangerous man—and may expect to hear from [me]."[6]

Attacks on the "turbulent few," however, were predictable. What is surprising and noteworthy is the sense of faith and confidence in the people's judgment that Federalists expressed. Along with this, some supporters took pains to stress that "the people" included not just merchants or aristocrats but the great body of Americans. The same editorial which decried those who worked perpetually to encourage sedition and undermine peace closed with the plea that only "the confidence of the people in the wisdom of the government" could keep the nation safely out of war. In other writings Federalists were even more direct in their praise, not only of the people's confidence in government, but of their good sense and wisdom more generally. "The American public is to be congratulated on the late expression of the general sentiments of the people." That they reached such a conclusion should not be a surprise, this writer maintained. Confidence in the judgment of the people "is well grounded, which calculates on the sober and solid principles of the citizens of the United States."[7]

John Fenno's *Gazette of the United States* praised the public effusively. "There is," he wrote, "an inveterate propensity in the people of the United States, to *see, think,* and *act* for themselves—to be governed by the dictates of sober reason, and calm reflection—to trust to the evidence of their own senses, and to express the honest unadulterated feelings of their own hearts." Fenno observed that the "revilers of public men" apparently misjudged the qualities of the people, leading them to make "iniquitous attempts" to disturb the public opinion. Fenno and other Federalists shrewdly differentiated between "the people" and those who, in their minds, tried to mislead or misguide them or wrongly rouse them to ill-considered action. Other administration supporters, confident of the response they were likely to get, wondered if it might be proper for "the *people themselves* . . . to come forward" and voice their opinion. The author acknowledged that such a call represented a serious departure from previously held ideas of the proper role of citizens. "I am not especially fond of resorting to such unorganized bodies of men," the writer conceded. But he had a special purpose for making such a call. Since "the *Democrats* of the southward tell us, [the proclamation] is all the work of an *Aristocratic junto,* I wish these disturbers of our public peace to know

. . . that it is the *people themselves* who, with *one voice,* applaud the President's proclamation." This piece both advocated appeals to the public and made the point—to be repeated by Federalists in later campaigns—that the people who backed the administration were not merely the merchant class but a much broader group of citizens.[8]

Federalists could praise the favorable attitude of the public toward them because they had been working diligently to cultivate that very attitude for several months. As "Wilcocks" and others had called for, supporters of the administration and neutrality launched an impressive newspaper and letter campaign which helped recast the public debate. Shifting the focus away from the question of whether a position of neutrality was a betrayal of France (the terms the opposition cast it in), Federalists exposed Genet's machinations and turned the entire question of neutrality into a referendum on President Washington, a proposition they knew they would not lose. By presenting the whole question as a stark choice—did the people trust Genet or Washington?—Federalists shrewdly fashioned and shaped the terms of the public debate, moving it to the nearly unassailable grounds of popular adoration and respect for Washington. This would be neither the first nor the last time in the 1790s that pro-administration advocates played their trump card. Variations on this theme were used in the debates over the Whiskey Rebellion and the Democratic Societies, as well as the Jay Treaty. But it was in the public squabble over neutrality in the summer of 1793 that this theme, which would do such consistently effective work for the Federalists, was first deployed.

Leading the Federalists' literary efforts, as he would do in the later crises as well, was Alexander Hamilton. Determined to seize control of the public debate and to find an effective counterweight to Genet's initial popularity, Hamilton took up his pen in late June and drafted a set of seven essays signed "Pacificus" which demolished the arguments against neutrality. Hamilton, in his usual methodical, prosecutorial style, addressed and then dismissed objections to the policy and built a strong case for not only Washington's right to issue the proclamation but the propriety of the policy itself. Hamilton argued that a declaration of neutrality was not an exceptional action, but, rather, a proper one for a nation to take to avoid conflict. Further, the executive branch, not the legislative, was fully and uniquely authorized to make such a declaration. As far as broaching previous treaties with France, the proclamation was not wanting there either, for Hamilton made a distinction between defensive treaties (which he argued the France–United States alliance had been) and the offensive war France had declared against Great Britain and Holland in February. In characteristic fashion, Hamilton also advanced the argument that the U.S. had an obligation chiefly to its own self-interest. It did not owe France any debt from their assistance during the Revolution and to make such a claim now failed to grasp the realities of the situation.[9] "Pacificus" was initially published in Fenno's *Gazette of the United States* and then widely reprinted. When joined with his nine "No Jacobin" essays, published beginning in late July, which publicized Genet's efforts to appeal over the head of the president directly to the people, the effect was quite telling and proved to be all Hamilton and the administration could have hoped for. The essays encouraged and comforted Federalists, who sensed that these writings helped swing public opinion solidly behind them.[10] Their response to the changed tenor of the public debate will discussed below.

Hamilton's work by turns alarmed and dispirited Republicans, particularly their leaders Thomas Jefferson and James Madison. In his oft-quoted letter of July 7 to Madison, Jefferson referred to "Pacificus" and implored Madison to act. "Nobody answers him, and his doctrine will therefore be taken for confessed. For god's sake, my dear Sir, take up your pen, select the most striking heresies, and cut him to peices [*sic*] in the face of the public. There is nobody else who can and will enter the lists with him." In the very next sentence, however, Jefferson suggested the dual nature of the Republicans' dilemma. As if the power of Hamilton's words were not enough, Jefferson recognized how his own position was weakened by Genet's careless and irresponsible actions. He blistered Genet, claiming that never "was so calamitous an appointment made. . . . Hotheaded, all imagination, no judgment, passionate, disrespectful and even indecent towards the P[resident] . . . talking of appeals from him to Congress, from them to the people." If Congress ever had reason to examine his communications, Jefferson warned, "universal indignation" would result. Summing up, Jefferson told his associate, "He renders my position immensely difficult." Acknowledging the potential for damage to rub off on the Republicans, Jefferson confessed to Madison in early August 1793 (in the coded language they frequently used in the event their mail was intercepted and read by opponents) that Genet "will sink the Republican interest if they do not abandon him." Jefferson's correspondence throughout the fall made it clear how uneasy he was about the political damage Genet might do the Republican interest.[11]

Madison took up Jefferson's challenge and responded in late July with his "Helvidius" essays, but he did so very reluctantly. He had "forced" himself, he told Jefferson, to reply. "I can truly say I find it the most grating [task] I ever experienced." Madison complained that he was not as familiar with the materials as Hamilton obviously was; furthermore, many of the books and source materials he needed were not with him at Montpelier as he wrote. Beyond that, Madison's task was far more difficult—and his position much weaker—than Hamilton's. Without showing the least sign of disloyalty to Washington or questioning the worth of neutrality as a policy, Madison had to argue for the unconstitutionality of enacting neutrality by presidential proclamation. In addition, he had to express support for the French Revolution but distance Genet from the Republican party at home. It was a tall order and, ultimately, not even Madison's prodigious talents could pull it off. The combination of these factors made "Helvidius" less than successful as a response to "Pacificus," a fact Madison dolefully recognized.[12] (Two years later, when Hamilton dashed off his powerful "Camillus" essays to build support for the Jay Treaty, Jefferson again enjoined Madison to take up his pen and answer Hamilton. Perhaps aggrieved by the results in 1793, Madison declined, and neither he nor Jefferson wrote any substantial response to Hamilton at that time.)

Reluctantly or not, however, Madison did mount a public response to Hamilton, placing the "Helvidius" essays in Fenno's *Gazette of the United States,* the same journal which published "Pacificus," and so entering directly into the fray. Despite their comparatively weaker and more problematic position, Madison's essays were designed to appeal directly to the people in a public forum, a tacit acknowledgment that the contest for public opinion was now carried on in the newspapers of the day. But Madison never expected a wide readership. He told Jefferson that an answer to "Pacificus," if undertaken, "ought to be both a solid, and a prudent one. None but intelligent readers will enter into such a controversy, and to their minds it ought principally to be accommodated." If anything, Madison and the Republicans seemed more doubtful of the wisdom and propriety of carrying on a debate in the public papers than did Hamilton and the Federalists; they were certainly more reluctant than their rivals to enter the fray. Nonetheless, Madison began drafting the essays on July 22, 1793 (the same day he wrote to Jefferson about the intended audience), and completed the last of five essays on August 20. Four days later the first number appeared in the *Gazette,* and the series concluded on September 18, 1793.[13]

In the essays, Madison stressed the constitutional dangers of an overpowerful executive branch (the pseudonym "Helvidius" came from Tacitus and referred to the first-century Roman who resisted imperial power). Madison focused not on Washington's proclamation itself nor the policy of neutrality more broadly, but, instead, attacked the justifications of "Pacificus" for a broad or liberal reading of the Constitution's grant of executive prerogative. Such an interpretation was far too close to the model of monarchical Britain and would admit of grave dangers down the road. A free and broad construction, warned Madison, cannot be curtailed once introduced. When such doctrines "make their way into the creed of the government, and the acquiescence of the public, every power that can be deduced from them, will be deduced and exercised sooner or later by those who may have an interest in doing so." Madison suggested that both human nature and the history of governments offered proof of the danger. "A people therefore, who are so happy as to possess the inestimable blessing of a free and defined constitution, cannot be too watchful against the introduction, nor too critical in tracing the consequences, of new principles and new constructions, that may remove the landmarks of power." Madison laid out the arguments as best he could, but his task was fraught with difficulties and the impact of the essays less than he had hoped for.[14]

Republicans made other efforts as well. The Republican press did what it could to challenge the Federalist arguments. Philip Freneau's *National Gazette* staunchly defended Genet, even after revelations of his efforts to recruit Americans and after the publicity of those efforts forced Jefferson, Madison, and other Republican leaders to distance themselves from the problematic Frenchman. Likewise, Benjamin Franklin Bache used the pages of his *General Advertiser* to support Genet even after party leaders disassociated themselves from him. Identifying with the French cause and looking for any opportunity to attack the Washington administration's seemingly pro-British definition of neutrality, Bache soldiered on, writing editorials and printing sympathetic letters which tried to excuse or explain away the French minister's troubling conduct. But the basic weakness of the pro-Genet argument rendered Freneau and Bache ineffective, and their persistence in the face of the distancing being practiced by Jefferson and Madison merely showed how independent (how little under the control of party leaders) were the leading vehicles of the Republican press.[15]

Troubled by the boisterous receptions Genet received and concerned by the seeming level of opposition to Washington's proclamation, Federalist leaders conferred as the newspaper campaign (including Hamilton's "Pacificus" essays) began to bear fruit. Oliver Wolcott, Jr., wrote to Noah Webster in August, praising his work and promising him that the enclosures Webster had sent "shall be used to promote the purpose you mention." It must make the president happy, Wolcott noted, that his measures "are approved by the discerning republicans of the country." He also made reference to other elements of the Federalist campaign. "The city address was exactly to the purpose, and will have a good effect here." Wolcott assured Webster that the people of Connecticut could distinguish between an individual and a cause and that they agreed "that a foreign influence will not be permitted." In a similar vein, Federalist activist Peter Van Schaak of New York wrote to Loring Andrews on the effects of the "Pacificus" essays. "You have doubtless seen Pacificus, which I trust will fix the Tone of the publick Mind." Van Schaak urged Andrews, a newspaper publisher, to do his part to popularize the Federalist position. "I wish you wo[u]ld contemplate a Republication in a Pamplet of some of the Papers of the Day. I will endeavour within my sphere," Van Schaak promised, "to promote such an object, if you approve." He also wrote that friends of the administration had to stand firm. "Let *us* fraternize (perverted as the word had been) in upholding the Fabrick we have raised, or if the Tree of Liberty is a better Image may it be like Virgils Oak. . . . But let its luxuriance be watched & pruned by the Steady Hand of a wise Government."[16] Van Schaak's call for Federalists to band together and defend the new government suggests that Federalists considered it important to be actively engaged in the contest for public opinion.

The need to take their argument to the nation was also expressed by Christopher Gore of Massachusetts, who wrote to Rufus King in early August 1793 that "all our seaports are hearty in their approbation of our neutrality" and that towns "from Penobscott to this place [Boston] . . . are making resolutions similar to those of Boston. From time to time as they come in," Gore promised, "they will be inserted in the public papers." Gore also noted the successful effects of Hamilton's pen. "The writings of Pacificus have done much good; others are producing a conviction with respect to the precise tenor of our national duties." A couple of days before Gore's letter, King heard from Massachusetts merchant George Cabot, who noted that he had received a letter from King. "I thought a publication of some of the ideas it contained . . . might be useful & therefore after giving them a little change of form and arrangement, have *set them off* for the press." Massachusetts congressman Fisher Ames wrote to Hamilton at the end of August, exclaiming, "I am happy to see the good effect of the exertions which have been made to keep our country from meddling with the war. . . . The public mind seems to be open to receive the truth," Ames remarked, noting that "Such periods occur rarely & ought not to pass away in vain." Satisfied for now, Ames nevertheless told Hamilton he looked "forward to the next campaign with concern. I wish nothing may be omitted to make the people understand the truth, so well as to disarm the faction who distorts it."[17]

But Federalists did more than simply insert pro-administration or pro-proclamation pieces in newspapers. They also organized and staged town meetings in support of the policy and the president. These meetings were designed to counter the enthusiastic receptions Citizen Genet had received. Boston merchant Stephen Higginson wrote Alexander Hamilton in some despair: why, he wondered, do "Individuals or Classes of men interfere, who have no authority to interpret Treaties . . . ?" If an honest government decided upon much reflection for a certain policy, then citizens should support that position instead of organizing against it. But, Higginson noted, the supporters of government in Boston had recently held a meeting "of the Trade & of the Town. It was a good opening to give a full approbation of the late proclamation, & to get the Citizens pledged in favour of neutrality & the measures of government, & to excite similar feelings & Voices in other Towns." Higginson concluded that the opinion of the Boston town meeting would be echoed in "the voice of a large part of the State, perhaps above a hundred Towns."[18]

A few weeks after Higginson wrote, Hamilton received a letter from his close friend Robert Troup in anticipation of a town meeting to be held that day in New York. Troup claimed that the meeting, held in front of Trinity Church, would be "the most respectable meeting for numbers—character—& property—ever assembled in this City." The purpose was to express "warm approbation" of the proclamation and the desire for peace. Troup boasted that neutrality supporters had "by pursuing a bold & manly line of conduct effected a complete consolidation of parties in favor of the great object of neutrality." He noted that Genet's reception the day before had been "noisy—but contemptible to an extreme," and remarked that, as long as Washington pursued his firm course of neutrality, he would "secure the continuance of that respect & veneration for him which reign in the hearts of all reflecting & good men." At the meeting, the assembled citizens adopted six resolutions supporting the Neutrality Proclamation.[19]

Probably the best known Federalist public meeting took place deep in the heart of Republican Virginia, in Richmond, on August 17, 1793. Organized by John Marshall and chaired by George Wythe, Jefferson's longtime friend and mentor, the meeting considered and unanimously adopted a series of resolutions which strongly endorsed the policy of neutrality, asserted the people's confidence in President Washington, and condemned Genet, though not by name. The meeting concluded with a resolution which saluted Washington for past service to the nation and for his dedication to keeping the country at peace. An account of the proceedings and copies of the resolutions adopted were then printed and circulated and soon appeared in papers around the nation, thus magnifying their impact.[20]

Republicans, not willing to cede the ground entirely and worried at the apparent impact of the Federalist campaign, struck back, even though they lacked the preparation and organization of their rivals. Madison and James Monroe, sometimes in contact with Jefferson and sometimes not, laid plans for rallies and began drafting resolutions at Monroe's house during the last two weeks of August. They worked in a mood of frustration. "The Country," Madison told Jefferson, "is too much uninformed, and too inert to speak for itself; and the language of the towns which are generally directed by an adverse interest will insidiously inflame the evil." He mentioned to Jefferson the possibility of a series of counter-meetings and resolutions, noting that "If these examples should be set, there may be a chance of like proceedings elsewhere." But Madison remained doubtful: "I am not sanguine however that the effort will succeed." Nonetheless, he and Monroe plunged into the work. The first set of Republican resolves drafted by Madison and Monroe was adopted at Staunton, Virginia, on September 3, 1793. A second set was then sent to John Taylor of Caroline, who arranged a meeting for September 10. The authors of the resolutions faced the same constraints as "Helvidius." Still, the Republicans managed to ignore the Neutrality Proclamation altogether, firmly praising France and celebrating the strong bond between the two nations even as they gently and indirectly chided Genet's missteps, trying in the process to gradually distance the problematic French minister from both the French and Republican causes. The sets of Republican resolutions were printed, distributed widely, and used as models for similar resolutions adopted in other places.[21]

By August it seemed clear that the Federalist campaign was paying dividends. The tactic of standing the imperturbable and heroic Washington against the aggrandizing and flighty Genet created an impassible barrier for opponents of neutrality. Federalist leaders who had been worried earlier in the summer, during the first weeks of the crisis, now took heart that public opinion seemed to be swinging toward them. Even as early as mid-June, Baltimore merchant and congressman Samuel Smith indicated to Alexander Hamilton that, in Maryland, "the more I inquire the more I am persuaded that they will Ardently Support the Government & that with One Voice they approve the Presidents Proclamation." George Cabot told Rufus King that people in Massachusetts were united in their desire for peace. "Excepting a few factious men in Boston & a *very few* in other places, they are united too in the Sentiment that the President is the proper Guardian of the public tranquillity, & that the measures he takes to secure it, are fit and proper & ought to be supported." Cabot lamented the industriousness of the "propagators of falsehood" whose "Jacobinical principles" seemed for a time in the ascendency. He went on to castigate fellow administration supporters for not doing more to shape public opinion. Until Hamilton's "Pacificus" essays appeared, the administration position was largely absent from the public journals, leaving the pro-French position unanswered. The fault, Cabot found, lay with the administration's advocates: "the friends of Government are as blameable as their adversaries." He closed by urging King that Federalists should not hesitate to take the merits of their case to the people. "It will be useful to rouse the sober part of the community & oblige them to attend to a subject, the discussion of which can no longer be avoided."[22]

Hamilton's various correspondents kept him posted on the apparent drift of opinion in their respective areas. Samuel Smith wrote again in mid-August, assuring the treasury secretary that "this state is right & except for half a dozen fools of no Consequence at Chester will Act right." South Carolina congressman William Loughton Smith, passing through Boston, wrote, "You will be delighted with the Anti-Gallican Spirit which has lately burst forth in this State & which breathes the genuine Effusions of Patriotism in nervous Resolutions, engaging to support our paternal President & those real friends of the Country who advise him, against the insolent Attempts of a foreign Incendiary & a rascally Crew of Demogogues." William Loughton Smith's letter captures the exact terminology Federalists deployed to characterize their own position and that of their opponents.[23]

Finally, David Ross commented to Hamilton on the effectiveness of his "Pacificus" essays in shaping public opinion. (Incidentally, Ross voiced almost exactly the same sentiments Fisher Ames expressed over two years later to describe the effect—and effectiveness—of Hamilton's "Camillus" essays in the Jay Treaty debate.) Ross suggested that "the object of getting publications signed 'Pacificus' is done away by the Sentiment becoming so very general here [Maryland] in support of the measures of Government—& from the little countenance the 'Democratic Society' is like to meet with even in Virginia." Ross also observed that Genet's conduct produced "a very lucky circumstance as it has been the means of proving so great a confidence of the People, in, and a desire to support the Dignity, of, their own Government exceeding the expectations of its warmest friends." Thus, Ross noted that Hamilton's essays—effective as they had been—were now becoming superfluous, with the tide of events moving so much in favor of the administration's position.[24]

Federalists were not the only ones who recognized the drift of public opinion. Republican leaders Thomas Jefferson and James Madison noted the same signs. Writing to Madison in August, Jefferson observed that while Genet had recently been in New York, "the vote of a full meeting of all classes was 9. out of 10. against him, i.e. for the proclamation and chiefly with a view to manifest their disapprobation of G[enet]'s conduct. Philadelphia, so enthusiastic for him, before his proceedings were known, is going over from him entirely." Madison commented acidly to Jefferson that it seemed to him that Federalists planned "to drag before the public the indiscretions of Genet; and turn them & the popularity of the P. to the purposes driven at." A week later, Madison noted along the same lines that the "Anglican party" was busy "in making the worst of every thing, and in turning the public feelings against France, and thence, in favor of England." Madison expressed hope that, with proper information, the country might still come around to the Republican position; but the towns, he warned, "are generally directed by an adverse interest."[25]

The main themes of the Federalists' campaign were reflected back to them in many of the petitions sent to President Washington. The merchants and traders of Philadelphia sent Washington in late May an address which stressed their support for the president and his administration's policy. Citing the need to "continue in peace, under their excellent laws and government," the merchants praised Washington for "the wisdom and goodness which dictated your late Proclamation." The merchants and traders insisted that "an unoffending conduct towards all the world" was the "the true policy of America," and they resolved not only to obey the measure themselves but "to discountenance, in the most pointed manner," those who might not. This address was signed by "about three hundred of the principal merchants and traders" of Philadelphia. A pleased Washington, grateful to receive such unequivocal support so early in the crisis, responded in like form, restating many of the key themes of the merchants' address while thanking them for their support. Washington noted that it gave him "pleasure to learn" that the proclamation had "given general satisfaction to the Citizens of Pennsylvania." He hoped, furthermore, that the U.S. would be as diligent about preserving peace as it was about defending their rights.[26] A similar exchange of addresses occurred between the merchants and traders of Baltimore and Washington, with the president writing that he took "no small degree of satisfaction to find that my endeavours to promote [neutrality] . . . have met your approbation."[27]

But it was not only the self-identified merchants and traders, but other groups of citizens as well, who sent Washington their sentiments. These petitions and addresses likewise reflected not only Washington's message itself but the central themes of the Federalists' campaign. Residents of Trenton, New Jersey, wrote to the president expressing "high satisfaction" with his "watchful care." Citing their belief that war would destroy the prosperity and flourishing economy the U.S. was then enjoying, they stated their support for the proclamation and their determination to insure compliance from their fellow citizens. This late July address also communicated a sense of broader public opinion: since the proclamation, the correspondents noted proudly, its ideas were met with "general acceptation" and expressed, they believed, "the common sentiments and the common language of the citizens of New-Jersey."[28]

The New York Chamber of Commerce added its voice of support for Washington and at the same time nicely encapsulated many of the principles and understandings regarding governing and the relations between leaders and the public that Federalists later articulated in the Jay Treaty controversy. The Chamber's address called the Neutrality Proclamation a measure to promote peace and further the interests of the nation. Such "watchful regard for the honor and prosperity of the nation" had "uniformly distinguished the administration of our first magistrate." The address then made an important statement about the role of the constituted authorities, in an oblique reference to Citizen Genet. The "President . . . is the only organ thro' which the national will can be made known to foreign powers . . . any attempt of said powers or their ministers to communicate with this country . . . [except] thro' him, is an indignity to our constitution, an offence to the nation, and ought to excite the apprehension and displeasure of all good and orderly citizens." That last statement, of course, directly skewered Republicans who still—or had once—championed Genet, and questioned their loyalty, or, at the very least, their orderliness.[29]

Throughout August a spate of meetings were held throughout the nation to evince support for Washington and the proclamation, and these were happily reported by pro-administration papers. Again, the language used is telling for its similarity of tone and content. John Fenno's *Gazette of the United States* published a series of resolutions under the heading, "The Voice of the People Is the Voice of God." Each of the addresses which followed echoed the same themes praising the policy of neutrality and Washington himself. One group in Springfield, Massachusetts, stated, "although we do not feel disposed to arrogate the right of approving or condemning the official conduct of the Supreme Executive . . . we cannot but express our gratitude." An address from Newark, New Jersey, resolved that the president's proclamation was "a declaration of the real disposition of these States." And citizens in Exeter, New Hampshire, called the principles of neutrality expressed in Washington's message "constitutional, wise, and patriotic" and condemned those who criticized Washington or the policy.[30]

The winding down of the conflict over neutrality roughly coincided with the outbreak of another deadly epidemic of yellow fever in Philadelphia in late 1793. In assessing party triumphs and setbacks, it might be fair to conclude that the Republicans, soundly whipped in the battle for public opinion while playing a losing hand, managed about as skillful a retreat as could possibly be imagined—and, in doing so, minimized potential long-term damage to their cause. Jefferson shrewdly set the tone for accepting such limited objectives when he wrote to Madison in August: "I believe that it will be true wisdom in the Republican party to approve unequivocally of a state of neutrality, to avoid little cavils about who should declare it, to abandon G. entirely, with expressions of strong friendship & adherence to his nation & confidence that he has acted against their sense. In this way," he concluded, fully aware of the twin dangers of losing public opinion *and* acting disloyally, "we shall keep the people on our side by keeping ourselves in the right."[31] The Republican resolutions that came in that fall seemed to follow Jefferson's advice, steering away from the precipice Republicans had found themselves staring over in the summer. Although it angered many Federalists (who saw this as an opportunity to gravely wound the Republican interest), Washington accepted the friendly resolutions from Republican meetings that seemed to echo those of Federalist meetings. A potential political crisis for the Republicans had been deftly avoided. Thus, both sides came away with important victories: Federalists won the contest for public opinion on the substance of the Genet matter and the issue of neutrality, while Republicans minimized the damage to their party, leaving it not much the worse for wear and poised to regroup for the battles yet to come.[32]

But thoughtful leaders on both sides saw matter for worry as they reflected on the debate. Several Federalists, while expressing satisfaction at the outcome of the Neutrality Crisis, nonetheless expressed concern over the obstacles still to be faced and wondered about the implications of popular mobilization. Fisher Ames took pleasure, in August, 1793, in exclaiming that Boston "is less frenchified than it was. Citizen Genet is out of credit. . . . I like the horizon better than I did; there are less clouds. I do hope and trust we shall keep at peace." But then he concluded his letter to Thomas Dwight with a warning. "As to faction, we must expect to sleep, if we can, while the ship is rolling, for no calms, except those which are portentous of storms, are to be expected. We may be safe; we must not hope to be quiet." He made the same point in his previously cited letter to Alexander Hamilton when he observed that he looked forward to "the next campaign with concern" and hoped that every effort would be made to place the truth before the public so as to offset the efforts of "the faction who distort it." In short, Ames knew that the anti-administration faction had been quieted for the time being but not squelched altogether, and that only by "plac[ing] the truth before the public" could Federalists hope to beat back opposition and win the contest for public opinion.[33]

Rufus King raised an even greater concern in an early August letter to Alexander Hamilton, when he described the actions taken in New York for and against the proclamation and warned of far more dire consequences. "[U]nless the Executive will quickly and vigorously exercise its *powers* in checking the influence of Mr. Genet, it may experience the mortification of seeing them perish in its hands." He noted that the New York Chamber of Commerce would soon pass a resolution supporting the proclamation—and, he wrote, "we are resolved to try the citizens for a like purpose. But this is altogether wrong." He noted that the Constitution vested the president with the power to see that laws were executed for the good of the nation and for its peace and security. "It was never expected that the Executive should sit with folded arms, that the government should be carried on by town meetings and those irregular measures which disorganize society, destroy the salutary influence of regular government and render the magistracy a mere pageant."[34]

King's words at once express his—and other Federalists'—dismissal of town meetings as an illegitimate theater of action, but also remark that, despite such reservations, the friends of the administration were going ahead with their own plans for a town meeting in support of the president's proclamation. His comments suggest that, even at this early stage of the factional conflict, Federalists realized the implications of the kind of public engagement they were undertaking, and saw its ramifications for rule by constituted authorities. They also reflect an ambivalence or unease about those very actions: King condemns the practice of popular mobilization in general even as he notes the plans being made for the express purpose of mobilizing the public in behalf of administration policy. Such ambivalence—decrying the act of popular politics even while engaging in it—came to mark Federalist activity in response to the Whiskey Rebellion and, especially, in the Jay Treaty debate.

For their part, Republicans made their own assessments of the contest. No doubt gratified and relieved to have broken the Federalists' considerable momentum and minimized damage to themselves, Republicans took advantage of the return to what Stanley Elkins and Eric McKitrick label "a kind of partisan equilibrium" in the aftermath of the campaign. Jefferson made his report on commerce as his last act as secretary of state before his resignation took effect at the end of 1793. Madison and congressional Republicans, armed with Jefferson's study, resumed their efforts to enact a policy of trade discrimination against British shipping. It was not entirely business as usual. Republicans knew that the Federalists had much more effectively managed the campaign to shape public opinion than they had. They also knew that in future clashes they would need to expand and strengthen their networks of newspapers, party operatives, and politicians who could put across their message swiftly and effectively in a coordinated fashion. Future battles for public opinion would be waged in the press and in public meetings, and the Republicans had catching up to do before they could match what the Federalist network of printers, party leaders, and operatives had been able to do in the neutrality controversy.[35]

As the calendar turned to a new year, many of the nation's political disputes in 1794 centered on the related issues of the Democratic Societies and the Whiskey Rebellion. The rebellion erupted in summer 1794 as farmers in western Pennsylvania, protesting the excise tax on whiskey, struck a pose of defiance toward the federal government. Echoing their forbears of the Revolutionary generation, crowds tarred and feathered excise collectors and turned on whiskey distillers who cooperated by paying the tax. Determined to put down this challenge to federal authority, Washington, Hamilton, and the Federalists mobilized over twelve thousand militiamen. When the army—with Washington and his treasury secretary at the head—swept into the area near Pittsburgh, they found symbols of defiance, such as liberty poles, but nothing in the way of actual rebellion. Cowed by this massive show of federal force, the whiskey rebels and their resistance collapsed.

The Democratic Societies predated the Whiskey Rebellion but played a role in that conflict. Over forty societies were organized between 1793 and 1800. Members defined themselves by their vigilance against government and its perceived encroachments on personal liberties. Often identifying with the Sons of Liberty, the societies quite consciously considered themselves as the torchbearers of the Revolutionary flame in the new republic. The societies further pledged that it was their duty not only to spread information and disseminate ideas, but "to *detect* and to *publish* to the world, every violation of our Constitutions, or instance of Mal-Administration." Thus, from the outset, the societies, nearly all of which formally adopted some variation on the preceding sentiment, presented themselves as watchdogs in opposition to the governing party from which such "mal-administration" was likely to occur. While not overtly affiliated with the emergent Republican party, the societies strongly shared the same political sympathies and outlook. As Stanley Elkins and Eric McKitrick put it, "there were very few Federalists in the Democratic Societies."[36] Small wonder, then, that Federalists, led by George Washington himself, were quick to condemn these organizations and linked the societies to the rebellion as nearly cause and effect. The president called the rebellion "the first *formidable* fruit" of what he denounced on other occasions as "self-created" societies.[37]

The societies proved highly contentious because they cut right to the heart of the debate over the proper role of citizens and their representatives in the new republic. When the German Republican Society addressed the Democratic Society of Philadelphia, its first resolve promoted a broad and expansive conception of the rights of citizens. The resolution called it "the natural privilege of every free citizen, to give his sentiments on all public measures, and not only on those which have operation, but on those also that are pending." In its response, the Democratic Society unanimously resolved that it "heartily concur[red]" in the resolutions of the German Society. This sentiment reflected the view held by many in the emerging Republican camp, that citizens had a right to instruct their representatives and to assert themselves in regard to public measures.[38]

Republican leaders shared some of these sentiments. While Jefferson and Madison both condemned the Whiskey Rebellion as a dangerous challenge to the supremacy of the national government, they were deeply troubled by the Federalist efforts to crush it. Initially, at least, they were far from concerned about the societies. In fact, Madison believed the societies were good examples of the expressions of local opinion he believed it necessary to hear, in order to gather public opinion. The two leaders, long determined to foster a watchful, even skeptical, eye toward administration measures, viewed the societies as a useful and healthy way to involve the public in the affairs of the nation. Fundamental to this project was finding a means, whether through newspapers like Philip Freneau's *National Gazette* or in other venues, of giving the people free expression without mediation. Republican leaders, especially Madison, saw the kind of political activity the societies were engaged in as not only desirable from the standpoint of party, but healthy for the republic. Viewed through Republican eyes, Washington's criticism of the societies themselves and the efforts by Federalists to link the rebellion to the societies were reprehensible and ominous.[39]

The administration's supporters saw things much differently. Once again they took to the newspapers to criticize the societies and those who joined or supported them, also using the occasion to reinforce their notions of the role of citizens and the need for them to trust and support duly elected officials. As they did in the Neutrality Crisis and would do later in the Jay Treaty controversy, Federalists encouraged the publication of pieces designed to influence and sometimes to mobilize public opinion on the administration's side. As they had and would again, the Federalists stressed the primacy of the constituted authorities and worked hard to discredit the societies and undermine the stance of the whiskey rebels, by portraying both as extra-constitutional if not unconstitutional bodies which were, despite their claims to the contrary, profoundly un-democratic and dangerous. As in the other controversies, Federalists during 1794 voiced and repeated several central themes in their writings, discussing the need to shape and influence public opinion in their private writings and developing public lines of attack and argument which meshed with their views of government and took ample advantage of the various symbolic images and actual advantages the administration had.

Federalist leaders, writing to each other, stressed the need to publicize their arguments to expose what they saw as the illogical and disloyal acts of the Democratic Societies. In an untitled piece, Fisher Ames denounced the hypocrisy of the societies but also addressed the need to educate the public. The administration would suffer if it did not make the case for its position because "the more ignorant the crowd, the more are they under the influence of the demagogues." Ames believed it essential to communicate. "The people must be very fully and repeatedly informed of their concerns. . . . Every federal man therefore should wish the national government and its proceedings should be kept in full view of the people." Once made aware of the situation, Ames thought, the public could choose wisely. Americans were distinguished for their "sober and orderly habits" as well as for "shrewd and penetrating sagacity." Thus, the American public, Ames believed, would "be able of itself to unmask its deceivers."[40]

In September, as the Whiskey Rebellion began to unfold, Ames, as he had done in the Genet matter, urged other Federalists to take their case to the public. The rebellion "cannot, I think, end badly for government, unless government flinches from its duty." However, he warned Massachusetts state representative Thomas Dwight that "Your papers should be kept right." Two months later, Ames again wrote to Dwight to discuss the recent debates in Congress about Washington's use of the term "self-created" societies, and the furor that ensued as the House debated whether or not to mention that phrase in its reply to the president. Again referring to the hoped-for impact on public opinion, Ames queried Dwight, "Would the insertion of the debates into your country papers have any good effect? . . . Every thing that will impress public opinion, as far as truth and decency allow, ought now to be urged, as the issue rests with the public, to hold up the clubs or the magistracy."[41] Of course, during the disputes of the 1790s Federalists made much of that trope—framing the issue as one of support either for some "other" (Genet, the whiskey rebels, the Democratic Societies, Jay Treaty opponents) or for Washington. But perhaps even more significant than the use of a time-honored framing device was the Federalists' recognition of the importance of taking their arguments to the newspapers, of keeping the papers "right," as Ames put it. Because different media reached different audiences—pamphlets reaching a smaller, more elite audience, newspapers and broadsides much larger ones—Federalists deliberately tried to carry their arguments through venues which would reach the most people. This awareness suggests that Federalists could be shrewd and sophisticated in their efforts to shape public opinion and in their understanding of how the process worked.[42]

Other Federalist leaders likewise emphasized the importance of putting their case before the public. In a long letter to Alexander Hamilton, former chief justice of the Vermont Supreme Court Nathaniel Chipman wrote that he had long been on record stating that in republics "the powers of government are supported, not by force, but by the sentiments of the people." Likewise, "it is necessary to cultivate a sentiment of attachment to the government." The Democratic Societies had perverted those principles. While they claimed to speak for "the people," they did not, could not, and could never claim to do so. Chipman distinguished between "simple democracy," in which all people met to enact laws—by nature a chaotic if not impossible practice which was very susceptible to passions—and "representative democracy," which provided an effective and organized means not only of gathering public opinion but of ensuring the protection of rights of life, liberty, and property. The clubs improperly attempted to voice the sentiments of the people, something which only a duly elected representative could do. The societies professed to spread political information, but, in truth, "they have assumed a dictatorial style in their resolves." "Like the demagogues of simple democracy," Chipman continued, "they have appealed wholly to the passions and jealousies of the people." Such improper influence must be countered by the friends of government. It was just as important, Chipman told Hamilton, "that the people should see and acknowledge the measures of government to be wise and good, as that they should be really wise and good." The only way citizens could form that good opinion was by having the information to judge properly. Thus, it was imperative that officials "render the reason of their measures plain and intelligible to the common sense of mankind."[43]

Federalists also worried that the democratic clubs were not being answered. Edward Carrington, U.S. Marshal for Virginia, wrote from Richmond in July that the societies were making a great deal of noise and were falsely assumed to be speaking for the people as a body. In fact, Carrington argued, the real problem was that "they speak loud in many places, & no one speaks against them, hence they claim a general concurrence of the people with them." Carrington noted, however, that whenever such bold presumptions were met with countervailing opinions, they could be put down, and that was precisely the course Federalists should follow now. "I have never yet seen an experiment tried of a counteraction, but it has produced good effects."[44] Hamilton himself, preparing to mobilize the militia to face down the whiskey rebels, wrote that the "friends of Government at Pittsburgh ought to rally their confidence and if necessary manifest it by Acts." Hamilton expected that the very existence of a beneficial government would produce "a most rigorous and persevering effort; in which the known good sense and love of order of the quiet body of the people" would lead to their support for the administration. Hamilton believed, like Ames, Chipman, and Carrington, that the key was to mobilize supporters of the administration to counter the opposing forces.[45]

As he did before in the Neutrality Crisis and would do again a year later in the Jay Treaty debate, Hamilton produced a set of essays designed, as so many Federalists had been advocating, to take the administration's case to the public and advance the Federalist cause. Although neither as long, as numerous, nor as well-known as his previous "Pacificus" and later "Camillus" essays, the four "Tully" essays Hamilton drafted in August and September 1794 had the same intent: to expose the errors of the opposition and to persuade and mobilize the public and bring them to support the administration. The first essay assured citizens that the author knew of their "firm attachment to the government you have established." It also urged them to "clearly discern" the true nature of the insurrection and to avoid giving credence to those whose sly yet unfounded criticisms of government could mislead. "Virtuous and enlightened citizens of a now happy country! ye could not be the dupes of artifices so detestable . . . ye cannot but remember that the government is YOUR OWN work," and that in supporting the administration's officials and their policies, citizens were in fact supporting their own representatives and their own power.[46]

Central to the Federalists' line of argument was the primacy of the constituted authorities and the need for the public to support them. John Fenno's *Gazette of the United States* stated very plainly, in March 1794, "The present is a critical period with the United States." In order to steer the ship of state through the crisis, the public had to support its officials. It all depended, warned the paper, on centering the "wisdom and firmness of Americans. Congress and the President form that centre; if we have not confidence in their decisions, *all is lost*—The ship must be under THEIR command or she will be wrecked." Administration supporters also contrasted the legitimacy of elected officials with the illegitimacy (in their view) of the societies and clubs. In February, Fenno's paper drew a contrast between a "*real patriot*" and a "*Pseudo-Patriot.*" The latter was given to addressing the passions and prejudices of the people and leading them hastily into measures they would later regret. Such pseudopatriots were given to "tickle our ears by flattering our pride," but such flattery was dangerous because it could "draw [away] from us the advantages we possess." In contrast, the real patriot "weighs deliberately the consequences of measures," puts aside momentary passions and intrigues, and "steadily pursues what his judgment and information indicate as the true and permanent interests of his country." Here the Federalists emphasized the need for careful study of and deliberation on public measures as well as the importance of putting calm reason over emotion, themes they consistently emphasized in all three crises.[47]

Federalists made the contrast between elected officials and the leaders of the clubs explicit. "The representatives of the people are known—but who knows the members of those clubs who have assumed the dictatorship of the United States?" asked one newspaper correspondent. The writer scoffed dismissively, "who would transfer their confidence from the representatives of the people, to place it on these men." Calling the presence of the democratic clubs a "competition for influence" with the duly elected representatives, this writer charged that such a power struggle would be death for American liberties. Other correspondents took up the same theme. If the nation's liberties were to be subverted, "no fitter instruments can be provided than self-created Legislators, who owe no responsibility to the people." The very notion of a self-created society threatened popular sovereignty, Federalists argued. "Do the people require intermediary guides betwixt them and the constituted authorities? . . . Are they [the clubs] chosen by the people? If not . . . I shall hereafter regard them as self-creators, as a branch, perhaps, of the Jacobin Society of Paris." Another commented that public men discharging their duty who are attacked by "the disorganizers of the day" should wear that criticism as a badge of honor: "uncommon *merit,* gives rise to this pointed abuse."[48]

As usual, Federalists drew a clear contrast between the people's true representatives and their purported friends in underscoring the centrality of the constituted authorities. Citizens spoke not in town meetings or in clubs, but at election time when they chose their officials. When "the *real* voice of *the people* is heard—as it most emphatically is, on the day of election, we are then *convinced* that the noise we have heard, was false and hollow." Federalists also tried to encourage support for the constituted authorities by calling on citizens to display their native "good sense." Here, too, just as they did previously in the Neutrality and Genet controversies and as they would do later in the Jay Treaty debate, Federalists claimed that the "good sense of the citizens" was naturally behind the government. If that good sense was "misled by lies and calumny" and public men and officials were attacked, that support could be undermined—but this tactic had its dangers, if opponents went too far in their attacks and affronted "the good sense of our people." When "calumniators" stretched their charges beyond credulity and beyond any strength of evidence, "the extravagance of their malice is in a considerable degree an antidote against its poison."[49]

Republican leaders were once again in a difficult position. Opposing the Whiskey Rebellion and having to be careful how they addressed the question of the Democratic Societies, lest they seem to be favoring extra-constitutional government, Jefferson, Madison, and others had to tread carefully. Despite being forced by Federalist attacks onto turf difficult to defend, Republicans fought back gamely, aiming to state their principled disagreement with Federalist policies and score points in the public contest, while minimizing any damage to their own interest so that they might still be effective in future contests. The correspondence among Republican leaders and their speeches in Congress suggest that the party took a two-fold approach: minimize damage to the Republican interest by distancing themselves from the rebellion and the societies, while still taking opportunities, where they arose, to articulate their principles and defend themselves from unfair or blanket accusations.

As the House of Representatives debated a response to the president's message on the western insurrection, Madison spoke artfully and found a way to avoid defending the societies (he barely mentioned them at all), a tactic which had the useful effect of distancing the Republicans from the clubs. At the same time, Madison's speech recast the problem in larger, general terms and, while not suggesting overt hostility, nonetheless directed some barbs at the administration's actions. Most importantly, Madison articulated broad principles which redounded as much to the benefit of the Republican interest as to that of the Federalists. "If we advert to the nature of republican government, we shall find that the censorial power is in the people over the government, and not in the government over the people." But the censorial power was really of little necessity. Having confidence in the "good sense and patriotism" of the American people, Madison "did not anticipate any lasting evil to result from the publications of these societies; they will stand or fall," Madison observed, "by the public opinion. . . . The law is the only rule of right; what is consistent with that is not punishable; what is not contrary to that, is innocent, or at least not censurable by the legislative body." Madison went on to comment that most Americans had been able to sort out the details of the insurrection and had the "proper sentiments" to condemn the insurgents themselves while not reproving innocent associations. "In a republic, light will prevail over darkness, truth over error." The genius of Madison's speech—many of the sentiments of which found their way into the House response to the president—was in its strategy of admitting without contest the error of the insurrectionists while seeking to limit the censure to those participants alone, and not to either the societies or the Republican party more generally. In addition, Madison's comments about law, about light prevailing over dark, and about public opinion being the arbiter of justice were sentiments to which members of *both* parties could nod their heads in agreement—even as the two sides could interpret his words in strikingly different ways and fill in his generalities with quite different particulars.[50]

But while Madison was careful and tactful in his public utterances, his private correspondence makes it clear just how disturbing he found the Federalist agitation on the matter. Washington's denunciation of the societies was "perhaps the greatest error of his political life," he told James Monroe. He noted that some were eager to seize on the crisis as a pretense "to increase the momentum of power," just as Madison believed had happened following Shays's Rebellion in Massachusetts in 1786. Thomas Jefferson was just as troubled. He told Madison, "The denunciation of the democratic societies is one of the extraordinary acts of boldness of which we have seen so many from the faction of Monocrats. It is wonderful indeed that the President should have permitted himself to be the organ of such an attack on the freedom of discussion, the freedom of writing, printing & publishing."[51]

While Jefferson and Madison wrote and worked behind the scenes, the Republican press, led by Benjamin Franklin Bache, kept up its own chorus of opposition to the administration. By October, Bache was regularly pillorying Hamilton in scathing attacks which, in the words of Bache's biographer, painted Hamilton as a "conspirator" against liberty and a "potential despot." Federalist editors fought back, and readers of the nation's papers followed an intense newspaper war in fall 1794. Much of Bache's firepower was turned to defending the societies from charges that they fomented the Whiskey Rebellion. Eventually, Bache seemed to settle on a strategy of condemning the excise tax and defending the right of the Democratic Societies to exist, but never going so far as to defend rebellious means of overturning the tax. Bache, like Madison and Jefferson, saw the Democratic Societies as a crucial vehicle for rallying and mobilizing public opinion and preserving the democratic revolution. He had learned from past skirmishes like the Genet controversy that spirit and zeal were not enough in the face of organization and determined pressure. But the failure of the Democratic Societies in the face of organized pressure from Federalists increased Bache's awareness of the importance of the press as a tool to rally the public and organize opposition to administration measures. Bache's partisanship and his sense of the importance of the work he and other Republican editors were doing for the larger cause increased throughout the 1790s and reached a peak with the Jay Treaty debate in 1795–96. In November 1794, Bache made all of this clear to the public. He added the word "Aurora" to his newspaper's title and articulated to readers his mission as he saw it: "The AURORA, as far as the editor's exertions extend, shall diffuse light within the sphere of its influence,—dispel the shades of ignorance, and gloom of error and thus tend to strengthen the fair fabric of freedom on its surest foundation, publicity and information."[52]

Throughout 1794, at the height of the controversies over the Democratic Societies and the Whiskey Rebellion, Federalists took dead aim at the clubs or "self-created" societies, excoriating them for their disloyal and extra-constitutional role in the nation and questioning the patriotism of those who organized and led the societies. From February to October and beyond, Federalist newspapers raged against the clubs and the threats they posed to representative government. These denunciations, joined with Washington's famous condemnation, influenced public opinion and helped turn the clubs into unpopular and disgraced enterprises. They subsequently lost their stature and gradually disappeared from the scene—but Federalists did not leave this to chance, and made a concerted effort to undermine the propriety and legitimacy of the societies. This campaign touched on themes common in Federalist appeals to the public in the middle 1790s and served as a rehearsal for the lines of argument they would deploy in the Jay Treaty debate.

One correspondent linked the current controversies back to the Neutrality issue, arguing that "our incendiary faction pretend to be on the side of the people, and they rail . . . at the creatures of the *court.*" However, these pretended voices of the people "found their doctrine overthrown by the people themselves. . . . Facts shew how little these wretches, respect the people, or are supported by them." Another raised the specter of French influence on American politics—a favorite Federalist trope—by asking pointedly of the societies, "if a man is bound as a good and true Mobocrat to hate and undermine the Republican Government of his own country, how happens it that you oblige him to swear to be faithful and true to an anarchy, nicknamed republican, beyond seas?"[53]

As attacks on the societies escalated over the summer, their themes were refined into increasingly effective instruments of assault. Federalists took great delight in skewering the societies by pointing to the growth of public opposition to the clubs, drawing a contrast between the people and their pretended spokesmen and linking the societies to France at every turn. "The disorganizers of this country who pretend to be the staunch friends of liberty, have long since forfeited all right to that distinguished character. . . . The real friends of the equal rights of man . . . regret excesses which not only tarnish the lustre of the best of causes, but put to hazard the eventual establishment of a free government."[54]

In a long critique addressed sarcastically to "the Great and Mighty Democratic Society of New York" and originally published in Noah Webster's *American Minerva,* "A Federal Republican" wondered what induced the society to print a long self-vindication. "Have you discovered that public opinion is against you; that you are dwindling fast into contempt; that the steady firmness of our government is like to defeat all your schemes; that elections do not go right. . . . The people of America are not so stupid as to be unable to discover the benefits of your institutions, if any such exists." He intimated that the society saw itself losing ground in the public war and felt the need to strike out in need of support. "A Federal Republican" dissected at length the hypocrisies and inconsistencies he saw in the New York club and contrasted its mode of behavior with that of the supporters of the duly chosen government. "We have no clandestine meetings to manage opinions, to concert plans, to frame resolutions. We reprobate all such practices. You on the other hand, with the most solemn professions of being friends to equal rights, form yourselves into a private club." Further, the clubs denounced the anonymous writers who took up pens against them yet thought nothing of dispatching their own to attack the leaders of government. Lest anyone mistake his inclinations, the writer assured readers that he was "no tory, no British agent, no speculator." He was a friend to farmers, had no connection to the Englishmen, never took part in the funding of debts, and was under no influence but that of "truth and integrity." Finally, he concluded that he knew the "general opinion of the midling class of people about the country, and he [knew] that they generally reprobate Democratic Societies; considering them merely as Genet's scouting parties."[55]

Republicans were frustrated but not fooled by Federalist tactics. In fact, they saw almost immediately what kind of game their rivals were playing against them, as Madison communicated to Jefferson and Monroe in almost the same terms. To Jefferson: "It was obvious that a most dangerous game was playing ag[ain]st. Republicanism. The insurrection was universally & deservedly odious. The Democratic Societies were presented as in league with it. The Republican part of Cong[res]s were to be drawn into an *ostensible,* patronage of those Societies, and into an ostensible opposition to the President." He told Jefferson it was not yet clear how this game would turn out, but warned, "If the people of America are so far degenerated already as not to see or to see with indifference, that the Citadel of their liberties is menaced by the precedent before their eyes, they require abler advocates than they now have, to save them from the consequences." In very similar language he explained to Monroe that "The game was, to connect the democratic Societies with the odium of the insurrection—to connect the Republicans in Cong[res]s with those Societies—to put the P[resident] ostensibly at the head of the other party, in opposition to both, and by these means prolong the illusions in the North—& try a new experiment on the South." The Republicans understood that the Federalists were trying to box them in by constructing a narrative designed to cast the activities of the clubs, the whiskey rebels, and the Republicans in the worst possible light. As one scholar has noted, the Federalists succeeded both in imposing their own narrow version of what constituted legitimate political action, and in destroying, by labeling as "subversive," the societies' claims that they spoke for or represented "the people."[56]

With the approach of fall and the perceived turn of public opinion to the administration's position, Federalists stepped up the attacks. "Nothing can be more laughable and ridiculous than to see little vagabond societies and committees throughout the United States . . . *Resolving* in the most pompous dictatorial style" against particular measures of government, noted "Order" contemptuously. These clubs fired off opinions and resolutions with little regard for the complexities and intricacies of the issues at hand. Congress, consisting presumably of men "eminent for learning and patriotism," spent great amounts of time deliberating on the key issues because they were important and difficult questions. "But the inhabitants of a township in Cumberland," he noted incredulously, "settle the matter at once, at a single meeting," where, he surmised, "some preternatural wiseman presided and *dictated*."[57]

A letter to Benjamin Russell's *Columbian Centinel* (Boston) in early October asked point blank, "What is the use and advantage of clubs?" and proceeded to answer with a scathing indictment of the presumption and underhandedness of the societies, underscoring all the central ideas of the Federalists' campaign against them. The correspondent argued that the clubs claimed they were formed to collect political information, then asked why they presumed that they had special access to information "which the people in general have not." This argument would prove a durable one for

Federalists in the 1790s as they practiced what might be termed triangulation: they posited the clubs as improperly coming between the people and their duly chosen representatives, in much the same way they would argue, in the Jay Treaty debate, that anti-treaty town meetings were improper interferences between the public and their chosen government. If the country's citizens wanted to meet to consult, "what better club can be desired than a town meeting, where all is day light, and the law has regulated the proceedings in such a manner as to secure to every man his fair and equal privilege." Hitting on another persistent theme of the Federalists, the writer noted that while the clubs "affect to be *popular*" societies, "They are not so. They are aristocratic," for they usurp the role reserved for the people's legislators in a republican government.[58]

Federalists stressed throughout the fall that "the eyes of the people are opened to discover, and detect, the gross fals[e]hoods which have been palmed upon them as facts for the last two years." Lamenting the establishment of anti-administration newspapers, this writer ("A Federalist") detailed the attacks on the administration and the efforts at undermining public confidence in the authorities. The public had but to "re-peruse in the hour of calm inquiry" the slanders against the administration to realize that the criticisms were "the most absurd and ridiculous." The writer took satisfaction in knowing that the public, in checking the veracity of such claims, would see the blatant lies and deceptions for what they were. The insurgents in western Pennsylvania surely realized as much themselves. The rebels "must be convinced from the readiness of the militia to march against them, that all attempts to overturn . . . the powers of a government, based on the hearts of the people, will be impotent." In short, the people as a body were now solidly on the side of the administration, not the insurgents, and this recognition along with the show of federal strength could not have gone unfelt.[59]

At least one of the societies fought back publicly, to Madison's great delight. The Baltimore Society flatly denied Washington's charge that the societies had in any way fomented the rebellion. Not willing to back down in the face of Washington's popularity and mounting public support, this society refused to silently accept the criticism being routinely poured out by Federalist pens. Madison observed that the Federalist attack seemed not to have been as sweepingly successful in disgracing the Republicans as it had been in undermining the societies. "You will see," he told Jefferson, "that the appeal is begun to the public sentiment, by the injured parties. The Republican Society of Baltimore set the example. That of Newark has advertised a meeting of its members." In other parts of the country there was similar resistance to Federalist abuse. Madison commented that in Boston, for instance, "the subject is well understood, and handled in the Newspaper on the republican side, with industry and address."[60]

Nonetheless, the newspapers that fall were filled with other forms of testimonial in support of the administration and its stance. Petitions and resolutions to President Washington offered support for his position while restating many of the themes Federalists had been using for weeks. When Washington himself headed the military force to western Pennsylvania, he was greeted enthusiastically. Large crowds turned out to see the extraordinary sight of the president leading an army to put down a rebellion which was now nearly nonexistent. On the evening of October 8 in Carlisle, Washington was met by a crowd of "federal citizens" who displayed large illuminated transparencies bearing the messages "Washington Is Ever Triumphant," "The Reign of the Laws" and "Woe to Anarchists." It must have been exceptionally pleasing to both Washington and the Federalists, who had hoped for and worked to create such a response.

Even more to the point was an address from the citizens of Carlisle the following Monday. Calling themselves "friends to good order, government and the laws," the subscribers praised the president for his virtues and leadership "at this critical period of impending foreign and domestic troubles." They denounced the rebellion, assured Washington of the citizens' "love of order, and attachment to the constitution and laws," and expressed their willingness to put down foreign as well as domestic insurgents who threatened that order. The address went on to lament the efforts by the opposition to mislead and misrepresent facts in order to "delude our fellow citizens." Noting that they "trust[ed] the efforts of the General Government, the combination of the good and virtuous against the vicious and factious," the subscribers concluded with a hopeful prayer for "our internal peace and stability of our government" and a long life for Washington.[61]

Having received praise and support for exactly the things Federalists advocated during the crisis, Washington could not have been more pleased, and he expressed his thanks in his reply to the Carlisle address. The president was gratified by the "enlightened and patriotic attachment which is manifested towards our happy constitution and the laws." He hoped that the recent "delusions," "murmurs," and "tumults" would not last and that "reason will steadily regain her empire, and the laws their full authority." "Let the wise & the virtuous unite their efforts to reclaim the misguided, and to detect and defeat the arts of the factious." Like the petitioners, Washington praised the stability of the government, invoked the need for internal peace, and spoke of the desire to establish "the authority of the laws in the affections of all, rather than in the fears of any," even if it required him as president to "raise the sword of justice" on occasion.[62]

As public opinion began to turn that fall against the whiskey rebels and their justifications for protest, as the nation seemed to be siding with the hero of the Revolution instead of with those who claimed to uphold the revolutionary legacy, Washington and his administration received support from some unlikely sources. This was a testament not only to Washington's unequaled stature, but to Federalist efforts to shape the campaign on their terms and and define it on their rhetorical turf.

On September 24 one group of citizens in Newark met and unanimously adopted a set of resolutions. They read as if they had been drafted by the administration's strongest followers. The document declared that an "essential ingredient" in republican government was that the will of the majority must govern. To profess otherwise "unhinges every principle of freedom, by setting up the will of the few against that of the many." At no time, the resolution claimed, had the government so needed to hear the voice of support from its citizens. It denounced the actions of the whiskey rebels, proclaiming that if they believed the laws were unjust they had selected the wrong method of appealing. Instead of violence and force, they should have relied on reasoned argument to make their case. Affirming their support for the duly constituted authorities, the signers declared, "To the wise and well constructed governments, we have cheerfully confided our lives and our prosperities, and pledge ourselves to our country to support as far in our power, their constitutional operations."

Nothing unusual in that. Only at the end of the resolution could one see something out of the ordinary. Stating that any attempt to stifle free investigation into the conduct of government was "as dangerous to civil liberty, as to rise in arms against its constitutional operations," the resolution advocated a moderate position, a middle ground which recognized the legitimate claims of both sides in the recent contest. The document closed, however, by echoing the Baltimore Society in declaring it unfair to condemn all Democratic Societies for the work of a few, noting that it was grossly unfair to blame the societies for the rebellion. The source of this set of resolutions? None other than the Democratic Society of Newark, New Jersey. One of the abominated "self-created" societies had been won over to the Federalist position, or at least had declined to leap into the abyss it saw other societies running towards. That one of the Democratic Societies would issue such a statement suggests not only the speed and certainty with which public opinion turned against the rebellion (and, to a great degree, against the societies as well), but how effective the Federalist arguments about trusting the constituted authorities, the sanctity of the laws, and the proper degree of reverence for Washington had become.[63]

As Republicans reflected on the debates of recent months in late 1794 and early 1795, at least one of them believed he saw a silver lining. While Madison was probably too much involved in the debates in Congress and on the front lines of the struggle for public support, Thomas Jefferson's detachment from the immediate conflict gave him a broader perspective, not to mention the leisure to take the long view. Despite the battering the Republicans and the societies had taken, Jefferson remained optimistic. In a letter to Madison, he first offered an overview of the controversy, but then noted, "However the time is coming when we shall fetch up the lee-way of our vessel," using one of his preferred nautical metaphors. "The changes in your house," he told Madison, "I see are going on for the better, and even the Augean herd [the Senate] over your heads are slowly purging off their impurities. Hold on then, my dear friend, that we may not ship-wreck in the mean while." Jefferson thus gave voice to the confidence and optimism he frequently showed during the 1790s, even as so many of the conflicts of that decade were seemingly going against his side.[64]

If Republicans—who had ostensibly lost the public debate over the societies and been embarrassed by the rebellion—were confident about the future in spite of such apparent setbacks, the victorious Federalists did not sound much like winners. If anything, they seemed strangely pessimistic for a group that had just won a substantial battle for public opinion. As friends of the administration assessed the uproar over the Democratic Societies and the Whiskey Rebellion, they recognized that a combination of factors had produced their success, even as they looked ahead to likely challenges and to ways they might minimize their effect. Perhaps no one summed up the matter more concisely than Fisher Ames, who wrote that "had not Harry Lee been Governor of Virginia, probably that region would have been *whiskeyed*. The State for a long time acted a whiskey part, till, by the zeal of New Jersey, the talents of the little Secretary [Hamilton], the weight of the President's name, and bad management among the rioters, the tide turned in favor of government."[65] Ames noted the instruments Federalists had deployed and the opposition weaknesses they had exploited in both the Neutrality and Whiskey crises: the written rhetoric of Hamilton, the labors to mobilize the public, the incomparable stature of George Washington, and the imprudent, unwise, or outlandish actions of intriguers (be they foreign in the case of Genet or native in the persons of the whiskey rebels) which put Jefferson, Madison, and other responsible opposition leaders in awkward and often embarrassing situations.

But to certain Federalists something still seemed amiss. Perhaps it was the tenuous and fortuitous ways in which circumstances unfolded to the Federalists' benefit in both instances, or perhaps it was their ongoing concern about the nature of republican government and the need for eternal vigilance to guard against usurpations of the constituted authorities. Whatever may have prompted it, some leaders sensed—even as they gloried in the successful resolution of the Whiskey Rebellion—that the celebrations might be short-lived, or were at least premature. In these forebodings, Federalists prefigured the nagging fears and doubts they would express again during the Jay Treaty controversy.

Fisher Ames, writing to Thomas Dwight in December 1794, granted that the government might seem to stand "on better ground than it ever did." But Ames wished "exceedingly that our sober citizens should weigh matters well. Faction is only baffled," he feared, "not repenting, not changed. New grounds will be found or invented for stirring up sedition." Unless the nation was "deeply sensible" of the recent dangers and, even more, "of the true characters of our public men, new troubles will arise." Ames looked ahead to the next election and could only hope that citizens saw matters clearly. "Will the people, seeing this pit open, approach it again by sending those to Congress who led them blindfold to its brink?" It was crucial, Ames believed, that the people "interpose in the appointed way, by excluding mobocrats from legislation." Ames had faith, he noted, "that very plain dealing with them [the people] would work a change, even in Virginia."[66]

Ames's concerns were echoed by others. Early the next spring, Jesse Appleton, president of Bowdoin College, also wrote with an eye to coming elections. He told his correspondent that he worried about lingering effects of the Democratic Societies on politics, and denied that they ever had been or ever could be truly democratic. Despite their appellation, they in fact behaved as aristocratic organizations for the intention of controlling elections. "Is it not a very serious thing, that some of the Jacobinical societies have been instituted . . . to superintend elections? . . . is it not plain, beyond contradiction, that their tendency is aristocratical? For what is aristocracy but for a few to engross the power of the whole?" Appleton lamented, too, that there were "many pliant people among us, who have a devout veneration for every thing that comes from France, & vary their own opinion, so as to comply with every new measure." Such a situation could only augur poorly for the future.[67]

Alexander Hamilton knew, also, that Federalists must be prepared to fight again, and soon. Despite the achievements to date, he believed the administration would be facing even greater challenges in the months ahead. Even as he was writing about putting down the rebellion (to Rufus King in late October 1794), he was struck by the ever-present potential for trouble. Hamilton was blunt. "The political putrefaction of Pen[n]-sylvania is greater than I had any idea of," he wrote. "Without vigour every where our tranquillity is likely to be of very short duration & the next storm will be infinitely worse than the present one."[68]

This was no mere premonition. Hamilton had been corresponding with John Jay on the status of Jay's negotiations with Great Britain. Knowing the details of the negotiations and the emerging outlines of what would become the Jay Treaty, able to anticipate the objections that would be raised and the furor that would likely result, Hamilton had ample reason to expect that the administration would not be in calm waters for long.

3 | The Firestorm and the Counterattack

First Soundings in the Public Debate

"TOWN MEETING—TREATY!" the handbill screamed, begging Philadelphia's residents to take notice. "CITIZENS, assemble at the State-House, on Thursday Afternoon, the 23 instant, at 5 o'clock, then and there to discuss the Momentous Question, viz: Are the People the Legitimate Fountain of Government. . . . *Attend!* Your rights are invaded!"[1] Those who attended the July 23 State House meeting "considered and UNANIMOUSLY adopted" a series of resolutions condemning the treaty and appointed a committee to prepare a memorial to President George Washington "respectfully but forcibly conveying the sentiments of the City of Philadelphia."[2] Two days later a large crowd assembled to cheer the reading of the anti-treaty memorial, which argued that the treaty, among other shortcomings, did not provide for the fair settlement of the outstanding differences with Great Britain and harmed U.S. relations with France. The memorial closed with the request that Washington "evince an exalted attachment to the principles of the Constitution . . . and an undiminished zeal to advance the prosperity and happiness of your constituents" by refusing to ratify the treaty.[3]

In meetings like these held throughout the country citizens turned out to hear and jeer the treaty. They listened to attacks on the measure, its negotiator, the administration that sponsored the mission, and the Senate that approved it. These meetings were often large, sometimes contentious, and always exciting, as they represented huge steps in the evolution of popular political participation. As citizens attended out-of-doors meetings, signed petitions, and read, discussed, and debated the printed versions of the treaty and the extensive newspaper commentaries on it, they became political actors on a scale not seen since the Revolution. With its increased involvement and growing presence, the public—or, more precisely, an imprecisely defined "public opinion"—was courted by both sides in the treaty debate. Not for the first time, but to a degree never previously seen, there was a widespread recognition on all sides of the crucial need to inform, persuade, and mobilize the public, and—once constructed as desired—to swing public opinion into the service of one position or the other. Appeals were made by both sides through a variety of means. All adversaries were aware that the battle over the treaty would be fought primarily in the arena of public opinion, and that to triumph in such a contest required using measures beyond the usual operating procedures. Because the treaty dealt with such clearly significant issues, the struggle over its passage became much more than a perfunctory exercise in public appeals. Indeed, the stakes were so self-evidently important to both sides that they justified what the participants themselves sometimes regarded as extraordinary actions. Some of these measures were undertaken only because necessity overrode discomfort with new practices, because the need to secure vital interests trumped the fear of the unfamiliar in the evolving politics of public opinion.

The first stage of the treaty debate took place during the summer and early fall of 1795. Following upon some anticipatory behind-the-scenes maneuvering, the July 1, 1795, publication of the treaty sparked the actual public debate. There was, first, a relatively brief but fierce contest to obtain—or discourage—a ratifying presidential signature on the treaty recently approved by the Senate. During this crucial six-week period, public opinion was being shaped by both sides so that it might be brought to bear on President Washington. Once word got out that the president had signed the treaty in mid-August, both supporters and opponents would regroup and plan for the next phase of the contest, while the public, stirred to such passions during the summer and soon to be aroused again, settled into a less turbulent fall and winter. But the calm was an illusion. Forces were gathering for one last fight on the floor of the House of Representatives, in the streets, and in the newspapers.

This chapter explores that first stage, the period of initial efforts to influence Washington's decision. It will cover the behind-the-scenes discussions, on both sides, over how public appeals should be made, as well as the start of the newspaper war. I begin, however, by examining the public meetings—largely against, but occasionally for the treaty—in some detail, so as to analyze not only *what* was being done and said, but *how.*

While scholars have taken note of the demonstrations, they have rarely dissected the crowds which turned out to oppose or, less frequently at first, support the treaty. By looking closely at the content of the demonstrations—what was done, what was said, how actions and speech were constructed, how they were reported—we can gain greater insight into the treaty debate itself, but also into the dynamics of the emerging public sphere of early national America. For in examining the individual meetings and rallies with an eye to their content, and not merely to the fact of their existence, we can discern some significant differences between the pro- and anti-treaty meetings which bear on the larger struggles between Federalists and Republicans.

One significant anti-treaty meeting, widely reported in newspapers around the nation, took place in Boston. When the treaty was published, a group of citizens petitioned the selectmen to call a town meeting "to know the sentiments of the inhabitants on this important question"; it was set for July 10th. On that Friday, a crowd of 1,500 gathered at Faneuil Hall, chose Thomas Dawes as moderator, and proceeded to discuss the treaty. Charles Jarvis criticized the measure, arguing that it contained no reciprocity for the United States, and asked his fellow citizens to state what could possibly be gained by adopting the treaty. A "Mr. J Hall" spoke next, declaring that he did not intend "to vindicate any part of the Treaty" but wondered about the propriety and constitutionality of the town meeting acting on the subject. Was it not, Hall asked, better to assume that the "respective departments of the Government . . . had acted from the best evidence before them, for the interest of the United States?" Hall was immediately answered by Jarvis and by Joseph Blake, who spoke out for the right of the people to express their sentiments "on all matters in which their interest was concerned."[4]

Someone next made a motion to read the treaty, but this was dismissed; since the measure "had been so universally read by the citizens, it would be a needless delay." A general discussion ensued, during which it was observed that the measure was "proved to the satisfaction of the audience" to be "ruinous and destructive to the commerce, rights, and interest of this country." The moderator then asked if the town approved of the treaty. Not a hand was raised, according to the account, but when negative votes were called for, all hands went up. "The spirit and order of the meeting," according to one proud observer, "was as great as ever appeared on any former interesting subject." Participants were outspoken in their opposition, and unanimity prevailed in condemning all parts of the document. Finally, a committee of fifteen gentlemen was appointed to summarize in writing the complaints against the treaty, and directed to present its report on the following Monday.[5]

That Monday, the committee presented its report to a reconvened town meeting which heard twenty resolutions against the treaty read, and then adopted them "without one dissenting voice." The preamble to the set of resolutions stated, as the "sense of the inhabitants of this town," that the measure, if ratified, would be "highly injurious" to the nation's commercial interests, "derogatory" to the national honor, and "dangerous" to the peace and happiness of its citizens. The reasons stated in the Boston resolutions would be echoed by other anti-treaty groups around the nation.[6] Listed first was the charge that the treaty lacked reciprocity, that it fully provided for assuaging the complaints of Great Britain while addressing only part of the problems on the U.S. side. The resolutions went on to condemn the document for making no indemnification to U.S. citizens for property lost during the Revolution, for not reaching agreement on the matter of British impressment of American sailors, for placing U.S. trade in an unfair and disadvantageous position relative to British trade, and offered other related complaints. They concluded with an appeal to George Washington, praising him and hoping his "prudence, fortitude, and wisdom, which have more than once been eminently instrumental in the salvation of his country, will be equally conspicuous on the present occasion, and that the reasons we have assigned will have their influence to withhold his signature from the ratification of this alarming instrument." The town meeting, after passing the resolutions written by the committee, voted to express thanks to Virginia senator Stevens T. Mason, whose leaking of the treaty led to its publication, "thereby giving an *opportunity* to the Citizens to express their sentiments on so important and interesting a subject."[7]

One interested observer of the Boston events was Dr. Nathaniel Ames, the brother of Massachusetts' Federalist congressman Fisher Ames. In contrast to his better known brother, Nathaniel was a staunch Republican and an acerbic critic of Federalists and their policies. In June, after an outline of the treaty had been published, Nathaniel Ames noted in his diary that the measure "is the highest insult on the feelings of Americans of anything that has happened this long time." His diary entry for July 4, 1795, noted approvingly that Philadelphians had celebrated Independence by burning effigies of Jay as well as copies of his treaty. Ames made a lengthier entry on the July 13 Boston meeting and on the U.S. Senate which approved the treaty: "Boston Town Meeting unanimously condemn it, and it seems strange that a majority and so large a majority of American Senators could be found so tainted with aristocratic notions as to approve it. If they had voted to reproclaim the right of the British Parliament to bind America in all cases whatsoever, I should not have been much more surprised! and the best celebration of the 4th July was to burn Jay's effigy and his Treaty." Throughout the summer Boston saw more crowd activity opposing the treaty. Some protesters hollowed out a watermelon shell, carved it in the shape of a man's face, and paraded it through the streets. Federalists like Fisher Ames denounced such gatherings as "mobs," and appealed to Governor Samuel Adams, who dismissed such shenanigans as "a mere watermelon frolic, the harmless amusement of young persons." Nathaniel Ames saw no reason to mention these protests in his diary that summer.[8]

Accounts of the Boston meeting quickly reached New York. On Thursday evening newspaper notices called readers to a meeting on Saturday, July 19, at 12 o'clock, for the purpose of "uniting their common efforts with their fellow-citizens of Boston" in denouncing the treaty. On Friday a handbill was circulated which expressed sentiments against the treaty, noting that it "yields advantages which we ought never to part with, but with our lives." This handbill also spoke of the treaty's principles as "dangerous to the liberties and happiness of the people, and destructive of our freedom and independence," and urged citizens to attend.[9]

New Yorkers gathered at noon, as appointed, in large numbers—between five and seven thousand people—in what proved to be one of the most tumultuous meetings held on the treaty. Confusion reigned as treaty opponents jousted with a group of merchants who favored the measure. Alexander Hamilton and the leading merchants were determined not to cede the field to their opponents. One Federalist dismissed the anti-treaty crowd, sneering that it consisted of "mechanics, laborers, cartmen with their horses, the hod men, the clam men." What followed was a scene of great tension and animosity. Leaders of both sides insisted on being heard and refused to back down. At one point Hamilton climbed the steps of a building and tried to speak at the same time anti-treaty advocates were calling for a chair for the meeting. Republican Peter R. Livingston called for the floor but Hamilton would not budge. Cries of "hear him, hear him" alternated with hisses from treaty opponents. Those opponents called for a vote but Hamilton insisted that they should discuss the measure first. Republicans insisted the crowd divide according to its opinion on the treaty but this only provoked further confusion while failing to resolve the issue. Hamilton then gave a written resolution to the chair which read, in part, "Resolved, That it does not appear necessary to this meeting to express any opinion on the Treaty . . . inasmuch as they have full confidence in the wisdom and virtue of the President of the United States, to whom, in conjunction with the Senate, the decision of the question constitutionally belongs." This met with predictable ire and scorn, and treaty opponents then insisted on appointing a committee to draw up a resolution condemning the measure. Hamilton retreated with his allies, but not before becoming the target of violence himself, being pelted with stones according to some accounts. This back-and-forth continued for ninety minutes. At 1:30 p.m., William S. Smith, who Republicans had chosen to preside over the meeting, called for adjournment until a committee could draft a set of anti-treaty resolutions. The adjournment did little to sooth the tension. Leaving the demonstration, a furious Hamilton encountered two political adversaries on the street and promptly issued two challenges to duel.[10] The New Yorkers—minus Federalists, who stayed away this time—reconvened on the following Monday and drafted a set of anti-treaty resolutions which condemned the measure in much the same language and on the same grounds as the Boston resolves had.[11]

Anti-treaty rallies in smaller towns took on many of the same features as those held in big cities. In Portsmouth, New Hampshire, in September 1795, according to one account, "about 300 of our patriotic citizens, formed a procession, and marched through all the principal streets of the town, with EFFIGIES of JAY and GRENVILLE drawn in a cart." The procession was accompanied by martial music and "proceeded to the Long Wharf, where they erected a large bonfire, and communicated their Highness's to the flames." Once finished, the crowd returned to their homes; the correspondent noted proudly that "every person was perfectly calm and no disturbance of any kind took place." The account of the demonstration concluded with a terse dismissal: "So much for Mr. Jay's Treaty."

The entire demonstration had been prompted by "a subscription paper, handed about by an active Aristocrat," claiming that the town's vote against the treaty in an earlier public meeting was not an accurate representation of its commercial interests. Another account of the same incident noted that the town "was in perfect quiet, all animosity having disappeared as to the treaty . . . when about 33 men came forward, some by co[a]xing, some by threats and some with some other motive, in favor of the treaty, against the unanimous voice of the town." This was too much for some of the citizens, apparently Revolutionary War veterans. "The honest old [17]75 Captains and his [17]75 soldiers could not brook the insult: they came out, but in a manner as orderly as was the processions in that town when the Constitution was adopted." Both accounts testified to the orderliness as well as the firm resolve of the anti-treaty demonstrators.[12]

These protests did not just arise spontaneously. Anti-treaty activists were busy up and down the eastern seaboard that summer, organizing opposition to the hated measure. Benjamin Franklin Bache's *Aurora* office "became the command center" of efforts to mobilize opposition to the treaty. Bache printed thousands of copies of the treaty in pamphlet form and took them with him to distribute as he went north to New York and Boston. He sent another courier south with more copies. Bache found warm welcomes from other Republican editors and party activists along the way, and together they helped to plan and organize anti-treaty rallies and protests.[13] While Bache and other editors were doing their best to mobilize opposition, U.S. House clerk and Republican political operative John Beckley was also furiously active, keeping up a wide correspondence and helping to organize the July 23 Philadelphia State House yard protest meeting. In a letter to Madison, Beckley detailed his efforts to spread the anti-treaty message. Despite being hobbled by a tumor on his leg, Beckley assured Madison that he did not "omit any endeavor to assist the common cause of republicanism & our country as endangered by the impending treaty." Then he informed Madison of the specifics of the activities. "A select few, move in concert with friends at New York; a regular correspondence and union of effort is maintained and we have already dispersed in Circular letters, all over the States, a petition to the H. of Represent[ative]s without, as yet, the smallest suspicion from our opponents: All our movements are kept secret until they have reached their ultimate destination, and we now meditate an address to the people in the same mode, developeing [*sic*], as far as may be proper, the insidious plan that effected a ratification of the treaty." Beckley took evident and justifiable delight in the strong outpourings of opposition to the treaty, and, no doubt, great pride in his own role in helping to direct the opposition efforts.[14]

Around the country, Federalist leaders were worried, even panicked, by what they saw, heard, and read. The initial reception to the treaty seemed entirely negative. The demonstrations, petitions, editorials, and letters overwhelmingly opposed the treaty and seemed to reflect widely held sentiment. Federalist leaders were particularly galled by the lack of response from pro-treaty advocates and administration supporters. Massachusetts congressman Fisher Ames wrote that the merchant class seemed to be sitting on its hands, cowed by the popular protests. "[A]lmost all of the merchants and steady men are said to feel the prevailing fever or to want courage to resist it. . . . I could neither repress my indignation, nor disguise my contempt for the blindness and gullibility of the rich men." Ames was fearful that the anti-treaty spirit would spread if not met and answered by treaty supporters.[15] George Cabot observed that the severity and promptness of the criticism with which the treaty had been met offered "new proof that our government cannot rely for support even upon good men in cases of emergency: for these very generally acquiesced in the censure without any examination of the subject." Writing from Brookline, Massachusetts, Cabot lamented that "Our good men here all presume that the President is too firm to be shaken, and therefore have all the more willingly indulged themselves in supineness."[16]

Other Federalists emphasized not only the gravity of the situation but the absolute necessity that Federalists make immediate efforts to reverse public opinion. "It is," wrote Henry Van Schaak to Theodore Sedgwick, "an important crisis—Government or no Government? . . . Although we are surrounded with the most gloomy Prospects, I cannot but hope that those Patriots, who have so often rescued this Government . . . will at this time save it also from the evil design of the disorganizers." Van Schaak also stressed that supporters of the treaty and the administration needed to take their case directly to the people. "Time must be taken by the forelock, that the People may be early impressed with right notions. The antis will be indefatigable in spreading every thing that may tend to militate against the Government—if so the friends to it ought to be, at least, as industrious to communicate facts to counteract the poison." Despite his very real fears, Van Schaak concluded on a hopeful note. "I hope and expect," he told Sedgwick, "that in this County, the great body of the People will be for supporting the Government."[17]

Federalists, while shaken, began to respond quickly. Although the full outlines of the Federalist pro-treaty counterattack would not become apparent for a while, two points are clear from the outset. Federalists—whatever the elitist beliefs many of them held—expressed early and often, in the summer and fall of 1795 (and again the next spring), a sense of faith in the public's ability to decide the matter rightly, if given time and the facts. And, from the beginning, they laid plans for a massive campaign to create public support for the treaty. Thus, even with their faith in the public, they were leaving nothing to chance. The Federalists, in short, took up the challenge of popular politics willingly, skillfully, and forcefully, even as they promoted a more established, deferential view of how leaders and the people should interact. The tension arising from the Federalist embrace of an older brand of deferential politics, at the very time that popular political culture was changing, will be more fully discussed in later chapters dealing with subsequent events. But at this early stage, Federalists clearly understood that passage of the treaty hung in the balance, and that their full effort and attention was required to ensure triumph.[18]

As early as July 3, just two days after the treaty was published, Federalists stressed their faith in the people. New York's *Daily Advertiser* carried a piece by "Fair Play" which noted that some newspapers already were clamoring against the treaty, fomenting opposition and seeking to undermine the government. "The good sense of the people will still preserve them from the arts of violent men—They will suspend their opinion till the treaty is truly and fully known—till it has been fully discussed." Continuing in the same vein, "Fair Play" counselled, "If they observe this dispassionate course, they will not fail, as on former occasions, to come to a just judgment; and the public opinion will correspond with the public interest."[19]

Throughout that summer, despite widespread newspaper accounts of anti-treaty demonstrations and petitions, and with public opinion seemingly entrenched against the measure, Federalists expressed faith in the people and in the decision they would ultimately make on the treaty. Most of these expressions of faith in the public were accompanied by stinging rebukes of the treaty opponents for "hasty proceedings" which led many to "oppose [the treaty] before they knew a word which it contained." Still, one correspondent was not worried. "Good sense and general information are too extensively diffused among the people, to permit their being imposed on by noise and clamour only: Frenzy may rage for a time, but cool and temperate reason will prevail. When the subject is fully investigated . . . it will appear that the interest of our country will be promoted by its ratification." Another writer excoriated those in the cities who attempted to force the issue upon a populace which, "busy in their occupations, want time to deliberate on momentous questions." Once they had sufficient time and information, the people were to be trusted. The "intentions of the people as a body are always pure—and they would never misjudge, were it not for the arts, and misrepresentations of designing individuals, who find their account in deceiving them."[20]

Federalists, in praising the good sense of the people, explicitly compared those who energetically—and hastily—demonstrated against the treaty in the cities and those in the countryside who seemed inclined to give the matter further study. "When so much *poison* is distilled from the seaports; the country EDITORS certainly deserve well of their country, to administer reasonable *antidotes.*" One writer noted that "*clamours* equally as *loud,* and *predictions* full as *gloomy* and *frightful* were made, when the *Federal Constitution* first made its appearance." Now, some of the same men were making the same noises about the treaty. The people should remember this, noted the writer, and "beware giving ear to clamours against the treaty equally as groundless."[21] Federalist leaders, writing to each other, voiced similar thoughts. Peter Van Schaak observed to Massachusetts congressman Theodore Sedgwick, "The Phrenzy of the towns, which . . . attempt to dictate to the Country & the Nation, I trust will not spread." Van Schaak lamented the conduct of the crowds in Boston and noted "perfect Tranquility" in the countryside. He also expressed anger at "the pains that were taken to distort the Public Mind by the Infusion of Prejudices" into the public debate.[22] Other writings elaborated on those same and other key themes of the Federalist pro-treaty supporters throughout the campaign. Federalists were sure that the public would support the treaty because it would realize that treaty critics were too quick to denounce the measure before it had been properly digested; because it would recognize that the measure helped promote peace; because the treaty was favored by the constituted authorities, most of all George Washington; and because it would protect prosperity for farmers as well as merchants. All of these became themes of the Federalist campaign; all, too, were reasons why Federalists maintained from the beginning of the campaign that the public would see the issue clearly and favorably if given time to consider it and reasons to support it.[23]

Oliver Wolcott, Jr., writing to his wife, described some of the early anti-treaty activity and noted that Philadelphia "feels keen sensations at this rascally business, which will however do no harm, except when the affair is misrepresented." Wolcott was confident that despite the efforts undertaken to inflame the passions, "The reason of the people will however prevail." Another Federalist leader wrote to Wolcott that, as the document became better understood, opposition had begun to dissipate. "The violent are ashamed to avow their errors, ignorance and prejudice, but all dispassionate and reasonable men are quiet and tolerably contented with the treaty which I am persuaded will become more agreeable as it is more understood."[24]

Despite this optimism, treaty proponents knew they could leave nothing to chance. They trusted the public would eventually decide in favor of the measure but recognized that, in the face of hostile opposition, citizens would need to have the treaty's advantages delineated and extolled. This required an immediate response in the face of such determined and vocal opposition. One of the first things Federalists did as part of their campaign was to urge other Federalists to action. "Quiet" warned his fellow citizens that Americans were "abused and insulted" by the machinations of the "Jacobins" working to oppose the treaty. "It is time for the friends of our excellent government, and of the Chief Magistrate . . . to come forward and boldly tell you the truth—to detect the insidious attempts of disappointed popular leaders to throw you into disorder."[25]

The inactivity on the part of gentlemen was especially alarming to treaty supporters. Just a few days after the treaty contents were published, Fisher Ames wrote, "The country is yet perfectly calm, but pains will be taken to inflame it. My hope is, that early attention will be paid to the merchants of New York and Philadelphia." If "Right impressions" were made there, then, "like a double brick wall," the effects of the Boston anti-treaty resolves would be offset. Ames also stressed how important it was that "temperate and masterly vindications of the treaty should appear in the gazettes. Better, if in a pamphlet."[26] Rufus King urged Christopher Gore to promote the treaty. "You must exert yourselves in procuring a right conception of the Treaty," he wrote. "[I]f understood, it will not be disapproved." Meanwhile, another of King's correspondents wrote him that the actions of the anti-treaty crowds "shou'd be counteracted by the *good people,* lest it shou'd be imagined that all are alike infected with the rage of disorganization."[27]

Other Federalist leaders, stressing the necessity of a published defense, urged each other to take up the pen and answer the treaty critics. They also noted with pleasure the early efforts then appearing in defense of the treaty. Oliver Wolcott, Jr., secretary of the treasury, writing to Noah Webster, editor of the New York paper *American Minerva,* underscored the confidence the latter should feel in the president. As Wolcott advised Webster, "do not therefore despond, but continue to enlighten the public and defend the treaty. . . . We have everything to hope from the virtue and reason of one part of the community, and everything to fear from the vice and turbulence of another." Continued publication of defenses of the treaty was crucial, Wolcott believed, to engaging and mobilizing the virtue and reason of the nation.[28] Another Federalist leader stated his belief that the former secretary of the treasury, Alexander Hamilton, "might still do great good by giving the public his luminous pen." William Vans Murray contended that the records and documents to which those near the center of power had access provided "a point of light" which no one in a remote area, even with intense study, could match. "In this country, unless this light is poured upon us in the most remote places, the friends of government and order will stagger about in the dark too frequently."[29]

By the time Murray wrote, Hamilton had long been actively engaged in just such a task. While Hamilton had officially resigned his position as secretary of the treasury on January 31, 1795, he continued to exercise considerable influence and power over government policies and actions because of his close ties to his successor, Oliver Wolcott, Jr., and, most importantly, his strong and deep ties to George Washington. From all the times the president called on Hamilton throughout the next year and a half, it must have seemed to Hamilton as if he had never left the administration. Like Washington, Hamilton had initial reservations about the original treaty. He disliked Article 12, dealing with U.S. trade with the British West Indies, and might have hoped for more concessions from England. Still, Hamilton found the treaty containing "many good things" and believed that, upon "mature reflection," it would be wise to ratify it while working to modify or eliminate Article 12. Hamilton thought it best to try to modify the offending article rather than either accepting the treaty without qualifications or sending it back in its entirety for a new negotiation.[30]

Like other Federalist leaders, Hamilton was concerned by the virulence of the anti-treaty protests and the generally hostile response which seemed to accompany even speculation about the contents of the treaty before it had been released.[31] As word continued to seep out about the contents, Hamilton urged the Federalists to launch a preemptive strike by publishing the treaty. "Indeed I am of opinion on the whole that all further mystery at present is unnecessary & ought to be waved for the satisfaction of the public mind." He further noted that the failure to publish the treaty was "working as I expected that is giving much scope to misrepresentation & misapprehension."[32]

As the anti-treaty protests gained momentum and fury, the Federalists were stunned at the rapidity with which their opponents took to denouncing the treaty and treaty supporters. But they also seemed momentarily hesitant about pushing ahead with support for a treaty about which they had misgivings themselves. Put in the unenviable position of defending a less-than-perfect treaty in the face of a raging opposition, the treaty's supporters were torn between their lack of enthusiasm for the treaty itself and revulsion and anger at the tactics of its critics. One observer noted, in the wake of publication of the treaty and the crowds protesting against it in Philadelphia, that "fear seems to be the Leading feature in the face of our most peaceful citizens."[33]

The most sophisticated, sustained defense of the treaty and best articulation of many of the themes of the Federalists' campaign for building support for it was made by Hamilton himself in his "Defence" essays signed "Camillus." Thirty-eight essays—all but ten written by Hamilton—were published over a six-month period from July 1795 to January 1796. Hamilton wrote the first twenty-two, published from July 22, 1795, through November 11, 1795—corresponding with the height of the first wave of the Federalists' campaign. Widely reprinted in newspapers around the country, the essays had three central purposes: to defend the treaty in general terms and assert its constitutionality; to proffer a detailed analysis of many of the specific articles of the treaty; and, lastly, to rebut the arguments made against the treaty by Republicans. Judged by nearly any standard, the "Defence" essays were a success.[34]

Since the issues discussed in the treaty were close to Hamilton's heart and the treaty itself was negotiated along the lines of his instructions to Jay, he had little difficulty writing a compelling and prompt defense of the document, even though he was disappointed in some of its aspects and its omissions. Hamilton in fact spelled out some of the themes he would develop at length in the essays in a long document he prepared for Washington in early July. Washington wrote Hamilton asking to have "the favorable, and unfavorable side of *each* article stated, and compared together; that I may see the bearing and tendency of them; and, ultimately, on which side the balance is to be found." In response, Hamilton prepared a lengthy work considering in detail each of the articles just as the president requested. This response served as something of a rough draft, providing the gist of arguments and positions which would be developed more fully for the "Defence" essays which followed.[35]

After discussing particular treaty articles in his response to Washington, Hamilton added what he called a "general view" of the treaty. The most important feature of the treaty, Hamilton wrote, was that it settled "on the whole as reasonably as could have been expected" the disputed points between the U.S. and Great Britain and kept the country out of the "dreadful" war in Europe. "Well considered, the greatest interest of this Country in its external relations is that of peace." Whatever might be gained through commercial treaties was less important than keeping the U.S. out of a war which would "give a serious wound to our growth and prosperity." Should the nation be able to avoid war for the next ten or twelve years, Hamilton wrote, "we may then meet it without much inquieture and may advance and support with ener[g]y and effect any just pretensions to greater commercial advantages than we may enjoy."[36]

Many of the early numbers of the "Defence" echoed his response to Washington. In number 2, Hamilton argued that the relative strengths of the U.S. and Great Britain meant that the fledgling nation was in no position to dictate terms to England nor to seek any kind of military redress of grievances. "A very powerful state may frequently hazard a high and haughty tone with good policy, but a weak State can scarcely ever do it without imprudence. The last is yet our character, though we are the embryo of a great empire." In number 3, Hamilton touched on a similar theme, observing that the agreement hammered out in the treaty "was the only one on which the United States and Great Britain could ever terminate their differences without war." Had John Jay persisted in trying to force his points on Great Britain, he would have proven himself a "diplomatic pedant, rather than the able negociator" and might have been fairly charged with sacrificing his country's peace solely because of obstinacy.[37]

In the last of his general introductory essays before discussing the specific articles and terms of the treaty, Hamilton made an impassioned plea to the public to "rally round your own good sense!" and dismiss the arguments of the anti-treaty activists. He launched an assault on those activists for their misrepresentations of the treaty and what he saw as the inconsistency of their arguments. Speaking to the concerns Federalist leaders had raised earlier, he discussed why many supporters had waited so long to respond to treaty critics. Hamilton explained that as long as anti-treaty arguments were merely polemical in nature it was easier for supporters to "prefer silence to contradiction," and ignore the "antagonists" of the treaty and their "habit of making random assertions." But now that "they have undertaken to become the instructors of their fellow citizens on a subject, on the examination of which they unite very superficial knowlege with the most perverse dispositions," it was necessary to respond. In an earlier number of "The Defence," Hamilton had criticized treaty opponents for concocting worst-case scenarios of what would occur if the treaty were to go into effect. He thought little of these overheated objections, regardless of the concerns they raised. "Experience no doubt will demonstrate that the horrid spectres which have been conjured up are fictions." Even if it took some time before the treaty's benefits were fully realized, "it will at least prove that the predicted evils are chimeras and cheats."[38]

The underlying thread of much of Hamilton's critique of the treaty opponents—indeed of so much of the Federalist response to critics—was that the opponents had not carefully studied the treaty or approached it with reason. This became another of the major themes of the Federalist campaign and was expressed in private letters, public writings, and the newspapers. Time after time, Federalists hammered away at their opponents for misrepresenting the treaty and repeatedly assured the public that, after careful study and reflection, all would see the merits of the treaty and reject the outcries against it.

With the very first number of "The Defence," Hamilton tore into treaty critics and lambasted them for deliberately inciting the country with unthinking critiques of the measure. Some men, he charged, "counting more on the passions than on the reason of their fellow citizens," were stirring up public discontent for their own ends. These opponents, because of their predisposition towards France and animosity towards Britain, were "disinclined to any amicable arrangement with Great Britain." Because of those prejudices and the actions they inspired, Hamilton noted contemptuously, it would have been "a vain expectation that the treaty would be generally contemplated with candor and moderation, or that reason would regulate the first impressions concerning it." In fact, for Hamilton, the unthinking opposition to the treaty was merely an instance of "a systematic effort against the national government and its administration; a decided engine of party to advance its own views at the hazard of the public peace and prosperity."[39]

Hamilton went on to remark that the anti-treaty demonstrations were organized hastily to spread "alarm and discontent" by the "leaders of clubs" anxious to "seize the passions of the citizens and preoccupy their judgments against the treaty." He noted that the treaty was published one day in Boston and a meeting organized to denounce it the next, "without it ever being read; without any serious discussion, sentence was pronounced against it." Could any one believe, he asked, that in such a short time a complex treaty could have been understood by those who turned out to condemn it? The result of the meeting could be considered little more than a "sudden ebullition of popular passion, excited by the artifices of a party." Further, the haste and intemperance which accompanied the calling of the meeting "prevented the body of merchants and the greatest part of the most considerate citizens from attending the meeting," and left those who did attend under the influence of a "set of men" who have been "the uniform opposers of the government."[40]

The opponents of the treaty, Hamilton continued, resisted all attempts at fair-minded, open discussion. For proof, he drew on his own recent experience in addressing a crowd gathered to debate the treaty in New York City. "[A] respectable meeting of the merchants" had also tried to promote "a fair discussion of the treaty." But the leaders of the "clubs" refused to allow any such discussion of the document on its merits. "It cannot be doubted that the real motive to the opposition, was the fear of discussion; the desire of excluding light; the adherence to a plan of surprize and deception." Hamilton then concluded the first "Defence" essay by proclaiming that to "every man who is not an enemy to the national government, who is not a prejudiced partizan, who is capable of comprehending the argument, and passionate enough to attend to it with impartiality," he promised to demonstrate in the following essays the advantages and merits of the treaty and the reasons why the public should support it.[41]

While the first essay in the "Defence" series laid the foundation for many of the criticisms and denunciations of the actions of treaty opponents, the charge that opponents were appealing solely to passion and not to reason, and the closely related admonition that with careful study the treaty would be seen in its true light, were consistent themes of Hamilton's in those early weeks of the Federalist counterattack. In an early August piece outside the series, Hamilton asked, "Why is it that the opposers of the Treaty so constantly appeal to our passions, and to convince us they are in the right endeavour first to make us angry? Do they imagine that we can only feel, that we cannot reason? Do they suppose that a man is best-fitted to judge in proportion as he is agitated and incensed? Or is it that they really dare not trust their cause to the sober result of fair discussion and calm reasoning?"[42]

Joining Hamilton in the production of pro-treaty essays was Noah Webster, editor of the *American Minerva* and the *Herald* (both of New York). Publishing the first of his pieces a few days before Hamilton began the "Defence" essays, Webster ultimately wrote twelve articles entitled "Vindication of the Treaty" between July 18 and August 5 which were reprinted in a number of newspapers in the weeks that followed. These essays, six of which were signed "Curtius," made much the same arguments that Hamilton made, defending the treaty against its critics, stressing what the measure would accomplish and, just as importantly, what it would avoid (war), and attacking critics for their unseemly haste in ranting against the treaty. "They excited a temporary clamor . . . and every effort is used to distort and misconstrue some passages. . . . But the clamor of the moment subsided on reading a correct copy of the Treaty," Webster wrote in the first essay. The treaty, contrary to the charges of critics, bore close examination quite well and the fact that it did was, he concluded, "a substantial argument in its favor." It was further proof, too, "of what we should all regret, that the *passions* of men outstrip their *judgement*."[43]

While Hamilton and Webster were excoriating the opposition for deliberately failing to consider the treaty seriously and for inflaming people's passions instead of appealing to reason, other Federalists took to print to advocate the benefits of a careful study of the treaty. Both Robert Goodloe Harper and William Loughton Smith of South Carolina wrote pamphlets criticizing treaty critics and asking citizens not to listen to others but to consider the treaty themselves. New York merchant James Watson urged restraint on the part of his fellow citizens, who were being summoned to a town meeting to denounce the treaty. Watson informed his readers that they were being called to meet the next day "not to consider and discuss the Treaty . . . and to express the conviction which shall arise from a fair examination of its merits, but to condemn and oppose it as a thing prejudged." But Watson urged readers not to be so hastily convinced. Assuring them that he and other merchants who would be most affected by the treaty had studied it closely, he concluded, "we have not yet been able to discover in the Treaty those hideous features which are alledged to exist, yet we are disposed to meet the rest of our fellow citizens and to promote with them a fair and rational discussion of the subject." Watson expressed his confidence that a reasoned, deliberate discussion of the treaty would save New Yorkers from having a resolution condemning the treaty "imposed upon them without due investigation."[44]

In a late July editorial, the *American Minerva* made an important statement, blasting some critics who had taunted treaty supporters for their perceived initial silence on the measure. "Be assured the treaty is not given up as *indefensible.* The friends of our government . . . delayed their defense of the treaty for the *noblest purpose*—that of *examining its merits.* It required time to investigate its various parts to compare it with other treaties and laws of the nation." This was the "*honorable motive* of delay." Contrasted with the "hurry and rashness and the tumult of [the treaty's] opposers, where is the man who will not admire this conduct of its advocates?" In short, anyone's early silence during what one Federalist leader later called "three more gloomy weeks [in early July] than I have ever known in our political hemisphere" should not be taken as evidence of abandonment of support for the treaty, but of wisdom.[45]

Whatever public perceptions may have been, the record shows clearly that many Federalists praised the advantages of the treaty from the outset. Even before Hamilton and Webster weighed in with their essays, newspaper editors and their correspondents stressed in the first few weeks of the public debate reasons for supporting the treaty which became part and parcel of the Federalist campaign. On July 4, when many celebrations of Independence Day metamorphosed into anti-treaty demonstrations, Boston's *Columbian Centinel* argued that the treaty "must be a source of pleasing sensations, and a cause of mutual congratulations, to all sincere lovers of their country," and then proceeded to delineate the measure's advantages. Chief among these was keeping the peace with Great Britain by removing "the seeds of dissension" through a "train of amicable adjustment." The ceding of the western posts and free navigation of the western waters would create "unbounded" commercial possibilities. American-claims for the seizure and spoliation of their ships would be heard by a tribunal whose members would be appointed by both nations. And the opening of the East India trade to American shippers would also represent a great advance. These were but some of the most "prominent features" of the treaty that would benefit the United States. Other papers carried similar early defenses.[46]

Another theme of treaty supporters in those first weeks of the debate was the assertion that John Jay had made every reasonable effort and produced the best treaty possible given the circumstances. The *Gazette of the United States* condemned the invective heaped upon Jay, calling the censure he was receiving "*unmerited* . . . proof that no eminence of former services can secure a man from *Ingratitude*." If the treaty was less favorable than some expected, it could hardly be blamed on Jay. "He has made the *best Treaty he could*," a line which would occur time and again in Federalist discussions. Likewise, "Americanus" claimed that Jay "obtained the best terms which he possibly could." This piece, like other early defenses of the treaty, stated that the measure secured all the important demands against the British and yielded concessions which were not at all unreasonable. This was decidedly preferable to following "the wild projects of certain hot headed or discontented politicians, whose plans, if followed, would inevitably have involved us in the calamities of War." Other writers struck the same theme: "We are persuaded, it is the *best* that can be obtained; and that it is . . . for the interest of the United States, to carry it into effect."[47]

Significantly, Federalists did not content themselves with pamphlets and newspaper essays alone. They also worked hard at assembling pro-treaty counterdemonstrations and rallies to offset Republican efforts. Whatever reservations they may have had about the propriety of politics in the street, Federalists did not simply yield this forum to their opponents. Instead, they engaged and mobilized themselves. While much of the content of these demonstrations, especially the petitions that stemmed from them, will be explored more fully below, a consideration of them here provides some important points of contrast with Republican anti-treaty protests already described.

In their own rallies, Federalists stressed the same themes as they did in their newspaper and pamphlet campaign and made their most direct appeals yet to the public. One of the more important pro-treaty meetings was called by New York merchants at the Tontine Coffee House on July 21. Already reeling from the disputatious town meeting at which Hamilton and others were driven from the scene, New York's Federalists regrouped. More than seventy members of the Chamber of Commerce, comprising what the recording secretary labeled "the most respectable meeting ever held," gathered, heard the treaty read, and then circulated and passed a resolution approving it. The measure was said to contain "as many features of Reciprocity, as . . . could reasonably have been expected." The treaty was "wisely arranged" for preserving peace and, if it should fail to be ratified, war might follow. After raising the specter of hostilities with Great Britain, the resolution expressed faith and "full confidence" in those officers in whom the Constitution placed the power to make such decisions. With its expression of the belief that this was the best treaty that could be gotten, that it would preserve peace, and that the constituted authorities knew best and should be trusted, this New York Chamber of Commerce resolution nicely summed up the central themes of the Federalist campaign.[48]

Another key pro-treaty meeting was held in Boston on August 11 at the Chamber of Commerce hall. The town's merchants and traders wanted to express their dissent to the anti-treaty town meetings held the previous month. Because some anti-treaty activists had suggested that merchants likewise condemned the measure, many now wanted to set the record straight. "[U]nwilling to be implicated in the number of those who approve of the doings of that meeting, and reserving to ourselves the right of expressing our opinion individually upon the merits or demerits of public measures," the merchants decided to hold their own.[49] Described as a "large and respectable meeting," the Boston Chamber gathering heard a motion to read and discuss the treaty article by article. However, it was argued that, since by this time everyone had read and knew the contents of the measure and reached a decision, reading it would be redundant. The meeting instead moved immediately to a discussion and vote on three resolutions. After little debate and unanimous or near unanimous votes, the Chamber sent a resolution to Washington praising the treaty as "wise and prudent." The Chamber also noted that it "cannot but lament and disapprove" the efforts of opponents to incite opposition among the people "and to detach their confidence from the government of the Union." In a free government, they observed, "a firm reliance of the people on the wisdom and integrity of those authorities which they have themselves constituted to manage their public concerns, and a chearful acquiescence in the decisions of rulers of their own appointment, are indispensable to secure the peace, the honor and the happiness of the community."[50]

Federalists in Philadelphia also organized merchants and the larger community to rally behind the treaty and the president. The address of the Philadelphia merchants and traders evinced support for both, and also reflected nicely, as did the Boston petition, the Federalist conception of government discussed above. The Philadelphia merchants first expressed their faith in "the wisdom, integrity and Patriotism of the Constituted Authorities." While noting that they normally would not offer their opinions on this important subject, the merchants had decided to speak out following the anti-treaty demonstrations and resolutions "lest our silence should be construed into an acquiescence in their opinions." The resolution also stated that the merchants considered the prospect of peace and the promotion of commerce to be principal advantages of the treaty which outweighed all objections. Washington responded with a warm message thanking the merchants for their "confidence in the constituted Authorities" and praising their "deliberately formed" sentiments. The president noted that he was especially glad to have the support of "men whose interests are more immediately concerned than those of any other classes of my fellow citizens."[51]

Much of the activity both for and against the treaty was designed to influence President George Washington, who finally signed it in mid-August. Washington himself was dedicated to a strict adherence to constitutional principles as he understood them, and throughout the Jay Treaty controversy he held to a consistently, even excessively legalistic view of the president's role and duties under the Constitution. At the height of the outbursts of opposition to the treaty, Washington offered a clear statement of his vision. In his most widely known reply to the petitions he received, this one from the selectmen of Boston against the treaty, he succinctly explained his conception of the president's role. "I have weighed with attention every argument which has, at any time, been brought into view. But the constitution is the guide which I never can abandon. It has assigned to the president the power of making treaties, with the advice and consent of the senate." Washington went on to note that this was "doubtless" done because it was felt that these two branches of government would have the greatest command of the pertinent facts. He warned against seeking the truth "through any channel but that of a temperate and well informed investigation." Washington told the selectmen that they were "at liberty to make these sentiments known as the grounds of my procedure." This was one of the first letters Washington drew up in response to the petitions, and its substance and form were repeated in many subsequent letters. Washington even occasionally sent his response to the Boston selectmen to other groups, claiming that it was applicable elsewhere.[52]

While all of this activity in the streets and the newspapers was going on, Republican party leaders gathered information, took stock, and assessed their options. James Madison and Thomas Jefferson, writing frequently to each other and also to other correspondents, spent the summer and fall collecting reports, monitoring public opinion, and expressing their dismay at the treaty and the tactics of its supporters. Both men received information on the treaty's reception and forwarded accounts of town meetings to each other. Robert Livingston wrote to Madison and warned bluntly, "Never my dear Sir was there a time that called more loudly for exertion. It may yet be possible to convince the publick & the president of the danger of a ratification. Write to them write to him shew the evils the unconstitutionality of the treaty in its true light." Livingston told Madison that he had just written Washington himself. Madison's reply to Livingston in early August suggested the direction that the Virginian's thinking was taking. Madison directly blamed Jay and his party. "Indeed the Treaty from one end to the other must be regarded as a demonstration that the Party to which the Envoy belongs & of which he has been more the Organ than of the U.S. is a British party, systematically aiming at an exclusive connection with the British Governt. & ready to sacrifice to that object as well the dearest interests of our Commerce, as the most sacred dictates of national honor."[53]

Madison elaborated on his criticisms of the treaty in an August 23 letter to an unidentified correspondent (probably Alexander Dallas or John Beckley) and in a draft of a petition to the Virginia General Assembly in September. He was particularly bothered by three facets of the document: what he called its "ruinous tendency" regarding the carrying trade, its "insidious hostility" towards France, and its failure to add to or protect the rights of neutral nations. In his draft petition Madison detailed those and other concerns and sought to show that the treaty lacked reciprocity and was manifestly unequal. Madison hoped that the petition he drafted might influence public opinion by communicating the clear sentiments of the Virginia representatives. Down the road, he hoped this petition might provide a rallying point for anti-treaty critics and give congressional opponents further support.[54]

Jefferson reached similar conclusions. While he declined to take part in the public campaign against the treaty, Jefferson remained active behind the scenes, sharing reports and information, encouraging others to participate, and concocting strategy with other leaders. Privately, Jefferson made it clear how much he despised the treaty and scorned both its negotiator and the administration which supported it. He wrote to Mann Page on August 30, mentioning the treaty itself only once but leaving little doubt about his subject. In an elaborate metaphor, Jefferson told Page that he did not believe, as some suggested, that fourteen of every fifteen men were rogues. "But I have always found that rogues would be uppermost" and would always try to insinuate themselves into positions "of power and profit." Once in place, the rogues then commence "with stealing the people's good opinion, and then steal from them the right of withdrawing it, by contriving laws and associations against the power of the people themselves. Our part of the country is in considerable fermentation on what they suspect to be a recent roguery of this kind. They say that while all hands were below deck mending sails, splicing ropes, and every one at his own business, and the captain in the cabbin [*sic*] attending to his log-book and chart, a rogue of a pilot has run them into an enemy's port."[55]

To other correspondents Jefferson did not bother to couch his contempt and anger in metaphor. In early September he observed to James Monroe that he had never witnessed so "general a burst of dissatisfaction." Those who understood particular articles of the measures condemned those articles, while those who lack a detailed grasp of the treaty denounced it in general as showing hostility toward France. Furthermore, he believed that the battle lines drawn over the treaty had exposed clearly how isolated "the monarchical party" was from the vast majority of the public: "The chamber of commerce in New York, against the body of the town, the merchants in Philadelphia, against the body of their town." This description calls to mind Jefferson's earlier metaphor of rogues; he believed that the treaty had been foisted on the public by an elite that was out of touch with and even hostile to the people's interests. Writing to Philip Mazzei a few days later, Jefferson noted that Jay's treaty "has excited a more general disgust than any public transaction since the days of our independence."[56]

As usual, Jefferson was most direct in his correspondence with Madison, explicitly condemning Jay, Hamilton, Washington, and the Federalists. Jefferson noted with a seething anger how even many merchants had originally been opposed to the treaty but were scared away from their initial opposition, and his response to Madison indicates just how firmly Jefferson believed that the Federalists were subverting popular government by any means necessary:

> But the general expression of indignation has alarmed them for the strength of the government. They have feared the shock would be too great, and have chosen to tack about and support both treaty and government, rather than risk the government: thus it is that Hamilton, Jay &c. in the boldest act they ever ventured on to undermine the constitution have the address to screen themselves and direct the hue and cry against those who wished to drag them into light. A bolder party-stroke was never struck. For it certainly is an attempt of a party which finds they have lost their majority in one branch of the legislature to make a law by the aid of the other branch, and of the executive, under color of a treaty, which shall bind up the hands of the adverse branch from ever restraining the commerce of their patron-nation.[57]

Jefferson closed by noting that he detected a pause in the public expressions against the treaty. This he attributed, in essence, to the Federalists' campaign: specifically, to the effects "of the desertion of the merchants, of the President's chiding answer to Boston and Richmond, of the writings of Curtius and Camillus, and of the quietism into which the people naturally fall, after first sensations are over."[58]

In the opening weeks of the controversy, treaty opponents hoped that the demonstrations, protests, and pamphlets attacking the measure might influence the one man who could still do something to prevent its passage: President Washington. Tench Coxe, writing to Jefferson on July 30, condemned the treaty and stated, "I do not know what are the prospects of the Business or even the present state of it. But," he observed hopefully, "I think the President is yet uncommitted—and waiting for information and argument." Earlier that month, during the initial outbreak of the controversy, Henry Tazewell informed Jefferson of the Senate's narrow and conditional approval (pending the suspension of Article 12). "This conditional ratification," Tazewell told Jefferson, "has produced some embarrassment in the Executive. The result is yet unknown." These letters evidently had an effect on Jefferson, since he spent a good deal of time that summer urging others to write critiques of the treaty and responses to pro-treaty arguments, while following closely the newspaper and pamphlet war then already under way. Hoping also that the president might be dissuaded from signing, Jefferson read the anti-treaty writings closely. He was disappointed in their quality and doubted that they would have the intended effect.[59]

Jefferson was at Monticello, away from the center of action, receiving news only after some delay, and reluctant to participate in the fray himself. He told Philip Mazzei, melodramatically, "I determine to take no part in the passions of the day, but to pursue my farm and my nailery, pay my taxes, and leave public measures to those who have longer to live under them." But he actively followed the debates and worried about the effectiveness of the anti-treaty efforts. In early September, writing to James Monroe, he surveyed some of the early literary efforts on the treaty. He noted that several supporters had written in favor of the measure but that "A more powerful one is *Hamilton* writing under the signature of *Camillus*." To Tench Coxe a few days later he observed that "Camillus may according to his custom write an Encyclopedie on the subject, but it is too obstinate to be twisted by all his sophisms into a tolerable shape." But to Madison he bluntly expressed his worry that the anti-treaty answers to date were no match for Hamilton. Jefferson suspected that the critical "Features of Mr. Jay's Treaty" was written by John Beckley or Tench Coxe (actually it was Alexander J. Dallas) and observed that the "antidote is certainly not strong enough for the poison of Curtius"; he was distressed that "honest sound hearted men of common understanding . . . were not able to parry the sophistry." His real concern was Hamilton, who he called "a colossus to the antirepublican party. Without numbers, he is an host within himself." Jefferson also worried that the Federalists had severely overstepped with the treaty, "got themselves into a defile, where they might be finished." But he blamed Republicans for being too lax and confident in the early outpouring of opposition and thus giving the effect of Hamilton's energies and abilities time to sink in. He pressured Madison to reply personally. "A solid reply might yet completely demolish what was too feebly attacked, and has gathered strength from the weakness of the attack. . . . For god's sake take up your pen, and give a fundamental reply to Curtius and Camillus."[60] Madison, perhaps remembering his less than successful efforts to combat Hamilton's "Pacificus" in 1793, steadfastly declined to join the battle.

Finally, on August 14, 1795, Washington put his signature on the treaty and brought a close to another phase of the conflict. The president had long been inclined in this direction, as his correspondence that summer indicates. His letter to the Boston selectmen certainly hinted that his reading of the treaty was more positive than that of the treaty critics, and in a July 29 letter to Hamilton, Washington made it clear that he supported the treaty even though he had some reservations. Washington's position had evolved. At first, he was disappointed that the instrument did not include more favorable terms and that it ignored several key issues, such as impressment. He was moving in the direction of seeing the measure as providing some crucial benefits and accepting the treaty, but had not, at the time of the selectmen's letter, made up his mind to sign. It is also quite clear from his letter to the selectmen that Washington was genuinely angry at the tactics and the presumption of the anti-treaty side. Thus, while he had not yet decided to sign, the opposition ruckus, far from persuading him not to, likely moved him farther along the path toward signing the instrument.

Before he did so, there would be one more prominent incident that placed him solidly in the pro-treaty camp. Secretary of State Edmund Randolph, who favored a delay in ratification until American vessels were guaranteed freedom from British interference, was accused by Secretary of War Timothy Pickering and Secretary of the Treasury Oliver Wolcott, Jr., of disloyalty. They charged that Randolph had been improperly involved with the French government, perhaps even passing secrets, and that he had received money for advancing French interests while in the United States government. The immediate source of the accusation was a letter from French minister Fauchet, intercepted by the British and given to Pickering and Wolcott by George Hammond, the British minister. The letter was far from conclusive proof of wrongdoing, and some historians have argued, as Randolph himself did, that he was unfairly accused. But Washington was disappointed by Randolph's reaction on being confronted with this evidence and apparently believed that it established at least the appearance of impropriety. It was enough to make him deeply suspicious of his fellow Virginian and long-time friend. Although the president had been leaning toward signing the treaty for several weeks, the Randolph allegations, which came to his attention in early August, sealed his decision, and in his anger and sense of betrayal he now steadfastly supported the measure.[61]

Although it has often been suggested that this evidence against Randolph converted an undecided Washington to the pro-treaty ranks, such an opinion disregards ample evidence that suggests that Washington had long been inclined in just such a direction. Biographer John Ferling suggests that the president's thinking was clear even before he learned of Randolph's alleged perfidy. In his letter of July 29 to Alexander Hamilton—written one day after the response to the selectmen—Washington "all but stated that he was prepared to sign Jay's treaty . . . he went on to suggest that the great virtue of the pact was that it afforded a chance for peace with London. Though his would be an unpopular act . . . he believed that once 'the paroxysm of the fever is a little abated' the 'real temper of the people' would change, endorsing his decision. Thus, by the time he departed Virginia, five days before he learned of the allegations against Randolph, Washington appears to have decided to exchange ratifications with [Great Britain]. The machinations of the Pickering-Wolcott-Hammond cabal, at best," concludes Ferling, "only hastened and colored the inevitable."[62]

Even before he announced a decision on what action to take, Washington saw pleasing signs in the public debate. He praised the "Camillus" essays to Hamilton (who published the first of thirty-eight numbers on July 22). "I have seen with pleasure that a writer . . . has promised to answer, or rather defend the treaty. . . . To judge of this work from the first number, which I have seen, I auger well of the performance." In this letter to Hamilton and in others that he wrote, Washington made it clear how crucial it was that able defenses of the treaty begin to appear in the public papers. Washington encouraged this practice. Speaking of "Camillus," he noted that friends of the administration should spare no effort to promulgate this and other pieces like it; otherwise, "a few only will derive lights from the knowledge, or labour of the author; whilst the opposition pieces will spread their poison in all directions." Ultimately the president feared that this "poison," left unchecked, would give Congress an unrepresentative sense of public opinion. And here, Washington drew an unmistakable distinction concerning the campaign for public opinion on the treaty, one that shaped his conception of the issue itself and determined the actions he took. At the close of his letter to Hamilton, the president cast in broader terms the nature of the problem before them, a problem that Washington doubtless thought applied to much of the partisan conflict that marked his administration. "The difference of conduct between the friends, and foes of order, and good government, is in noth[in]g more striking than that, the latter are always working, like bees, to distil their poison; whilst the former, depending, often times *too much,* and *too long* upon the sense, and good dispositions of the people to work conviction, neglect the means of effecting it." In fact, Federalists had already launched—with the president's full backing—just such a campaign to win support for the treaty; they would not "neglect the means of effecting" such support. Washington's comments, considered alongside those of Jefferson, Madison, and Monroe discussed previously, make it clear that by the summer of 1795, at the height of the treaty debate, both sides believed that they were opposed by a "party" or "faction" which threatened constitutional government and independence.[63]

Washington's decision to ratify the treaty on August 14, 1795, capped a furious six-week interval of efforts designed by both sides to sway the president's mind. His decision ended the first stage of the treaty debate and had a powerful effect on both supporters and opponents. Some critics took Washington's signature on the treaty as a sign to cease combat or at least to desist for the time being while the struggle shifted to other venues. Alexander J. Dallas, the author of the anti-treaty "Features of Mr. Jay's Treaty," stopped his writings after learning of Washington's decision and considered the matter closed, a testimony to the president's influence and stature even among opponents. As for the president himself, whatever doubts and reluctance he may have had initially about the treaty had long since vanished. Concerned by the outpouring of opposition, furious at the tactics used by treaty opponents, troubled by the Randolph implications, and gradually convinced that the treaty was the best that could reasonably be obtained, Washington, once he decided to sign the measure, was energetically and actively engaged in the campaign to bring it to fruition. Having carefully deliberated, weighing pros and cons, Washington was fully and decisively committed to the treaty and played a crucial role in bringing about public and congressional acceptance.[64]

But if Washington's signing led to a drop-off in activity for Dallas and some Republicans, it simply deepened the disillusion which others felt. Few were more blunt than Nathaniel Ames, who noted in his diary that

"Washington now defies the whole Sovereign that made him what he is—and can unmake him again. Better his hand had been cut off when his glory was at its height, before he blasted all his Laurels."[65] And few were more dogged than Philadelphia's Benjamin Franklin Bache, who practically declared open war on Washington in his paper, the *Aurora,* and filled its pages with diatribes that summer and fall. Editions of the *Aurora* contained bitter, often sarcastic attacks on the treaty and its supporters. Bache tried to foment talk of impeachment, and made a sustained argument that the government, by supporting the treaty, was disregarding the democratic will of the people. In December, in the face of mounting evidence to the contrary, Bache—spurred by the possibility that the House of Representatives might refuse funding for the treaty—tried to argue that a new wave of anti-treaty spirit was sweeping the nation.[66]

The pro-treaty petitions which were sent to Washington and then widely republished not only reflected the orchestrated efforts to mobilize support, but suggested what seemed to many observers on both sides to be a gradual shift in public opinion. Just as Jefferson had detected a "pause" in the protests, some Federalists believed they could sense this change as early as late summer of 1795 and continuing through the fall. George Cabot noted that the "respectable people" in Salem, Massachusetts, were "acquiescent, and many of them approve." The leading merchants of Newburyport were also happy with the treaty and efforts were being made to make their opinion known. Cabot concluded that, while some were still reluctant to express their opinion, "the sober and discreet part of even our seaports, and still more of our country towns, feel a great anxiety lest the treaty should by any means miscarry."[67]

Another Federalist leader, Fisher Ames, reported in September that the accounts he received from Newport indicated that the treaty protests had been so overheated that the general public took little notice and even the "anti-treaty men are ashamed of the business." Such violent protests would have the effect, "by outraging the feelings of those who abhor all excesses, to turn the public mind more forcibly than it would otherwise go, from the views of the seditious." Ames also observed that he had recently visited a number of country taverns and concluded from his conversations that "the yeomanry are yet right. They say the men in the government know best what to do, and the President will not see the country wronged, much less wrong it himself." The public seemed to display "confidence in, and almost adoration of the President" and a strong determination to support the government. "On the whole, it depends I think, on the spirit and firmness of the government itself, to keep the country right. . . . Now the contest lies between the mobbers and the government, and if there should be no want of spirit, the eventual triumph of the latter may be expected." Along those lines, Ames closed by noting that Washington's response to the Boston selectmen (widely reprinted and sent in response to other resolutions as well) "is greatly extolled, and I believe has done more towards calming the country, than all the good pieces published in Webster and the Sentinel."[68]

Other Federalists, commenting on the sentiment in their areas, stressed again the significance of Washington's stance on the treaty and the continued importance of strength and firmness on his part. Christopher Gore believed that any deviation by Washington from a firm and steady course "will give strength to our disorganizers, and confirm and encrease the hold they now have on the prejudices and passions of the people." But Gore wrote that "So far as I can learn the temper of the country on the treaty, it is right." As long as Federalists remained firm, there was little danger of Massachusetts being won over by treaty opponents. William Vans Murray was concerned that some southern states would violently declaim against the treaty but maintained that, in Maryland, "by nine-tenths of the gentlemen collected from all the counties the treaty was approved, and the fiat of our good President the order of the day." Vans Murray observed that while the "people in the towns may mob and rouse . . . those in the country cannot soon be brought to the service of sedition. It will be all talk and writing."[69]

Throughout the fall Federalists continued to express—to each other in letters and to the public in newspapers—their belief that opinion had changed. In October, George Washington, responding to an anti-treaty petition from Petersburg, Virginia, noted that "It would have been pleasing to me to have found a universal concurrence of my fellow-citizens in the same opinion; and I flatter myself, that what diversity of sentiment exists, will daily diminish." As judged by other Federalists, at least, Washington was correct. "A Farmer" noted, "I sincerely think a great majority of the people are perfectly satisfied with the act of the President and Senate, believing they have the best information, and will act for the public good."[70] By December, Federalists were more fully confident that public opinion had shifted. Noah Webster's paper declared that because it had been asserted so frequently that the people of the country were against the treaty, it was necessary to offer evidence to the contrary. In a long editorial which measured known public opinion state by state, Webster asserted that "The truth is ascertained beyond all controversy, that a great majority of the people are well satisfied with the Treaty and with the measures of the administration." Anecdotal evidence from other party leaders seemed to confirm his judgment. Christopher Gore wrote from Boston in December that "a very different sentiment of the treaty prevails in this town from that which was circulated by the inhabitants in their town meeting," and elaborated a few weeks later: "there is a most pleasing alteration in the Sentiments of our fellow citizens. . . . The Scene is brighten[e]d."[71]

Perhaps the best gauge of the success of Federalist efforts was the frustration evinced by Republican leaders who saw the anti-treaty spirit ebbing in the face of the concerted Federalist campaign. In his letter to Madison in late September 1795, Jefferson noted bitterly that the delay in responding to Hamilton had been detrimental to the Republican cause. He lamented that anti-treaty writers had attacked first, which gave Hamilton "the advantage of answering them," and that he had, for the longest time, been "unanswered himself." He lamented, too, that Hamilton's essays had been "too feebly attacked and [had] gathered strength from the weakness of the attack." This dynamic, added to Washington's influence, seemed to turn the tide of the debate.[72]

Madison, too, noted with mounting frustration the success of the Federalists in his correspondence with Jefferson. The Federalists' strategy Madison wrote in early December was "to blazon the public prosperity, to confound the Treaty with the President, and to mouth over the stale topics of war and confusion." Later that same month Madison revealed both his frustration with the course of events and his shrewd recognition of Federalist tactics when he wrote to Jefferson that the "situation is truly perplexing. It is clear that a majority if brought to the merits of the Treaty are agst. it. But as the Treaty is not regularly before the House, and an application to the P[resident] brings him personally into the question with some plausible objections to the measure, there is great danger that eno' will fly off to leave the opponents of the Treaty in a minority."[73]

By December, George Washington and other Federalist leaders were more convinced than ever that the tide of public opinion had indeed turned. John Jay wrote the president that the public was becoming more sanguine about the treaty. In a reply, Washington concurred. "My information with respect to the general disposition of the people accords with yours and I have little doubt of a perfect amelioration of sentiment after the present fermentation (which is not only subsiding but changing) has evaporated a little more. The dregs, however, will always remain and the slightest motion will stir them up." In the last week of the year, Alexander Hamilton and Fisher Ames expressed much the same thoughts. "I greatly miscalculate," Hamilton wrote to Washington, "if a strong and general current does not now set in favor of the Government on the question of the Treaty." Ames observed, in a series of letters, "The country is cooling, and as far as multitudes can be said to see, it is opening it's eyes," and "Let our three branches keep duly united, and the efforts of the party will be impotent, at least for a time. The people are coming right." Convinced of the direction of public opinion and impressed by Federalist moves to shape it, Ames believed that Hamilton's efforts in particular now represented overkill. "I have read two Camilluses on the constitutionality of the treaty; so much answer to so little weight of objection" Ames found odd. Hamilton "holds up the aegis against a wooden sword. Jove's eagle holds his bolts in his talons, and hurls them, not at the Titans, but at sparrows and mice."[74]

Well into 1796, Federalists noted with pleasure—and, surely, with relief—the change (or at least the cooling) in public opinion. One letter writer noted, "Many have said to me that they were sensible they had taken up the business of the treaty *too hastily, too warmly, and unadvisably* . . . that 'it was the best treaty which could be obtained, and that its ratification was preferable to seeking redress for our wrongs by arms.'" An editorial claimed the opposition to the treaty "made the usual progress of silly things—it was begotten in cabal—supported by knavery operating on the passions or honest credulity of the multitude in a few great towns—and has fallen before the power of reason and mature reflection, into general contempt." Both pieces reflected the growing influence of the themes the Federalists had been hammering away at for months.[75]

In all of this Washington's stature grew apace. Late in February, Washington and the First Lady went to Ricketts' Amphitheatre. "[I]t was the first time he had been in public since the late noise and disturbance on account of the treaty." As soon as Washington came forward to his seat in the presidential box, "an instantaneous loud and general plaudit took place—a second—and a third, still louder: when these were over, an honest sailor, in the sincerity of a generous full heart, called out, 'Damn me if that is enough for the Old Fellow, let's give him three cheers.'" At that, the entire audience, "gentle and simple, old and young, most heartily joined. It must have given the President pleasure; his benign countenance and graceful demeanor shewed his sensibility and the goodness of his heart. I verily believe he is more sincerely admired and beloved at this moment than he ever was."[76]

A few days later, convinced of the change in public opinion and viewing with favor the results of the Federalists' campaign, Washington declared the treaty in effect and submitted it to the House of Representatives, at long last, on March 1, 1796. But neither Washington, the Federalists, nor the treaty would be out of the woods just yet. The anti-treaty critics had long since fastened on a strategy of trying to defeat the measure in the House of Representatives by denying funding for the commissions the treaty called for. But the House could not take action on this until Washington formally submitted the measure for its consideration. The president, shrewdly waiting for the recent pro-treaty and pro-administration sentiment to gather, had waited to send it to the House. Once he did, however, the final, climactic struggle over the treaty ensued, touching off passions equal in intensity to those of the previous summer. But before we turn to those debates, before we continue the story into the spring of 1796 in the House of Representatives and back in the streets, it remains to spend more time with the summer and fall 1795 debates, with the writings and speeches and activity both for and against. By examining some of these matters more fully, we can gain greater insight not only into the Jay Treaty debate itself but about some of the larger issues of political culture and the fight to shape public opinion in the United States.

4 | The Words of Tongue and Pen

The Rhetorical War over the Jay Treaty

"Damn John Jay! Damn every one who won't damn John Jay. Damn every one who won't put lights in the windows and sit up all night damning John Jay!" read the message chalked on a wall by a treaty opponent in New York.[1] Such visceral anger was seen elsewhere from other anti-treaty activists that summer. On July 25, 1795, angry Philadelphians gathered in a mass meeting in the yard of the State House, a traditional site for gatherings going back to the days of the Revolution. On this Saturday, the crowd, consisting of members of the Society of United Irishmen and other opponents of the treaty, was sizable and angry. They were stoked even further by Blair McClenachan, the president of the Democratic Society of Pennsylvania. McClenachan seized a copy of the treaty and waved it in the air, exclaiming with fury and contempt, "What a damned treaty! I make a motion that every good citizen in this assembly kick this damned treaty to hell!" At McClenachan's urging the crowd stuck a copy of the treaty on a pole, marched first to the home of the French minister, and then proceeded to the home of the British minister, where they burned the offensive document with evident disgust. For good measure, some in the crowd then broke the windows of some leading Federalists.[2] Many of the early written statements about the treaty were no less acidic. "Atticus" wrote in early July, "At length the illegitimate imp, the abortion of Liberty, has crawled from its skulking place, and contrary to the wishes of its *parent* and of it *godfathers,* has peeped into day. Divested of the darkness which encompassed it, we may now behold and examine the foul blotches that overspread it, and trace a pestiferous malady oozing from every pore."[3] Clearly, the public disdain for John Jay's work drew rhetorical flourishes of unprecedented passion.

Accounts such as these have long provided colorful anecdotes for brief discussions of the Jay Treaty because they characteristically exemplify rabid public opposition to the measure and capture a sense of the depth of feeling against the treaty and its negotiator. But while these certainly illustrate that broader theme, the harsh, violent commentary of McClenachan and the anonymous sidewalk graffitist also provide a window into another critical if little-studied facet of the Jay Treaty debate. When considered in a different context—and when contrasted with the statements and writings of pro-treaty advocates—they reveal much about the differences in rhetoric used by the two sides and offer another key for exploring and contextualizing the Jay Treaty debate. To the extent to which these rants predominated in the anti-treaty denouncements, they not only stand in stark contrast to the Federalists' speeches and writings, but also help to explain a crucial dimension of the debate: the role of rhetoric. This dimension is not merely aesthetic; it played a determining role in the way the debate unfolded and in how it was received by the various publics involved.[4]

The Republicans' vituperative attacks on the treaty created the context for the Federalists' very different, measured modes of response, but they also suggest an important point about the leadership of the Republicans on the treaty issue. While the Federalists called on their top-rank leaders —Washington, Hamilton, Webster, King, and others—in battling for public support of the treaty, many of the Republicans' leading lights absented themselves from the debate. Jefferson remained at Monticello, an increasingly distraught but idle observer. His most concerted efforts were directed—unsuccessfully—at getting James Madison to engage Hamilton by responding to the latter's "Camillus" essays. But Madison, too, remained largely silent and inactive. Even as Jefferson lamented the poor quality and ineffectiveness of much of the anti-treaty writing, neither he nor Madison took up their pens to challenge the Hamiltons, Kings, and Websters who wrote so effectively for the measure. This curious absence of top Republican figures and the generally unremarkable essays produced in their stead by secondary party figures will be discussed below. A key part of my argument is that, not only were anti-treaty efforts hampered by the absence of the leading literary and oratorical talents of the day, their absence foisted such men as McClenachan, Benjamin Franklin Bache, John Beckley, and others forward into the gap—sorely mismatching their skills against Hamilton's *and* decisively shaping the content and the tone of the rhetoric used in the debate. The conspicuous absence of Jefferson and Madison harmed the anti-treaty effort both rhetorically and politically. The very nature and demeanor, not to mention the tone, of the anti-treaty campaign was shaped by the words and speech of those who stepped in to fill the void. And, since the debate was a dialogue, the rhetorical tone and stance initially taken by the Republicans in turn created the context in which Federalists responded, shaping *their* rhetorical choices in the oral and textual debate.[5]

Treaty opponents, especially in the early weeks of the dispute, laced their writings with the same kind of vitriol and animosity that McClenachan and others made popular in their spoken commentary. They attacked the treaty's defects in harsh language and excoriated treaty supporters. Opponents furiously decried the document itself and personally savaged those most closely associated with it—Jay, George Washington, and Alexander Hamilton. Some writers even threatened secession rather than compliance with the instrument.[6] These writings joined with the verbal broadsides to set the tone for anti-treaty rhetoric. But the prevalence of this kind of material, which dominated in the first weeks of the public debate, did more than make for colorful accounts of political protest. It created the context in which Federalists would work when they weighed in later.

As Republican newspapers got hold of the treaty, their denunciations were filled with exclamations, capital letters, and italics.[7] One newspaper reprinted a handbill circulated in Portsmouth, Virginia, telling citizens that "*Your all is at Stake.*" It urged them to demonstrate with "spirit, against [Washington's] signing a Treaty, which will be the *Death Warrant* of your *TRADE*." Another paper spoke in distraught tones of the "Death of Independence," noting that "this extraordinary man" was born in Philadelphia July 4, 1776, and died there June 24, 1795, the date of the Senate approval. "In the early stages of his life, he was a child of the most promising hopes, as to both morals and hopes." While the "wicked men" who were the "instruments" of this death might be temporarily ascendent, "the friends of patriotism are numerous, & determined" and would punish those responsible. Another piece described the angry and violent manner with which the treaty was received in Charleston, South Carolina. The document "was immediately thrown into the fire to purify it, and prevent the citizens of a free state from being poisoned by that venomous present of the British Cabinet." One unfortunate "aristocrat" who attempted to speak in favor of the measure against "the will of thousands" met with a rude reception: he "was dragged to the pump and there completely ducked." Refusal by any other "tories" to renounce their allegiance to "the former tyrant of America" would force loyal citizens to resort to tarring and feathering: "a royal mantle and plumage of that kind, would fit the abettors of royalty in America admirably."[8]

Republicans pounced quickly on the early Federalist efforts to defend the measure. "How despicable and inconsistent are the hireling tools of the faction," began one editorial in the *Aurora* which mocked the Federalists for their comparisons of anti-treaty town meetings to Paris mobs. But such attacks were to be expected, since those meetings reprobated the treaty, "that favourite instrument of aristocrats and anglo Americans." It was little wonder that anti-treaty meetings were "held in detestation by the minions of an expiring faction." A few weeks later the same paper observed that supporters no longer bothered to defend the measure on its merits but instead argued in favor of it "because it has been negotiated by men who have *once* done service to us." This was an "insidious defence of an instrument, which is the universal execration of Americans!"[9]

Other attacks centered on those who wrote to defend the treaty. Supporters, according to some papers, had enlisted "a few mercenary Printers" or "hirelings" who, while "personally insignifican[t]," took license to "abuse every character" who opposed the measure. Such men used every trick they could summon and resorted to "sophistry to persuade the people that they ought to accede to the Treaty." Still, "the good sense of the YEOMANRY will teach them." Further, Federalists, who found their views opposed by the vast majority of the public, found it necessary to "degrade" the people by showing contempt for their opinions and even to "dispute their capacity in judging their own interests."[10]

The strongest attacks, however, were saved for those the Republicans believed were directly responsible not only for the treaty defense but for the orchestration of the measure itself. Benjamin Franklin Bache's *Aurora* went hard after Alexander Hamilton. One writer to the paper found that the "Camillus" essays, of which "the *ci-devant* Secretary of the Treasury has been publicly and uncontradictedly said to be the author," refuted very few of the many objections made to the treaty. If it was indeed true that Hamilton was the author, "we need not wonder at the flowery diction and sophisms of an essay, that proves *nothing.*" Another writer, "Atticus," was even blunter. He noted that Hamilton was deploying "his usual weapons, sophistry and seduction, but not with his accustomed success." As Hamilton's character became known to more people and more fully understood, his influence on the public "has become as harmless . . . as a toad or a cock roach, and like those animals, he excites sensations which are those of aversion more than of dread." As many Republicans would throughout the debate, "Atticus" excoriated Hamilton for raising the cry of war, and warned his fellow citizens that Hamilton expected "by his hideous yells, to terrify you . . . into an abandonment of your rights." Still another attack on Hamilton that fall scorned him as "*President would be;* alias, Alexander Catiline," whose "soporific and copious dozes, instead of lulling free-born Americans asleep, only tend to spread the detestation of Jay's treaty."[11]

Bitter attacks on Hamilton, a fierce partisan battler himself, could be expected. What was more shocking was the quickness and firmness with which Republican newspapers, principally but not exclusively Bache's *Aurora,* attacked George Washington. Beginning in the summer and escalating into the fall, the anti-treaty side launched unapologetic assaults on the president for his elitism and disregard for the people and for public opinion, and denounced the fact that many seemed all too willing to follow blindly wherever Washington chose to lead. The ferocity of these writings is striking because it shows not only how quickly the no-holds-barred style of partisan conflict had developed, but how Washington, once a virtually untouchable figure standing above partisan division, became enmeshed in and identified with those very divisions.

Bache's *Aurora* unquestionably led this assault on the president, but that paper was by no means alone, joined as it was by others across the nation. As early as August 22, 1795—just eight days after Washington signed the treaty—Bache's paper, which had entertained the hope that the president might be induced by the public opposition to the measure not to sign the document, launched a full-scale attack. With no hope of persuading Washington, the *Aurora* declared war, providing more examples of the vehemence and intemperance of the anti-treaty side. The immediate source of disagreement was the contrast between Washington's response to a petition of merchants and traders favoring the treaty and those from various citizens opposing it. Bache was unsparing and unmodulated in his criticism. "His answer would lead us to suppose that he was the omnipotent director of a seraglio, instead of the first magistrate of a free people. He thunders disdain upon the people." Bache then declared up front what Washington should expect from citizens: "as he has treated us with disrespect, he must expect to be no longer viewed as a saint; as he has spoken daggers to their feelings, he must no longer expect a blind devotion to his will."[12] A different piece in the same paper was even more pointed. "Are the Merchants a privileged order that the petition of four hundred should outbalance the decided voice of the majority of the citizens? Are *they* alone concerned in the operation of Laws?—Is the constitution to be violated with impunity because four hundred merchants and traders approve of the violation?"[13]

Another *Aurora* writer, "Hancock," accused Washington and treaty supporters of elitism and class politics, claiming that the president had "introduced a *distinction* among the people, not warranted by the government under which we have associated, utterly repugnant to the equal rights of freemen, and contrary to every principle of republican liberty." The author noted that the thousands of people who signed petitions in Boston, Philadelphia, and New York, as well as other parts of the country, had been answered "*in the lump*" by Washington, whereas a mere four hundred merchants and traders in Philadelphia "have been graciously honored with a specific reply." "Hancock" concluded that, examining that reply, "we should forget ourselves so far as to imagine that it was the Royal George with whom we have made a treaty graciously replying to his loyal and dutiful subjects."[14]

In Boston, Thomas Adams and Isaac Larkin's *Independent Chronicle* skewered Washington as well, denying that the president had any defensible reason for signing the treaty. It especially found fault with him for signing even while fully aware of public opposition. "Had his signature been given immediately after the adjournment of the Senate, and before an universal expression of disapprobation of it had taken place, ingenuity might have found a cover for him; but the public mind seems to have designedly wrought up to the highest key of expectation, that the contempt of it might be more strongly disclosed." Washington was excoriated for substituting his own will for that of the people and for trampling on the Constitution: "Is the President to receive more reverence than our Constitution, and more devotion than liberty!" Echoing a theme raised by other writers, the piece asked, "Are freemen to be treated with the most marked contumely, and to be passive under it like slaves?" Most importantly, this essay and others raised—as early as the summer of 1795—the possibility of continuing the fight in the House of Representatives, which became the Republicans' ultimate strategy. So strong was the dismay over and opposition to Washington's actions, however, that this piece and others raised the specter of impeachment, an idea which would have been unthinkable just a few years—or even months—before. "Atticus" asked incredulously, "Are we to establish a political infallibility, and consecrate a political Pope in our country! . . . If so, I will preach up a reformation, and dare to be Luther in politics. I will strive to unmask the idol we have set up, and show him to be a man. . . . As our application to the President has been treated with scorn, let us make our appeal to that Body, which has the power of impeachment, and we shall not find in the *Step-fathers* of their country. . . . Let us then, my fellow-citizens, rally round our Representatives, and we may still be free."[15] Such criticism, not to mention the implication of future action, suggests just how extreme some critics were in voicing their disapproval of the measure and the administration.

Republican newspapers also attacked Washington for elitism more broadly (that is, beyond the specific issue of the Jay Treaty), and his administration for cultivating the trappings of monarchy. "Pittachus" noted bluntly that Washington started his political career "as if he had inherited a kingdom. . . . His first step was to impress the people with *awe*." Could the president be a true friend to republicanism and to the people if he had introduced "*a pageantry*" to government? Would the people never see "the magistrate of their choice but in *a coach and six,* or at a *levee?*" Washington and "*a complying Senate*" assured that constitutional violations that "merit impeachment and disgrace" had been considered "as a wise and judicious construction." In fact, not only was the Constitution subservient to Washington, "the laws which he himself sanctioned, appear to have ministered to his convenience and to his gratification." Such behavior likely foreshadowed his conduct in the Jay Treaty matter. "Pittachus" wondered whether Washington's answer to the merchants and traders was "dictated by a reverence for *wealth*" and whether it was "*poverty* which chilled his sensibility, when he haughtily told the people of Boston, New-York, Philadelphia &c. that he would 'not substitute the sentiments of others for his own conviction.'"[16] Other critics believed that Washington's actions on the treaty were part and parcel of his administration's conduct and showed very clearly his derisive attitude toward public opinion. After Senate approval and the publication of the treaty, the president expressed a wish that the public voice could be heard. But once the public weighed in opposing his administration's measure, Washington made his own decision which not only slighted the views of those citizens who were against the measure but "*insults* the public voice." In short, critics argued, Washington asked for public opinion but then plainly rejected it. "The plain language of all which is, first, 'I am at a loss how to act, I know not which alternative to chuse, then let the public voice determine.' Afterwards, 'I have made up my mind; hold your tongue, think you I am to listen to you.'"[17]

For Bache and many other Republicans, Washington's high-handed, imperious behavior exemplified a deeper problem which treaty opponents would have to overcome if they were to convince many Americans—among them even some treaty opponents themselves—of the need to reject administration policies. The problem as many saw it was that Washington was still too awe-inspiring and powerful for American citizens to suspect ill of or oppose. Some Republicans noted this fact bitterly and bluntly. "One Eye Shut" compared Washington to a despot by suggesting he simply wanted Americans to follow him blindly and stop demonstrating against the treaty. The author took heart that Americans were not shy about opposing Washington and were not backing down timidly under his glare. "[T]he idol both walks and talks, rather more unheeded, than when that confidence was merited; that a conduct delineating the strong features of a despot," he wrote, "has at last roused them to a feeling of their wrongs and a search for a remedy to the evil." Others were even more blunt. Neatly encapsulating the problem for treaty opponents, one writer asked, "as long as George Washington is President, can it be expected that the people will deliver their sentiments freely? The fear of offending, with many, will prevent their passing their opinion, when it is in opposition with the President's. . . . Who can oppose him?"[18] But while opposing Washington did take some effort and courage, Republicans—with Bache leading the way—were doing so more often over the treaty. Their denunciations of the president comprised an important element of the anti-treaty campaign and shaped the broader dimensions of the debate.

For their part, Federalists responded to such sharp and hostile rhetoric with derision, scorn, and mockery. While they occasionally resorted to answering Republicans in kind, they mostly concentrated on criticizing their coarse, hyperbolic language, on attributing the protests to

Jacobinism and French influence, on denouncing the most outspoken opponents as disorganizers and malcontents, and on mounting a strong defense of George Washington and the constituted authorities.[19]

But the Federalists also had another powerful tactical advantage in the rhetorical war, in that they knew what the Republicans' themes and modes of attack would be and could shape a counterattack based on that knowledge. Because Republicans overplayed their hand initially, Federalists could seize on the most outrageous actions and writings denouncing the treaty, publicize them widely, and attack opponents for hyperbole and rhetorical excess while positioning themselves as the voice of calm reason. Ironically, even though Federalists criticized themselves for waiting so long to engage in the public debate, the delay served a useful purpose: when they did weigh in they could exhibit a stark contrast in style, tone, and language to that of the Republicans and they could both call for, and exemplify in their own writings, a calm, rational, considered position.

Federalists reamed the anti-treaty side for the harshness, violence, intemperance, and hyperbole of its rhetoric. John Fenno's *Gazette of the United States* led the way. "FIRE, FIRE, FIRE, HELP," he began one editorial mocking the alarmist rhetoric, "the town is on fire—the world's on fire—we shall all be burnt up alive—roasted, baked, to make a dinner for aristocrats." Fenno counselled treaty opponents to stop attacking the measure but did not think that was likely to happen: "nothing can stop the mouth of a fool, especially if he is a wicked one: he cries on FIRE, FIRE, FIRE. . . . Such, and so absurd, is the clamor against the late treaty." "But what," he lamented, "can appease determined discontent?" At the same time as he ridiculed the overheated rhetoric of treaty opponents, Fenno—writing in early July 1795—stated one of the central themes of Federalists in their campaign to win backing for the document: that it was the best treaty possible and that John Jay had got as much in the way of concessions and recognition as one might fairly expect. After all, Americans should bear in mind that when dealing with a nation like Great Britain, "we must not expect that our desires are to be the terms of negotiation. . . . If Mr. Jay had been treating with a nation of id[i]ots or children, he might have cajoled the poor creatures out of any thing he could have asked."[20]

The *Gazette* suggested that the rash and immediate attack on the measure "is an evidence of the continuation of the unrelenting spirit of party and faction. . . . To effect its object and multiply its partizans, misrepresentation and misconstruction are called in aid, and truth is sacrificed," all in an effort to "prejudice the public mind." Fenno repeated in other editorials his condemnation of the excessive rhetoric of those opposed to the treaty. In one, he observed that it was by "*mutilated speeches, misrepresentations and exaggerations* that men of a certain description are enabled to raise and inflame the passions of the people, and hurry them to commit outrages against the officers and the measures of government."[21]

Other papers took up the same theme. "Nestor" wrote acerbically that the merits of the treaty were not being discussed with moderation and objectivity. "Contemptuous and abusive language does not bring conviction, but inflame the passions, and produce mutual hatred and jealousy." He found the writings of "Cinna" (Brockholst Livingston) particularly offensive in their overraught tone and their animosity toward Jay and toward Hamilton as the author of the "Camillus" essays. "Nestor" made it clear he did not object to "Cinna's" writings merely because they were critical of the treaty. "I blame him not for writing against the treaty, but for his irritating expressions. The treaty admits of discussion, let it be done with ingenuousness and temper." Some Federalists went so far as to argue that the more extreme anti-treaty writings should be published widely, believing that their exaggerations and overstatements would, conversely, win backers for the document. "Valerius" was especially singled out for contempt. "The more generally, therefore, they are circulated, the more extensively of course, will the parricidous designs of the authors be exposed to the observation of the people. It is, therefore wished, that all the printers would publish *Hancock* and *Valerius*." The author believed that "much good" would arise from publication. Noah Webster editorialized that the popular disturbances were so great in part because opponents misrepresented the document: "The worst features of the treaty are first exhibited and exaggerated," he wrote. But this had a good effect; the denunciations would prompt a closer examination and a rational consideration. Once people had a chance to do so, they would discover for themselves that the measure was not as opponents represented it. "The people as a body," Webster wrote, "have always honest views—they therefore never do wrong, but through delusion. The moment their delusion is removed, they return to principles of order, and leave their deceivers in the lurch." Webster recounted other times in the previous decades when public opinion changed dramatically and argued that this dispute would follow the same pattern. Eventually, he believed, the public would "bless the President and Senate and despise the Jacobins who have misled them."[22]

Webster's prediction points out a second leading theme of Federalists as they wrote against the hyperbolic, violent rhetoric of their opponents: Jacobinism. From the early days of the public debate Federalists used the term in their assault on opponents. Webster in particular raised this theme repeatedly as a favorite rhetorical weapon, often in point-blank, unsubtle ways. It was curious, he noted, the rise and fall of popular ferment, "and how the tide of popular censure and declamation in the United States, resembles the inflamatory proceedings of the Jacobins in Paris." Closely examined, the segment in America calling upon "Antifederalism, or more recently Democracy," would be found "perpetually in action, and operating successfully on great numbers of weak, credulous minds, and drawing them into the turbulent vortex of party." The "materials" of Jacobinism, according to Webster, were "inflammable passions" which make "a violent blaze for a time and then gradually expire." But Webster also noted that "Steady wisdom always gets the better of this frantic enthusiasm" and believed he already saw signs of a settling of the treaty furor. As the treaty was more widely read, it was more fully understood, and "many men who execrated the treaty before they *had read it*, now say, 'it is not as bad as they thought.'" Even so, he noted a few months later that real damage had already been done. The Democratic clubs, modeled, he believed, on French societies, had produced many ill effects and would likely do so for some time to come. "[T]here is little doubt that the late Jacobin intrigues of France have laid the foundation for serious trouble in America that will last for many years to come."[23]

Webster attacked Jacobinism directly in the twelfth and final number of his pro-treaty "Curtius" essays. Having discussed and defended the instrument in its particulars, Webster declared his intention to close the series by addressing some more general concerns. He asked, rhetorically, why Americans had not left the treaty business to the constituted authorities and answered the question by declaring that citizens had been deceived and misled "into rash opinions, and violent measures" by the foes of government. Worse, these foes were creating societies "formed on the plan of the Jacobin Society in France." Now, the U.S. was similarly threatened. Opposing the measure was not the ultimate goal of the disorganizers; rather, it was merely "a convenient instrument for them to wield" while the real reasons for opposition to government lay deeper. It was just as well, Webster concluded, that the contest between government and the Jacobins was out in the open, for "One or the other must prevail, and on the final prevalence of one or the other of these parties, are suspended the peace, prosperity and happiness of the United States."[24]

When Federalists were not attacking opponents as Jacobins they were denouncing the various anti-treaty public meetings for their violence and primacy of passion over reason and logic. In this way, too, Federalists positioned themselves as the voices of reason and calm while castigating Republicans as dangerous malcontents and disorganizers. Commenting on the New York meeting where Alexander Hamilton was attacked, the *Gazette of the United States* dismissed the meeting as being full of men who "arrogate to themselves the names of *Republicans*" and denied the right to speak to anyone who was not "avowedly of their party." Further, these opponents "hypocritically preach up the necessity of *a full investigation of public measures*" while they shout down speakers who try to discuss the treaty dispassionately. "Many were heard in the meeting to abuse the President, execrate the Senate, and damn the law. To believe that such men wish to support good government," the paper concluded, "requires faith so that we may move mountains." Other editorials condemned the "tocsin of confusion" rung by opponents of the treaty in the cities, who "pronounced [their] hasty anathemas against the Treaty without discussing it." Still, this was no more than was to be expected from such "turbulent and designing" men who had showed "opposition and malevolence" from the inception of Jay's mission to England. The *Gazette* also called on citizens to study the document carefully for themselves, to prevent "being imposed on by the intriguing enemies of our peace, prosperity and excellent government" whose "intemperate zeal to disorganize and weaken every public measure" had been manifest from the outset.[25]

And Federalists wasted little time in responding to assaults on George Washington, defending the president's honor and questioning incredulously whether the hero of the Revolution would ever so readily sell out his nation's interests to the British as some critics charged. Regretting that the debate had prompted "every knave to come out from his lurking place and insult the public, by setting himself up for a *patriot*," "Nestor" distinguished between real and pretended patriots. "The American public will not easily forget the services the virtues, and the patriotism of their old and tried friends . . . they are not so pur blind as to mistake calumny for patriotism, nor so ignorant of their own interests as to place confidence in men whom they have long been accustomed to despise." Others struck similar notes. "An American" wrote that "even the actions of our Chief Magistrate are decried. . . . To suspect virtue so well tried, is surely the height of ingratitude"; were such suspicions widely held, it would be a disgrace. However, in "the warmth of zeal against public measures, which some of our citizens indulged, they have been blind to the prosperity they enjoyed." Once people calmly reflected on the matter, however, they saw things more clearly and the "gross fallacy . . . bec[a]me obvious." All of this proved a useful lesson; it reminded "our restless citizens, that in the future they [should] examine [issues] with more modesty, and suffer not their confidence in good men to be susperseded."[26]

While Federalists sometimes responded to Republican anti-treaty acerbity in kind, the entire tone, tenor, and substance of their campaign in favor of the measure were different. The writings of Hamilton, King, and Webster in particular, as well as other newspaper writers, set a high standard which anti-treaty Republican writers tried but failed to match.[27] With Jefferson and Madison electing not to contest "Camillus" and the other pro-treaty writings, Republicans by default had only second-tier figures to rely on for their literary efforts. Brockholst Livingston (writing as "Decius" and "Cinna"), Robert Livingston ("Cato"), and Alexander J. Dallas (who wrote "Features of Mr. Jay's Treaty") took up their pens to combat Jay's work.[28] Even though some of these essays made—with more evidence—the same points raised by less restrained treaty foes, the writings could hardly be judged even a qualified success, much less a match for "Camillus" and "Curtius." Partly this was because some of the essays, especially those by the Livingstons, still contained exaggerations and injudicious contentions. Dallas's "Features" was the most eloquent attack on the treaty, but it was legalistic, lacking in real forcefulness, and even Dallas' biographer has called the twenty-two-thousand-word document "pretentious."[29]

In short, despite the talents of those who wrote against the Jay Treaty, the work they produced lacked the cogency of Hamilton's. Jefferson ruefully noted as much when he tried to cajole Madison into writing against the former treasury secretary. Jefferson told Madison that, although there was speculation that the "Features" had been written by Tench Coxe, he believed it more likely that John Beckley had been the author. In any case, the essay failed to do the trick. "The antidote is certainly not strong enough for the poison of Curtius." Jefferson also noted that he had even tried to encourage "honest sound hearted men of common understanding, and they were not able to parry the sophistry of Curtius." Because of the strength of Webster and especially Hamilton—Jefferson wrote, famously, "Hamilton is really a colossus to the antirepublican party. Without numbers, he is an host within himself"—the Monticello statesman implored Madison to write. "We have had only midling performances to oppose to him. In truth, when he comes forward, there is nobody but yourself who can meet him." Jefferson also shrewdly noted the problem of timing Republicans faced as they tried to combat Hamilton. "His adversaries having begun the attack, he has the advantage of answering them, & remains unanswered himself."[30] Madison, unhappy with the way he had measured up against Hamilton in his "Helvidius" essays of 1793, declined, and the Republicans never did find anyone who could match the Federalist leaders rhetorically. The absence of the anti-treaty side's leading lights proved very costly in the public debate. In the contest of heavy hitters, the Republicans' best weapons were never unsheathed, meaning that the pro-treaty writers stood all the more forcefully astride the rhetorical landscape by comparison.

Jefferson's and Madison's decisions not to engage Hamilton directly manifested not only in the absence of any strong writings to match his, but in their general approach to the Jay Treaty debate. Significantly, the anti-treaty campaign was led, not by the authors of the Declaration and the Constitution, but instead by the Livingstons, Dallas, Carey, Beckley—and the McClenachans of the street. Beckley in particular did yeoman work to get copies of the treaty printed and distributed, circulate petitions, gather writings, and build grassroots opposition to the measure. He received encouragement (if little actual help) from the party's main leaders, but Beckley was "the stage manager of a ferocious assault on the Federalists." As a recent student of his party activism has noted, with Jefferson retired and Madison back in Virginia, "the leadership of the emerging party fell almost by default to Beckley and his fellow militants."[31] While that default leadership reflected a shift that Jeffrey L. Pasley pinpoints as the social origins of campaigning, it also left the anti-treaty side at a loss, in a war of words, at a time when the power of the printed word still counted for a great deal.

The war to sway public opinion stretched well beyond the learned pamphlets and essays, however. The verbal battle also extended to humor. Writers on both sides produced an array of doggerel, verse, and sarcastic attacks on what they viewed as the hypocrisy, inconsistency, foolishness, and simple wrongheadedness of the other side. In significant ways, these writers nicely reflected the central themes of each side's arguments, articulating in a lighter way the same points others made more straightforwardly. In fact, the sarcasm and humor in many of their writings actually gave an even harder, more acerbic edge to the arguments, and reinforced with added bite the very same themes and articulations. Rather than being dismissed as mere lampoons, these writings can be profitably examined for additional insights to the rhetorical war.

Treaty opponents used sarcasm and humor to berate the Federalists for the same faults they accused them of in more serious writings. Bristling at being denounced as a "detestable faction," one Republican wrote that perhaps he was part of a detestable faction and suggested, tongue in cheek, that he and others had no reason to recoil at the charge. He proceeded to list ten reasons why Republicans might be a "detestable faction," all having to do with their opposition to the treaty and each concluding with the phrase, "We are a detestable faction": "2nd. Because we cannot discern a single advantage which America derives from this infamous compact. . . . 3rd. Because we believe that its ratification thus far was brought about by mere strength of party. . . . 4th. Because we dare to exercise our own opinions, and decently express them to the President of the U.S. . . . 9th. Because we watch with jealous care, and oppose with republican freedom every attack of administration upon our excellent constitution," the piece avowed, "we are a detestable faction."[32]

Republicans also mocked by sarcastic overstatement what they saw as the high-handed manner of the Federalists in dismissing opposition to the treaty, and contrasted the "*manner* and *stile* of the President's answer to the common people of Philadelphia, New York, Boston, &c." to his tone in answering the merchants and traders of Philadelphia. "Do *the people* mean to put themselves upon a par with *the merchants & the traders!* Are *five thousand* of the *common mass* of citizens of Philadelphia to weigh against *four hundred merchants and traders?*" Continuing in the same sarcastic vein, the writer exclaimed, "Ye swinish creatures are not to approach the presidential sanctuary with your gruntings. Is he to be pestered with your impertinent opinions, and to have his delicate nerves unstrung by your advice!"[33]

Other Republicans mocked the secrecy of the Federalists. One printed several choruses of a piece titled "Mr. Jay's Treaty Disclosed by Stephens

Thomson Mason," which played on the Virginia senator's role in leaking a copy of the treaty to Benjamin Franklin Bache:

> When the Senate, assembled had shut up their door,
> And left us no clue their designs to explore,
> The people were anxious, & whispered their care,
> But their voice was too weak for the dignified ear
> Ye are down, down, down, keep ye down. . . .
>
> But the rabble had nothing to hear or to view,
> Says the *twenty,** the secret's too sacred for you,
> Ye are down, down, down, keep ye down.
>
> But Stephens T. Mason, a man we revere,
> With his name bid the infamous treaty appear,
> 'Twas the act of a freeman, who join'd with the TEN,
> To save us from tyranny, rank us with men,
> Altho' down, down, and like to be down.
>
> He gave his assistance; enlightened our eyes,
> And a cloud from all quarters begins to arise,
> *Vox Dei, Vox Populi,* truly but one,
> Shall tell dark designers—*our will shall be done,*
> Till you're down, down, *twenty* times down.[34]

Treaty opponents also sarcastically mocked the supposed arrogance and pretension of its advocates. A long story printed in the *Jersey Chronicle* in September 1795 had a "plain countryman" urging a group of citizens to come to a town meeting on the treaty. At this point a "speculator in certificates" stopped to listen, but soon interrupted the countryman, "assuring him that 'it was impossible common people, like him, living in an obscure village, could understand the treaty; and that therefore he, or any of his neighbors, ought not to presume to give any opinion on it.'" The countryman responded with outrage, denouncing the instrument's "obscurity of language." He exclaimed that "Truth and honesty evermore speak in plain language, intelligible to the meanest capacity, and comprehensible by the mind of rusticity itself. Imposture and deception

* The Senate voted 20–10 for the treaty.

deal in double meanings and obscure phrases and, like the witch's prayer, as read forward or backward, will utter blessings or curses." This harangue continued at length, with the citizen dismissing contemptuously the notion that those who lived away from the merchant cities could indeed understand the measure, and attacking the speculator and his friends. "Ought we to have any treaty, sir, that, in its general features at least, is above the comprehension of the plain yeomanry of the United States?—Are lawyers and merchants, British agents and trimming pettifoggers the only men that are gifted with ideas and the common intelligence of men?" After continuing the put-down of the speculator at some length, the plain countryman listed all the qualifications one must have to pass judgment on the treaty, ridiculed the pretension of the speculator and his allies, and disposed of his views forcefully. "The speculator in certificates rode off—and lo! all the people set up a loud laugh!"[35]

Republicans mocked treaty advocates for exaggerating any bit of good news in those early months after it became public, and for the presumption that the opinions of a few Federalist gentlemen were more important than all others. One newspaper report noted that "a small number (about 36 out of 130)" of the Boston Chamber of Commerce met to discuss the treaty and prepared resolutions supporting the measure. "We should be happy to have given these resolutions to the public," noted the *Aurora* sarcastically, because "they must be very important and patriotic—the opinion of 36 must certainly weigh down the voice of 1500, and may have a great weight with the President."[36]

Bache's paper also took aim at Alexander Hamilton's "Camillus" essays, seeing the prolific detail of the pieces as a detriment. "Oneirophilus" poked fun at Hamilton's verbosity in a long piece entitled "The Dream." The author noted that he had been engaged in reading several of the "Defence" essays one evening when "a sudden and irresistable drowsiness came upon me, and I fell asleep in my chair by the fire." In this slumber he was soon transported into a dream in which he was witness to a trial arraigning Hamilton. "The prisoner immediately put himself into the attitude of an orator," when the judge sternly cut him off and spoke to him:

> CAMILLUS, this court is not at leisure to listen to one of your prolix *Defences:* neither *rhetoric* or sophistry will here avail. This court listens not to harangues calculated to disguise truth, to veil its opposite, and to give false colourings to facts. We proceed only upon evidence, and that

> evidence is collected from the offender's own confessions. Listen therefore to the questions propounded to you by the court, and presume not to answer in any other manner than by a simple negative, or affirmative; and, for the first time, learn to *obey*, instead of presuming to *dictate*.

The prisoner seemed taken aback by this charge and fell uncharacteristically silent as the judge put a series of thirty-nine questions to him, designed to uncover Hamilton's identity as the author of previous essays and other writings, which, the accusations charged, evinced a love of monarchy and Great Britain. The questions also blamed Hamilton for creating a party and faction, and for orchestrating all the actions of that party. The final question read, "Hath not your whole political conduct, had for its objects a RE-UNION with GREAT BRITAIN; the *subversion* of the present *limited* constitution; the ESTABLISHMENT OF THE MONARCHY; and the eternal ANNIHALISM OF REPUBLICANISM, & A REPUBLICAN FORM OF GOVERNMENT?" Just as the judge was about to pronounce sentence, the author, "struck with horror at the scene," started awake. This piece thus managed to strike at Hamilton with the usual charges, but in a mocking and humorous fashion.[37]

During the spring of 1796, as the Federalists' campaign to win public support was in full swing, the *Aurora* ran a sarcastic piece which mocked what Republicans saw as the extreme lengths (and lies) Federalists resorted to in order to persuade the public. The paper contained an "Advertisement Extraordinary" promising a $1,000 reward to any man who could invent a story to help the treaty win passage in the House of Representatives. "From past experience," the advertisement noted, "the bugbear of a war is likely to prove most efficacious. But as this story is worn rather thread-bare, it will require somewhat of a new dress. Much pains need not be bestowed on the subject, as, from the present favourable disposition of the public mind, they seem disposed to swallow any thing, how monstrous or impossible soever it may be." Applications for the reward could be made "at the sign of England triumphant, next door to Jay's-Court, in Treaty Lane." A few weeks later the paper printed a response to the advertisement which was headed "WAR! WAR! WAR!" and offered a fantastic story of five different wars that would break out, in addition to other horrors that would follow, if the treaty were not approved. "A Friend to the Treaty" asked Bache if he was not fully entitled to the reward money for his story. "I have invented lies enough to terrify all the old women in the Union into an acquiescence in the Treaty." The author noted that he had, as the advertisement suggested, stressed "the very successful topic of war, and have given it 'somewhat of a new dress,'" but, because it seemed that any old tale would do, he "thus had not taken great pains in this undertaking."[38] Such writings were at once humorous ways of mocking the Federalists' actions on behalf of the treaty and expressions of Republican frustration at the success supporters were enjoying, through what opponents considered unfair and antidemocratic, if not wholly illegitimate, methods.

But Federalist papers got in their own humorous digs at Republicans, skewering the impropriety of their actions as well as the wrongheadedness of their positions. Federalists ridiculed the improper, extra-constitutional conduct of the town meetings, portraying them as the seedbeds of faction. Noah Webster's newspaper published a piece purporting to be the proceedings of a "general meeting of Disorganizers" held at "Club-hall" with "Citizen FACTION in the Chair." The mock meeting drafted several resolutions, including one holding that treaties should be ratified by town meetings "in any irregular way that any one disorganizer shall see fit to propose." When any treaty was ratified by the Senate it would be the duty of the club to "prejudice the public mind against it" by calling meetings before the treaty was published and making sure the treaty was "damned before it is read." Furthermore, "if anybody offers to discuss the Treaty, we will stone him or hiss him down. We can do this much better than we can *argue* and *reason,* and besides it will not take half the time to decide questions by stones, as it will by arguments." Amplifying the Federalists' stinging critique of the town meetings, another newspaper correspondent wrote that he believed he had, while recently considering the workings of government, hit upon a better and less expensive way of managing affairs. "Sir, we can do without a President," he wrote to the editor, "and without a Congress, too . . . whenever things begin to get wrong, there are a few people in every City who are always ready to set them right—they can prepare business all ready to our hands, and then will have nothing to do but to call a Town Meeting, lay the state of things before them, and take their votes by shew of hands." It was little use giving men time to consider or study matters fully because "it serves to puzzle them, the more they think."[39] Such retorts both attacked the anti-treaty side and underscored the Federalists' commitment to the constituted authorities.

Another undercurrent in most of these Federalist writings is the sense of faith and confidence that the American people are either on the Federalists' side, or will be, once they can be persuaded to dismiss the harmful and dangerous anti-treaty diatribes. One essay ridiculed activists who "tried to keep up their own [opposition] by addresses and town-meetings, and scribblings and blackguardings, and actually would have knocked the Congress and the Constitution, *and all that,* in the head, if they had not been afraid of the people; for I overheard one of these wise men saying to another wise man, 'The Game is lost, *the people wont join us.*'"[40]

John Fenno's *Gazette of the United States* printed a lengthy work in mock-Biblical tones which damned the anti-treaty side for a variety of sins. The piece included fifteen verses which told the story through the saga of the counsellor "Jayham" and the covenant he made with the "king of the Albionites." This piece is best excerpted verbatim rather than paraphrased.

> 3. And behold, when Jayham returned from his embassy, and made a report of all he had done, the chief ruler [President Washington] and the elders of the people [The Senate] agreed therewith; but the sons of Belial and Anarchites were sore displeased.
>
> 4. And they said unto Jayham, why has thou done this? Thou has kissed the hand of the Queen of the Albionites, and has bowed thyself down before her. And Jayham replied, and said, I have done so, and so, that you, and your wives, and little ones might eat bread; and we might have peace in the land all our days.
>
> 5. But the sons of Belial and the Anarchites waxed wroth against him. And they took unto themselves a block of wood from the yards of the ship-builders, and they made an image like unto Jayham, and they burned it with fire. Now this happened without the walls of the city, about the first watch of night.
>
> 6. And they made a league also with the Atheites, who had sworn that they would smite the Albionites with the edge of the sword, until none should be left alive.
>
> 7. And they all took counsel together, how they might raise an uproar in the land, and set at nought the covenant, which Jayham the counsellor had made with the Albionites: but the wisdom of the chief ruler and the elders of the people prevailed against them.

> 8. Then the sons of Belial, and the Anarchites went together into the dark places of the city, and they drew up a writing filled with all manner of falsehoods, and revilings against the covenant which Jayham had made, and against the chief rulers and the elders of the people.

But ultimately, the "Sons of Belial and the Anarchites" were stymied, and "their counsels became confused; and there was a great tumult." All the actions of these "Anarchites" were for naught and their unruliness in opposition to the laws of the land stood "as a warning to our children and our children's children."[41]

Another humorous piece in Fenno's paper, published in November 1795, lampooned the anti-treaty side for its general tendency to assume the worst of the adminstration as well as its alarmist tendencies, not just on the treaty but on other matters as well. Under the heading "Federal Ship News," the essay noted that the good ship "*Federal Government,*" under the command of George Washington, continued on her voyage with "safety and success" notwithstanding the nearly constant second-guessing and cries of danger:

> For some time past a gang of land lubbers, who were entered on board as ordinary seamen, have been frightened at some flocks of Mother *Carey's* chickens, which have hovered about the ship, and have been continually bawling out *Rocks, Rocks a head—look out for breakers,* and other outcries equally as vociferous—The old seamen at the bows, whose duty it is to con, has seen nothing of the reefs, and the seamen in the chains continually cry, *no soundings.* But notwithstanding these, and the Capt. always at the helm, these land lubbers are always on the cry of *Rocks and Breakers* when on deck; and when between decks as constantly insinuate the Capt. means to run on the breakers and destroy the vessel. The Mates and Old seamen laugh at the swabbers; and to quell their fears, ask them if the Commodore would destroy himself and ship for the sake of drowning such animals as they are? This stops their jaws for a moment; but the instant their watch is called, they continue the old tune; and the honest tars can scarcely sleep in their births [*sic*] for the noise.[42]

While this piece was written with the obvious intent to poke fun at nervous Republicans and amuse Federalists, the sentiments it voices—even in humor—reflect the very essence of the Federalists' argument about the role of constituted authorities and the "proper" role of citizens (to trust and follow said authorities), as well as the contempt in which the anti-treaty activists were held by the Federalists.

A final example, which appeared early in 1796 in Noah Webster's paper, also underscores many of the main points of the treaty advocates—both in its stinging dismissal and ridicule of Republican leaders and their arguments and in its expression of faith in the people, the citizens who would come around once again to back their leaders and their administration. "Guillotina," addressed to the readers of the *Connecticut Courant,* recounted in verse the anti-treaty activities of the previous summer and fall while poking fun at those who participated. Ridiculing the efforts of Bache and others to foment opposition to the document, this piece decried the publication of the "half-false Treaty" which "came in print; For telling truth so long had stray'd, From Bache, he had forgot the trade." Leading anti-treaty voices (including Massachusetts governor Samuel Adams) were lampooned, as in the case of Blair McClenachan and his famous opposition: "At Philadelphia Blair the great, That Irish guardian of the State, Rais'd his hard foot to give the blow, And cry'd 'to hell the child must go.'" But the work concluded on a hopeful note, as the public seemed to reject such arguments against the treaty and supported the measure, the administration, and especially President Washington. "Bold FREEDOM feeds her Vestal Fires, And every heart and tongue in-spires; While, still in Courts, as once in Fields, Great WASHINGTON her Glory shields; Long may his Sun unclouded Shine, And set 'full-orb'd.'"[43]

Both sides in the debate thus used humor and sarcasm to needle the opposition, ridicule it for perceived outrages, and lampoon the emptiness or disingenuousness of its arguments. The Federalists—whose print campaign was massive and widespread—especially used sarcasm as a way of advancing their positions and underscoring with humor the same claims and positions they advanced in their serious writings.

Further analysis of the rhetorical campaigns for and against the Jay Treaty can be done, but as even this brief examination has shown, the words deployed—written and oral—reveal a great deal about the nature of the contest. The tone of each side's argument was shaped by the personnel engaged in the debate and by the decision of some to sit on the sidelines. Further, the language used by the anti-treaty side in its initial soundings undermined its position and enabled the treaty defenders to cast their position in a far more favorable light. But there is a larger consideration as well. The debate also illustrates the way in which print and oral culture—the written word and the spoken word—worked together, and often, as Sandra M. Gustafson has recently argued, were mutually reinforcing.[44] Rather than print culture displacing oral culture, the two overlapped, and the treaty debate provides a glimpse into the ways that process of overlapping and reinforcing took place. But the debate also confirms the lingering power of written discourse, a field in which Federalists were experienced, comfortable, and largely successful.

5 | Petitions, Instructions, and the Duties of Citizens and Representatives

Daniel Buck, a Federalist congressman from Vermont, sat down in January 1796 to respond to a resolution sent him by a group of constituents. Those citizens from Bennington County urged Buck to investigate the constitutionality of the controversial treaty which had been denounced in the streets and newspapers the previous summer and was sure to come before the House of Representatives that spring. The clear implication of the resolution was that the citizens opposed the treaty and that Buck would be wise to follow their wishes. The petition noted that the citizens of Bennington had "unanimously condemned" the treaty and resolved that "it would be eligible for the people of the county of Bennington to appoint a convention . . . to confer on said treaty—to instruct the representative from the western district of Vermont in congress . . . to urge by every means in his power a strict inquiry into the constitutionality of that instrument in the ensuing session of congress."[1]

While the Bennington petition gave voice to a newer, expansive conception of the rights of citizens, the duties of their chosen leaders, and the degree to which citizens could and should try to instruct or influence their representatives, Buck's response harkened back to an older, more deferential notion suggesting limits to such involvement. He assured his constituents, "I cheerfully listen to the voices of my fellow citizens and friends . . . upon the subject of the treaty." He went on to acknowledge that Vermonters did and should follow public issues closely, and to say that he appreciated their sentiments. However, Buck declared, he did not subscribe to all the sentiments expressed in the petition. Although "I am placed here as one of the representatives of the state of Vermont . . . my own judgment must be my guide." The citizens of Vermont had "confided to me a trust, and delegated to me a power to act, I must faithfully exercise that power, according to my best judgment and ability." Once he had investigated and studied the matter and made up his mind, "I must decide and act as I should rationally conclude my constituents would do, were they acting with integrity and uprightness, under the same impressio[n]s and view of the subjects as I myself at the same time possess." Buck concluded with a postscript which acknowledged that many in Vermont had made up their minds on the treaty, presumably opposing it, and promised his constituents, "if I should have the misfortune in finally making up my opinion to differ from them in sentiment, I will do myself the honour to send you a statement of the reasons on which I found my judgment."[2]

Later that same spring, as the Jay Treaty debate concluded with the House of Representatives voting to make appropriations for the measure, another group of citizens, this one in Newberry County, South Carolina, sent a petition to their congressman, Robert Goodloe Harper. They stated that although they did not like every component of the treaty, "we consider the many superior advantages you enjoy of national information, we conceive it places you in a capacity of judging these things much better than ourselves." The address went on to praise Harper for exercising his prerogatives as an elected official, a "constituted authority" in the phrase of the day, instead of bowing to the first expressions of the public will. After Harper was informed "both publicly and privately, that near nine-tenths of your constituents were pointedly opposed to the ratification of the treaty," the petitioners noted admiringly, "you did not sacrifice your feeling, in joining them to secure your popularity, but like a brave hero entered the field of national politics; and . . . by the dint of your pen, have given cogent reasons for a contrary opinion; which reasons have had their happy influence on the minds of a number of your fellow-citizens."[3] These South Carolina petitioners, unlike their New England brethren, evinced a deference to elected officials absent in the Vermont resolutions. The attitude of Harper's constituents toward the duties of a representative—that he should not simply follow or transmit public opinion but should, if his superior knowledge and information warranted a different judgment, attempt to persuade citizens—contrasts significantly with the Vermont petitioners who wrote to Buck. By gently responding that he hoped he would be of the same mind as his petitioners, but reserving the right not to be, Buck prepared his readers for such an occurrence—and his response suggests that the conception held by the South Carolina memorialists of the proper relationship between citizens and congressmen was shared by a number of elected officials, even though they might receive resolutions and instructions to the contrary.

The petitions from Vermont and South Carolina, drawn from crowds at public rallies and demonstrations, express very different conceptions of the nature of representative government. They thus highlight a vital if little studied dimension of the treaty debate, and, further, suggest a revealing yet previously unexplored function of the town meetings which produced them. In numerous petitions, memorials, resolutions, and instructions, citizens across the new nation informed President George Washington and members of Congress of local sentiment on the treaty. They also expressed a firm belief either in their rights as citizens to not only petition but instruct their representatives (as in the case of the Vermont petition), or their deference to the informed judgment of the duly constituted chosen authorities (as in the case of the South Carolina petition). By examining some of the petitions and the responses to them by elected leaders like Buck, we can see two very different perspectives on the rights of citizens and the duties of elected officials in the early republic. Each corresponded neatly (but by no means in all respects) to the views held on the two sides of the treaty debate, and to those of each of the two nascent political parties: of Federalists, who largely supported the document and the constituted authorities, and of Republicans, who generally opposed it and invoked the right to instruct representatives. Still, the ambiguity or unpredictability of some of these petitions underscores one of the key themes of this book: the evolving, work-in-progress nature of political conflict in the 1790s. An examination of the views expressed in the Jay Treaty petitions provides great insight into these still-forming conceptions of rights and obligations.

More significantly, the early protests clearly expressed attitudes on the part of the crowds concerning not only their right to petition, but their expectation of an active role in the political public sphere. These petitions, then, not only served to denounce the treaty; they also voiced, strongly and lucidly, a newer conception of the roles and duties of citizens. Such conceptions, still emerging and developing, pushed at the edges of what was acceptable in the highly fluid political culture of the 1790s, and constitute the subject of a fascinating and significant smaller debate taking place within the context of the larger debate on the treaty. Thus, the battle over the Jay Treaty was only partly about the document itself. It was also a contest between a fading yet still firmly rooted notion of limited public involvement and an emerging yet not fully formed idea of political activism, with this contest mirroring some of the larger battles of the 1790s and beyond. A closer examination of the treaty debate along these lines will reveal the highly fluid and seriously contested nature of the political culture of the 1790s and provide a fuller understanding of the changing perspectives on public participation in politics and, specifically, on the role of crowds and public displays in that process.[4]

Petitioning authorities was not, of course, a new development in the 1790s. It had a long Anglo-American history, particularly in colonies like Virginia and during the extended Revolutionary crisis. In fact, Edmund S. Morgan has concluded that "by 1795, petitions had become in America as in England one of the rituals of popular government."[5] But scholars of the Jay Treaty have not focused on these important products of crowd activity. Most of the historical literature on the role of crowds in the debate has emphasized the angry, violent demonstrations, the inflamed rhetoric, the burnings in effigy of John Jay, and other colorful highlights of the demonstrations themselves. By focusing only on the histrionics, scholars have overlooked or downplayed the *substance* of the anti-treaty protests, and, especially, the message contained in petitions opposing the treaty. Examined closely, however, the memorials, resolutions, and petitions sent to President Washington and later to Congress reveal another crucial dimension to the debate. These writings clearly articulate the role many citizens claimed for themselves in a battle for inclusion in the political nation. Convinced of their rights as citizens to declare their sentiments to their political leaders, members of these crowds asserted a newer, more modern understanding of the public's role in matters of political policy, an understanding which swept away older notions of deference to authorities and proclaimed instead the citizenry's desire to take an active role in the political public sphere. This newer understanding starkly contrasted not only with traditional practices, but also with the expectations and conceptions of Federalist pro-treaty advocates concerning what constituted proper civic behavior on the part of citizens in the political process, as explicitly expressed by those on the pro-treaty side.

A fascinating element of this debate centered on the advisability of citizens instructing their representatives on important public matters. The First Federal Congress had addressed this matter in August 1789, during the debate over amendments to the Constitution. In the discussion of the proposed first amendment's clause about the right to petition and assemble, Pennsylvania congressman Thomas Hartley argued that constituents should have faith in their chosen representatives while they were in office. "[T]he people ought to have confidence in the honor and integrity of those they send forward to transact their business; their right to instruct [Congress] is a problematical subject," he declared. Hartley noted that when passions were stirred, "instructions have been resorted to and obtained, to answer party purposes; and although the public opinion is generally respectable, yet at such moments it has been known to be often wrong." Fortunately, Hartley noted, governments filled with "men of firmness and wisdom" could ascertain and resist erroneous or misguided popular attitudes. He also registered a practical objection. Since small groups of citizens from particular areas of the country would necessarily have only "local or partial" views, they would not always be able to discern the common good. Instructions under such circumstances would merely "embarrass the best and wisest men. And were all the members to take their seats in order to obey instructions, and those instructions were as various as it is probable they would be, what possibility would there exist of so accommodating each to the other as to produce any act whatever?" But, speaking next, Virginia representative John Page took a different tack. Page argued that it would do little good to grant the people's right to "consult for the common good" if they then lacked the ability to instruct their representatives. "Instruction and representation," Page stated, "in a republic appear to me to be inseparably connected." To deny the people the right of instruction would be dangerous and would give citizens just cause for alarm. As he put it later in the debate, since the people have given a part of their authority to their elected representatives, "To pretend to refuse them the power of instructing their agents, appears to me to deny them a right."

Such talk disturbed Pennsylvania's George Clymer. "Do gentlemen foresee the extent of these words? If they [the people] have a constitutional right to instruct us, it infers that we are bound by those instructions. . . . I presume we shall be called upon to go further, and expressly declare the members of the Legislature bound by the instruction of their constituents.

This," declared Clymer, "is a most dangerous principle, utterly destructive of all ideas of an independent and deliberative body, which are essential requisites in the Legislatures of free Governments." Georgia's James Jackson worried that binding instructions might reduce Congress to a set of factions. He was for nonbinding instructions. "I am willing to leave both the people and representatives to their own discretion on this subject. Let the people consult and give their opinion; let the representative judge of it; and if it is just, let him govern himself by it as a good member ought to do; but if it is otherwise, let him have it in his power to reject their advice."

Not even James Madison was prepared to admit that instructions from constituents should be binding on representatives in Congress. Madison wondered about the predicament a representative might find himself in if instructed by constituents to vote for a measure which violated the Constitution. What would be the implications of voting in accordance with constituents but against the Constitution? Or of turning one's back on the people back home in order to uphold the Constitution? Further, Madison expressed doubts that any particular group of citizens could speak for the whole. "I do not believe," he observed, "that the inhabitants of any district can speak the voice of the people; so far from it, their ideas may contradict the sense of the whole people; hence the consequence that instructions are binding on the representative is of a doubtful, if not of a dangerous nature." Later in the debate, Massachusetts' Elbridge Gerry reflected on the discussion to that point, and noted that he believed the matter of instructions to be moot. "I do not think we shall be much troubled with instructions; a knowledge of the right will operate to check a spirit that would render instruction necessary."[6]

The views on instructing representatives sketched out above indicate the range of opinion on the matter in 1789, at the outset of the new federal government. Some of those positions would evolve and some of those who held them would refine or modify their views in reaction to the events of the 1790s, as political debate sharpened and the abstract hypotheticals of 1789 were replaced by the concrete particulars of partisan conflict over the next decade. In any case, it is clear that the aspect of the Jay Treaty debate that concerned the right of citizens to petition and instruct their representatives—and the "duty" of those representatives to obey those instructions—had a long-standing history independent of the conflict over the treaty. In short, when pro- and anti-treaty forces argued over instructions in 1795–96, they linked the controversy over the treaty to a much larger and longer-running one already under way, one which was given a new shape and focus by the circumstances of the mid-1790s

This fundamental underlying conflict over the proper role of citizens in a republic can be seen at work in one of the best known and documented of the town meetings. Bostonians gathered on Friday, July 10, 1795, to discuss the Jay Treaty, first published just a few days before. After denunciations of the terms of the treaty, one speaker questioned whether it was proper for the town even to address the treaty matter, suggesting that it was the duty of citizens to support the duly constituted departments of government and to "suppose that they had acted from the best evidence before them, for the interest of the United States." This speaker emphasized that he did not support the measure; rather, he worried only about "the propriety and constitutionality of the town acting on the subject."[7]

Other speakers quickly rose to assert "the right of the people, more especially of a town in their corporate capacity, to assemble to express their sentiments." The right to assemble and express opinions was a privilege allowed by the Constitution, and it "was an inherent principle in a free government, for the people to exercise this right." Furthermore, the people had a right to assemble and register an opinion not merely in support of government policies but in opposition to them as well. During the controversy over President Washington's Neutrality Proclamation in 1793, administration supporters had called out crowds to support the measure and the president and administration. It was hypocritical for some of the same people who called forth the public on that occasion to support a government policy to oppose and denigrate a town meeting called to express opposition to such a policy. "[I]f the people then had a right to *approbate*, they now had an equal right to *disapprobate*." Hearing the opinions of the people in the town meeting, some declared, whatever they were, should be "agreeable" to the president. Because he acted "for the general interest, he could not be displeased at their expressing their sentiments on so interesting a question."

The meeting then concluded with a vote to determine the crowd's opinion on the treaty. According to the newspaper account, not a single hand was raised in favor of the measure. In fact, "unanimity prevailed in condemning the document in all its parts. The only question was the right of acting, and this was the objection of but ONE MAN." The account noted that "the people felt themselves degraded in the suggestion, and spurned with a manly indignity, at the revival of a sentiment agitated during our struggles against the arbitrary measures of George the Third." Convinced of the unanimity of opinion, the attendees then appointed a committee to put its sentiments in writing; the public was asked to reassemble at a future date to hear the report of the committee.[8]

Treaty opponents made much of what they saw as the two-faced nature of those treaty supporters who implied that it was proper and fitting for the public to assemble and voice opinions supporting the administration, but somehow improper, unconstitutional, and dangerous to do so in opposition. In a long letter, "Atticus" spelled out many of the same opinions voiced on this matter in the Boston town meeting. He asked rhetorically, "Is ours a government of the people, or of the officers of government? If it is a government of the people, they certainly have a right to say by what rules they will be regulated. . . . If it is a government of the rulers, then our system is changed, and instead of a republic we are an oligarchy." Just as some at the town meeting had done, "Atticus" contrasted the Federalist administration's actions on the Jay Treaty with its activity in 1793 regarding the Neutrality Proclamation. It was considered proper then for Philadelphia merchants to hold a meeting, prepare an address, and march to the president's house to formally deliver to Washington their resolution in favor of the policy. "If aggregate opinions were not improper at that time, by what rule of ratiocination will they be condemned now?" Indeed, the author believed more than simple hypocrisy was at the root of Federalist objections to the anti-treaty meetings and protests. "As argument fails recourse must be had to other means to make the treaty acceptable, and hence the proscription of town meetings, the calumnious epithets of jacobin and antifederalist, and the appeals to our fears and to our affections. Artifices like these, fellow citizens, you will be on guard against; they are designed to seduce your understandings and your *American* feelings, which must ever rise up in judgment against an instrument abhorrent to every true friend of his country."[9]

Similar beliefs about the propriety of citizens addressing the president and other leaders were expressed by Americans around the nation and became a consistent and significant (if scarcely noted in the scholarly literature) facet of the anti-treaty protest. A variety of petitions, resolutions, memorials, and grand jury charges made the same bold claim for the rights of the public to assemble, protest, voice its opinion, and present that aggregate opinion to authorities. Stressed over and over again in the statements against the instrument, these ideas present a clear conception of a newer interpretation of citizens' rights and duties. That the propriety of such actions was under public debate and was being questioned by pro-treaty advocates at the same time it was being advanced by anti-treaty critics suggests that the Jay Treaty debate took place at the fault line of a deeper disagreement which went to the heart of the changing political culture of the early republic.

Some petitions took pains to express this newer conception in unapologetic yet still respectful language. A grand jury charge in Chatham County, Georgia, stated that, while recent protests and resolutions in Savannah showed "a proper respect for the government," they also revealed "a due attention on the part of the people, to the preservation of [its] inestimable privileges," reflecting a belief that citizens had a clear right and duty to assemble and speak out on government policies. Other petitions, scrupulously polite and correct in their language when addressing President Washington, made the larger point exceedingly clear. A petition signed by "Citizens of the State of New Jersey" argued that upon "due consideration" the subscribers were convinced the treaty would be harmful if ratified. The petition assured Washington of "a sincere respect and esteem for you, flowing from a recollection of numerous and eminent services, which gratitude hath indelably engraven on our hearts," but concluded by insisting on the right of the petitioners to inform the president of their position. Noting that they believed opposition to be "the prevailing sentiment of the citizens of New Jersey," they wrote that such a situation "renders it a duty incumbent on us to represent the same for your information, least our silence on the occasion might be construed into an approbation of the said treaty."[10]

Some memorialists and petitioners sketched out a middle ground, claiming the right to petition or address their leaders but granting the prerogatives of the constituted authorities and acknowledging some limits to petitioning. A Philadelphia memorial assured Washington that his constituents "entertain a proper respect for your constitutional authority" and "will faithfully acquiesce in the regular exercise of the delegated powers of the government." Still, the citizens stated that on such a "momentous question" they hoped Washington would "not deem it improper or officious in them, thus anxiously but respectfully, to present a solemn testimonial of their public opinion, feelings and interest." Even some pro-treaty petitions expressed a similar view, in similarly moderate language, of citizens' responsibilities. One example is a York, Pennsylvania, resolution supporting the measure which stated that, "although we consider it the constitutional right of the Citizens of the United States to address the President by way of Petition, Memorial, or Remonstrance, on any subject . . . there may be certain situations in which it would be exceedingly improper, and inconsistent with their duty, so to do." Having thus staked its claim to the right of petition, the York assembly nonetheless deferred to the president. "[W]e consider the present occasion as one of those, on which it would be highly improper to advise the President not to give his affirmative to the pending Treaty, as such conduct would seem to be interfering with the constituted powers, which ough[t] never to take place but in cases of the greatest necessity."[11]

Other petitions were much more blunt. A Camden, South Carolina, town meeting resolved unanimously "That it is the duty, as well as the right of freemen, on all great public occasions, that concern the honor and welfare of the republic, to come forward and declare their sentiments with freedom and firmness, to the end that those who are entrusted with power, may be admonished to use that power only for the good of the people who have placed it in their hands, and beware to violate the sacred trust." Likewise, a memorial from a Richmond, Virginia, town meeting, taking note of the present "crisis of American affairs—hold it not only their right, but their bounden duty, to express their sentiments to the chief magistrate of the United States."[12] A Morris County, New Jersey, resolution condemned the treaty and began by stating a basic theme of the protests: that it was the "duty of the citizens of the States to watch with a jealous eye, and carefully to guard against every attempt to destroy and infringe the rights, liberties, and privileges of the good people of this country." Such jealous attention to the public good required active citizen participation. The Philadelphia meeting against the treaty adopted a set of resolutions, the first two of which resolved that "it is the constitutional right and patriotic duty of the Citizens of the United States, to express on every important occasion, the public sense of public measures," and that "it is peculiarly the duty of the citizens to express the public sense, upon an instrument so novel, and so momentous as the Treaty with Great Britain."[13]

Republican party leaders evinced similar democratic thoughts, echoing the statements of the rank and file in the crowds. James Madison, who had declined Thomas Jefferson's entreaties to answer Alexander Hamilton's "Camillus" essays, nonetheless drafted a petition to present to the

Virginia General Assembly. Dated October 12, 1795, Madison's draft noted that George Washington's decision in August to ratify the treaty made any further applications to the president useless. Still, Washington's evident refusal to consider the clear sentiment of the people on the treaty made addresses to other governing bodies entirely appropriate and worthwhile. Madison observed tersely that the president, in his replies to various petitions which evoked the older, deferential conception of proper public activity, "virtually refused to view the representations of the people as a source of information worthy of his consideration" in deliberating on whether or not to ratify the treaty. "It is we deem important, when such inattention to the public voice is manifested, that the people should boldly exercise their right of addressing their objections to all other constituted authorities within the United States, who possess any agency relative to this highly interesting subject." Thomas Jefferson, too, was disturbed at Washington's apparent dismissal of public opinion. Referring to the same document Madison did in his general assembly petition—Washington's reply to the Boston selectmen—Jefferson observed acidly that the damping of the initial furor over the treaty owed much to "the President's chiding answer to Boston and Richmond." Both leaders expressed dismay at Washington's rejection of such clear expressions of the public will and his concurrent unwillingness to accept their legitimacy; the president's response reflected a clear gap between what treaty advocates and opponents conceived the citizen's role to be in public debates.[14]

Madison's thinking on the proper role of citizens and representatives evolved during the 1790s and was shaped by his response to Federalist actions in both the executive and legislative branches. To get a sense of his evolution, we must recall Madison's skepticism, during the 1789 congressional debate over constitutional amendments, about the wisdom and practicality of constituents instructing congressmen. By late 1792, he had seen the administration and its friends in Congress engage in what he believed to be plainly un-republican conduct, and he felt the need to respond. Madison fought back by drafting a series of essays for the *National Gazette*. A December 22, 1792, essay asked, "Who Are the Best Keepers of the People's Liberties?," a question which he answered unhesitatingly, "The people themselves." Constructing the essay as a dialogue between "Republican" and "Anti-republican," Madison insisted that citizens should not simply elect officials to government and then sit back and blindly submit to being governed. Rather than being passive and powerless observers, "the people ought to be enlightened, to be awakened, to be united, that after establishing a government they should watch over it, as well as obey it." Madison then had his "Anti-republican" charge that it was far more likely that the people would "fly off" from the government rather than the reverse. The solution for "Anti-republican" was simple: "to the people never pronounce but two words—*Submission* and *Confidence*." Madison's sharp words here can scarcely be read as anything but a direct criticism of the Federalist concept of deferring to the constituted authorities. The real danger, Madison perceived, came from the gradual augmentation of federal power which would come from such notions of deference and, ultimately, do grave harm to liberty. "What a perversion of the natural order of things!" exclaimed "Republican, "to make *power* the primary and central object of the social system, and *Liberty* but its satellite."[15]

By the end of the 1790s, Madison would even more explicitly condemn the idea of trusting the constituted authorities, seeing it as a doctrine which had misled many citizens into giving their tacit assent to policies harmful to national and personal liberty. In a lengthy 1799 newspaper essay entitled "Political Reflections" and signed "A Citizen of the United States," Madison considered the examples of both the American and French republics. Now furious after a decade of Federalist abuses, he was as blunt as ever. He spoke out emphatically "against the doctrine so ardently propagated by many, that in a republic the people ought to consider the whole of their political duty as discharged when they have chosen their representatives." He also spoke against the idea "that the people ought at all times to place an unlimited confidence in rulers so chosen, applauding the wisdom of public measures where they can see it and assuring themselves that it is equally the foundation of all others, where nothing but folly or mischief may appear on the face of them." In fact, recent history had taught that the people must be eternally vigilant: "in no case ought the eyes of the people to be shut on the conduct of those entrusted with power; nor their tongues tied from a just wholesome censure on it, any more than from merited commendations." Madison was not yet at this point of vehemence and dismay by the time of the treaty debate. But he was clearly striding forcefully in that direction, as even this brief survey of his evolving thought during the 1790s shows.[16]

Washington's reply to the Boston selectmen serves as a convenient bridge from the discussion of Republican views on petitioning to a consideration of Federalist ideas. The "chiding" statement to which Jefferson and Madison replied and which so disturbed them was Washington's letter to a group that opposed the treaty and petitioned the president to that effect. Washington's response was a classic exposition of the Federalist view of the relative rights and duties of citizens and elected leaders. He stated that his job was, in every act, to seek "the happiness of my fellow-citizens," and "to confide, that sudden impressions, when erroneous, would yield to candid reflection: and to consult only the substantial and permanent interests of our country." Washington went on to note that while he had read and weighed the writings against the treaty, "the constitution is the guide, which I never will abandon." The Constitution specifically placed treaty-making power with the president and Senate in the belief "that these two branches of government would combine, without passion . . . those facts and principles upon which the success of our foreign relations will always depend: that they ought not to substitute for their own conviction the opinions of others; or to [expect] truth thro' any channel but that of a temperate and well-informed investigation." Washington closed by observing that it was "Under this persuasion, [that] I have resolved on the manner of executing the duty now before me. To the high responsibility, attached to it, I freely submit." As for the approbation of the country, Washington said, "I can no otherwise deserve it, than by obeying the dictates of my conscience." The president's words—bold, firm, confident, and unapologetic—expressed the Federalists' view that the treaty issue was beyond the realm of public action and that citizens should trust that their constituted authorities, in possession of full information and wisdom, would make the right choices. Washington sent copies of his reply to the Boston selectmen to other groups who wrote to him protesting the treaty. As his address circulated, it formed a crucial early defense of the way the treaty issue had been handled, which Federalists would elaborate on in their other writings.[17]

The president's replies to anti-treaty petitions not only suggest his reasons for ratifying the measure but also articulate the key tenets of the Federalists' views on citizens' rights and representatives' duties. The Federalists clung to an older notion of the proper role of citizens in the public sphere. While they believed it was improper and subversive for the public to demonstrate *against* duly chosen government leaders or the policies they enacted, they found it entirely proper to show enthusiastic support *for* leaders and policies. Federalists believed that citizens should elect leaders, trust them to exercise their best judgment, and then, if dissatisfied with those judgments, choose a different set of leaders at the next election.[18]

Time and again during the debate, Federalists implored citizens to respect and trust the "constituted authorities" and reacted with dismay at the demonstrations against the treaty and the efforts by Philadelphia's Blair McClenachan and others to incite the public. Then, seeing no hypocrisy or inconsistency in their actions, they undertook to mobilize the public and called for equally vociferous expressions of support for the treaty and the administration. According to Federalist beliefs under an older and narrower conception of the public sphere, it was all right for the public to mobilize when called out by Federalists to support the administration; it was dangerous and improper for them to be mobilized by others against the administration. The very practices which Republicans denounced as hypocritical followed perfect logic to Federalist minds.

Noah Webster remarked in one of his "Curtius" essays that Americans had until now always shown "confidence in the constituted authorities." They were content to leave matters of commerce and dealing with foreign nations in the hands of those thought best able to negotiate treaties. In short, they "trusted to the men appointed for this purpose." Webster closed by arguing that most Americans simply did not possess the knowledge or expertise to judge a complicated treaty. "The great mass of people are not competent to decide what is, or is not our public interests, in complicated negotiations and national compacts." With an eye on the present as well as toward the future, Webster warned, "unless they repose confidence in public characters, we shall forever be embroiled with factions."[19]

Federalist newspapers made the same points in their editorials and lambasted the Republicans for their supposed factional behavior. "The principle pressed on the public mind by those jacobins, 'That the people have a right to deliberate, discuss, and decide, on the proceedings of public men in their public capacities,' is a most dangerous one—tending to subvert all governance, and introduce anarchy and confusion." How is it possible, this editorial asked, for town meetings in a matter of hours to digest and comprehend what duly constituted legislative bodies, with all relevant information before them, took weeks to consider? "It is morally impossible. The idea is futile and absurd to the last degree, when tried by the test of reason." A constitutional form of government was instituted precisely in order to entrust to representatives, who had access to special knowledge, expertise, and insight, the power to make crucial decisions. "We shall also be convinced," the editorial concluded, "that a part of the people has not a right to meet to do, or to undo, any thing that the representatives of the whole, chosen by the whole, may do or have done for them."[20]

Part of the reason for the vehemence with which the Federalists denounced the unofficial town meetings was that these meetings were, in their minds, not only improper but unnecessary. "The administration of the commonwealth is in the hands of men of approved wisdom and virtue. . . . What necessity therefore can there be to disturb or interrupt this safe and enviable state by the convulsive operations of town-meetings; where neither order, wisdom, or safety can be expected."[21] Federalists never tired of stressing that Washington was acting in close accord with the Constitution and was fully within his rights not to be swayed "by irregular unauthorized meetings."[22]

Soon, Washington received a bevy of petitions in favor of his decision to ratify the treaty and opposing the hasty actions of treaty critics. Federalist leaders encouraged and organized these petition drives, which were key to the pro-treaty counterattack. The Boston Chamber of Commerce met August 11 and sent a resolution to Washington praising the treaty as "wise and prudent." The Chamber also noted that it "cannot but lament and disapprove" the efforts of opponents to incite opposition among the people "and to detach their confidence from the government of the Union." In a free government, they observed, "a firm reliance of the people on the wisdom and integrity of those authorities which they have themselves constituted to manage their public concerns, and a chearful acquiescence in the decisions of rulers of their own appointment, are indispensable to secure the peace, the honor and the happiness of the community."[23] Federalists argued, in essence, that their legitimate authority came not from town meetings or extra-constitutional conventions, but instead from their position as duly chosen, democratically elected government officers. In that position they, not the people in the streets, were the real defenders of the people's government.

During the fall of 1795 and especially in the spring of 1796, as the public debate resumed, pro-treaty petitions either to Washington or the House of Representatives echoed the main points of the Federalist campaign. Citizen petitions specifically stressed the Federalist conception of governance, that is, that citizens should trust the judgment of their elected representatives. One Georgia petition captured this sentiment nicely when it admitted, "we are not in possession of all the documents necessary to form a decided judgment on the merit or demerit of the Treaty." However, the petition stated, since it had been ratified "by those Branches of Government which are appointed for that purpose, we think it the indispensable duty of all good citizens . . . to do whatever depends on them to carry it into effect." Another petition from western Pennsylvania made the same disclaimer: "Waving all question of the merits of the Treaty with Britain, it has acquired the sanction of the American Constitution, and our national faith is pledged to the world." Thus, Federalists and their supporters believed, once the constituted authorities had acted and exercised their judgment based on their better access to information, the country should trust those officials and support their decisions.[24]

The similarity of the language, phrasing, and content of such petitions suggests an orchestrated effort by Federalists to shape and mobilize public opinion. Although they may have been more circumspect about gathering petitions, they recognized that this was simply how the political game was being played—and they competed, albeit with more reservations than their opponents felt. "But why, it may be asked, petition at all?," asked one Federalist paper. "Ought we not to tell our representatives, that the execution of the British treaty is necessary to our safety? . . . We are sufficiently apt to censure our representatives, when their conduct displeases us; is it not better then, beforehand, to inform them of our wishes, and, if by our request we can, prevent their opposing them." Lest this statement be misconstrued, the editorial clarified its stand. "This is not overawing, or over-ruling their judgement, but declaring ours." Furthermore, "A free and honest communication of sentiment between constituent and representative is an useful thing in a republican government. . . . It is therefore proper for constituents, who are of no party, and are equal as to all, unbiassed by this prejudice, to express their sense of the general interest."[25] Again, it is noteworthy that Federalists did not oppose expressions of public opinion in principle, but distinguished between statements of *support* for government policies—legitimate and appropriate in their eyes—and statements of *opposition* to such measures —illegitimate and improper, even dangerous.

In gathering signatures for their petitions, pro-treaty advocates followed much the same procedure as the anti-treaty side did. Details of a petition circulated in Allegheny County, Pennsylvania, in March 1796 suggest the model followed by many treaty backers elsewhere. The local court adjourned its regular business after learning of the pro-treaty petition in order to find out the opinion of those present. The petition was read, approved unanimously, and signed by all those present who had the opportunity. But the advocates wanted to get as many signatures as possible and proposed that the meeting should be adjourned until the following Friday when more could, with advance notice, assemble and voice their opinion. In the meantime, one hundred copies of the petition were printed and disseminated to the surrounding townships in time for the forthcoming township elections, in order to gain the signatures of those who would be present to vote. Additionally, treaty supporters arranged to have the petition and proceedings printed in the local papers.[26]

Federalists also organized demonstrations of their own which showed support for the treaty, the administration, Washington, and, invariably, "the constituted authorities." Petitioners in Trenton, New Jersey, offering a dissenting view to an anti-treaty resolution adopted by the town, declared "their entire satisfaction and confidence in the constituted authorities of our country." Similarly, residents of York, Pennsylvania, sent Washington a petition stating that citizens had a right to petition the president on matters of national concern but that such an entreaty on this matter would be improper, "as such conduct would seem to be interfering with the constituted powers, which ough[t] never to take place but in cases of the greatest necessity." Residents of Portsmouth, New Hampshire, in a counter-petition to the one from their town condemning the treaty, spoke in favor of the commercial benefits it would provide and observed that "we rely on the wisdom of those to whom the Constitution of *our country* has committed the determination of questions of this kind."[27]

Federalist newspapers picked up on these themes early in the debate. John Fenno's *Gazette of the United States* condemned the petitions and town meetings against the treaty and asserted that "the administration of the commonwealth is in the hands of men of approved wisdom and virtue; to whom the constitution has delegated powers adequate to, and co-extensive with the public welfare." Fenno criticized the notion that citizens had a duty to address officials. He did not doubt the right of citizens to express opinions, "but that it is [a citizens'] *duty* on all important occasions to do so, is not quite so clear; for I believe there are important occasions, on which it is his duty to be silent."[28]

An early pro-treaty document, the resolution of the New York Chamber of Commerce of July 21, 1795, nicely articulates most of the key themes of the Federalist campaign, anticipating the language of the petitions, the pro-treaty writings and pamphlets, and the "Camillus" essays. The resolution noted the misrepresentations of the treaty which had served to "excite and irritate the public mind." It stated the belief that the measure contained as many features of reciprocity between the United States and Great Britain as could be expected and pointed to the benefits concerning permanent trading rights and the like. The Chamber's resolution also warned that if the treaty "should fail to be ratified, we should apprehend a state of things which might lead to hostilities." The resolution concluded by saying that the members of the Chamber were content to "chearfully" rest ratification of the Jay Treaty "where it is placed by the constitution; in full confidence that the wisdom and firmness under which our independence has been promoted beyond a parallel, will in this instance determine for the best interest of this country."[29]

The sentiments of the New York Chamber of Commerce were echoed by the Chambers of Philadelphia and Boston. The address from the Philadelphia merchants and traders placed trust in "the wisdom, integrity and Patriotism of the Constituted Authorities" and stressed the value of the treaty to commerce and peace. The Boston Chamber lamented the efforts to oppose the instrument and weaken confidence in the government. "[I]n a government like ours, a firm reliance of the people in the wisdom and integrity of those authorities, which they have themselves constituted to manage their public concerns, and a chearful acquiescence in the decisions of rulers of their own appointment, are indispensable to secure the peace, the honor, and the happiness of the community." These rulers, chief among them Washington, could hardly be construed as being like the irresponsible British ministers of the Revolutionary crisis. Such expressions of faith drew predictably warm responses from Washington. He wrote to the Philadelphia merchants thanking them for "expressing your confidence in the constituted Authorities, and the concurrence of your opinions with their determinations on this highly important subject."[30] Not to be overlooked, of course, is that the publication in newspapers of these petitions and Washington's responses to them further spread the word, both providing a model for other towns to use in their petitions *and*, through republication in smaller, local papers, serving as evidence of a rising countercurrent of pro-treaty opinion.

Individual town petitions touched on these same main themes. Petitioners from Rutland, Vermont, commented that even though some of their countrymen objected to various articles of the treaty, "they will undoubtedly abide by the decision of that body of men, which the American people have ordained to be constitutional authority and government." Citizens of Trenton, New Jersey, supported the constitutional authorities in general and their own representative in particular. They wished to "declare our entire satisfaction and confidence in the constituted authorities of our country, and our determination to acquiese [*sic*] in such measures as have been or may be finally adopted relative to the said treaty by such constituted authorities." New Jersey senator Frederick Frelinghuysen was also praised. "Resolved, (*without reference to the merits of the said treaty*), That the meeting have the fullest confidence in the honour, virtue and integrity of *Frederick Frelinghuysen.*" The grand jury of Rensselaer County, New York, condemned "wicked and disorganizing" critics and avowed its happiness under the Constitution and its recognition of the "necessity of due submission to the constituted authorities."[31]

Petitions were also sent to individual members of Congress. The contents of these petitions—and the response of congressmen to them—shed a great deal of light on the Federalist position and illustrate significant points of contrast with the Republican view. The Newberry County, South Carolina, petitioners of Congressman Robert Goodloe Harper, mentioned before, expressed the same thoughts Federalists had voiced for months. While admitting that they did not like every aspect of the treaty, they stated that "when we consider the many superior advantages you enjoy of national information, we conceive it places you in a capacity of judging these things much better than ourselves." The South Carolinians especially praised Harper for his steadfastness earlier in the debate, in the face of anti-treaty resolves from their fellow citizens. After Harper was informed "that near nine-tenths of your constituents were pointedly opposed to the ratification of the treaty . . . you did not sacrifice your feeling, in joining them to secure your popularity, but like a brave hero entered the field of national politics; and with a manly firmness and integrity . . . by the dint of your pen, have given cogent reasons for a contrary opinion." These opinions, the petitioners noted, had "their happy influence" on a number of Harper's constituents. The petition concluded with more praise and the wish that Harper, "as a national centinel . . . [might] watch over our rights with a virtuous jealousy, becoming the magnitude of the subject."[32]

Pro-treaty petitions did not only praise congressmen who refused to bow to popular pressure when they disagreed with their constituents. They also consistently echoed the Federalists' more conservative views of the role of citizens in public affairs. This is demonstrated even in pro-treaty petitions sent to *anti*-treaty congressmen. An April 1796 memorial from citizens in Williamsburg to Virginia's Republican congressmen John Page and John Clopton, both of whom ultimately voted against the measure, expressed the standard Federalist understanding of constituted authorities and the role of citizens. The treaty, it stated, was formed under the guidance of George Washington and ratified by him, "a man, whose wisdom and whose virtues entitle him to the unbounded confidence of his country." Such considerations, they wrote, led the petitioners to "desire a prompt and faithful performance" on the treaty question. However, despite making their wishes on the treaty clear to Page and Clopton, the petitioners were careful not to claim more than they could nor to overstep their bounds as they saw them. "We do not pretend to impose this communication on you as the sense of your district, but it contains the sentiments of a part." Had the petitioners had the time to convene a more general meeting, however, "we have reason to believe that the sentiments of a great majority of them would have been the same as with ours." Finally, they made an important concession to the congressmen. They did not expect "to controul your vote by this expression of our opinions, but in giving them we discharge what we think our duty on so important a crisis . . . and we leave it to your own judgement to determine what ought to be the effect."[33] Thus, this petition—even while informing congressmen of constituent opinion—still shows Federalist reservations about instructing or interfering with the duly chosen constituted authorities.

Just as this petition offers an interesting take on the question of instructing congressmen, John Page's reply also struck an ambivalent note when he wrote to acknowledge the memorial and explain his vote against the treaty. Page conceded, as Republicans argued throughout the proceedings, that constituents could instruct representatives. "I acknowledge the right of instructing representatives; that I am well pleased with the exercise of that right by my constituents; even when they differ from my own sentiments; that whenever a majority of them shall think proper to instruct me, I shall obey their instructions." Page appeared to be reading from the Federalists' book, however, concerning limits to how far congressmen should follow constituent opinion, when he then began listing exceptions to his stated rule. If a popular action violated the Constitution or if the rights of the U.S. would be injured, he reserved the right to dissent from his constituents. But Page, consciously or not, echoed a Federalist position when he next noted that he would make a further exception "when I may be certain, that if my constituents knew all the circumstances respecting the case, they would either leave me to the exercise of my own judgment, or would instruct me to vote in the very manner I intended." By adumbrating these exceptions, Page made it clear that not all Republicans were willing to blindly follow the public's wishes, and that he claimed some of the same advantages (such as better information and more time for study) that Federalists cited as a primary reason for trusting in the constituted authorities. His response also suggests that he was distancing himself from some of his stronger statements in the House debate of 1789 discussed earlier. In that exchange, Page had stated bluntly that to refuse constituents "the power of instructing their agents, appears to me to deny them a right." By 1796, tempered by experience in office and in the political conflicts since 1789, Page had modified his stark position of seven years earlier, much as other participants in that earlier debate had done. Such exchanges emphasize the shifting, evolving, work-in-progress nature of the emerging political culture of the 1790s and the danger of assigning absolute or rigidly consistent characterizations to either emerging party. As ever, shifting context and particular, concrete issues led participants to clarify and sometimes modify their positions in the political debates.[34]

A series of petitions and responses between Maryland Republican congressman Samuel Smith and his constituents further illustrates the ever-changing nature of political culture. A group of Baltimore citizens wrote to Smith in mid-April 1796, at the high point of the spring debate. The petitioners expressed their fervent wish that Smith vote for appropriations, and their hope that he would not only obey these instructions but exert every effort on behalf of the treaty. Other petitions from other citizens made much the same request. One group of petitioners stated that they "do therefore solicit, request, and instruct you, as our representative, to use your best exertions in Congress" to fund the treaty.[35]

Smith's reply expressed his satisfaction that his views accorded with those of his constituents; he hoped they recognized the harmony between their instructions and his conduct. But Smith also noted that while he was glad in this case that his vote corresponded to the wishes of the petitioners, the whole matter of petitions and instructions was fraught with danger and a certain double-edged dilemma. Smith wondered what might have been the case had he received a petition from a different group of citizens with an equal number of signatures "directing me *not* to give my consent to . . . carry the treaty into effect." He queried, "would you have thought it my duty *to have obeyed?* I presume not; *and yet it is my duty to know no distinctions!* Instructions are of a very delicate nature," Smith warned, "and ought not to be given without previous notification, being well digested and understood. In the present instance they have done but little harm." But Smith worried about the implications and cautioned, in closing, that "an example *thus set* may hereafter be turned to very improper influence over their and your Representative." As Smith's comments show, the issue of instructions was no less thorny than it had been in the 1789 congressional debate. If anything, it was probably more fraught at the time of the treaty contest, since it was no longer merely an abstract matter. This debate-within-a-debate over instruction raised many crucial questions about the duties of both citizens and their representatives, and suggests the larger significance of the Jay Treaty contest.[36]

To end the chapter where it began, both Daniel Buck and Robert Goodloe Harper were ultimately among the fifty-one congressmen who voted to fund appropriations for the treaty, as against the forty-eight who voted "no," the latter group including James Madison and John Page. Both Buck and Harper were reelected, although Buck chose not to serve. Public opinion seems to have shifted in Vermont. When Buck returned from Philadelphia after the session ended, he was praised in editorials and resolutions and feted by his constituents, as well as by some approving citizens in neighboring New Hampshire.[37]

As this discussion has shown, there was far more at work in the summer 1795 debates over the Jay Treaty than sentiment against the measure. While the treaty itself was the ostensible focal point, it was also a catalyst for addressing much larger and deeper issues. During the debate, both sides revealed much, not only about their positions on the document itself but also—and perhaps more importantly—about conflicts being engendered by the new nation's developing political culture. Coming at a transitional time marked by the emergence of a new conception of the proper role of the public in political matters, the Jay Treaty debate, while in its content explicitly focused on the terms of the treaty, implicitly engaged much more than Jay's negotiations. With government and citizenry each trying to define and assert its role in the new era, it led Federalists and Republicans to declare how they conceived those roles in the emerging political culture of early America.

If Federalists managed through a variety of factors to win the debate over the Jay Treaty, they lost the contest over the conception of the public's role. Eventually, the kind of engaged citizen involvement in public affairs advocated by the treaty's opponents supplanted the older, deferential notions of the Federalists, sweeping away the vestiges of their increasingly antiquated political culture, which became seemingly more untenable with each passing year. However, as the Jay Treaty debate makes clear, support for those older Federalist ideas about public participation still resonated deeply with many Americans who were ambivalent as to the proper workings of a still emerging political culture.

6 | The Final Push

The Debate in Congress and Out-of-Doors

On Wednesday, April 20, 1796, Massachusetts Federalist congressman Dwight Foster of Brookfield rose and "took several turns" around the State House yard at Philadelphia. He "inhaled the Fresh Breezes of the Morning which I find," he declared, "very pleasant & Salubrious." Three days later, on Saturday, he again rose "at an early Hour" and wrote some letters. After attending to some business, he took a walk, spent the day with friends and his brother Theodore, had dinner, and then retired to his room to read and write in his diary. At the time of these entries, Foster was engaged, with other Federalists, in the bitter and protracted struggle against Republicans over the Jay Treaty, a conflict which surely tested his "pleasant & Salubrious" state. For the past several weeks in the House of Representatives, Republican opponents had pressed a final assault on the measure, just as Benjamin Franklin Bache and others had long urged. Once President Washington submitted the treaty to the House, opponents worked diligently to try to secure enough votes to defeat it in a roundabout way, by denying appropriations for the commissions required for its fulfillment. The battle was a week away from its climax, that Saturday night when Foster turned to his diary. "The Jaco[bin]s of our House are much agitated," he commented. "The public Sentiment sets strongly against them," and pro-treaty forces "Shall yet be supported." But Foster remained cautious. "[O]ur struggle is not over—We must remain cool, firm & Steady. . . . 'Perseverando' must be our Motto and by Perseverance we shall carry our Point."[1]

The same Saturday that Foster spoke of the tough times ahead and counseled perseverance, another Federalist also took up his pen, this time to write a friend. Jesse Appleton, president of Bowdoin College in Brunswick, Maine, wrote a letter to Dartmouth College professor Ebenezer Adams concerning the raging debate in the House. "I dare say you read the papers with great anxiety," Appleton wrote; the debate over the treaty was of surpassing importance. "It is unless I am very much out the most important period which has passed since the adoption of the federal government." Appleton hastened to add that "People this way are very federal," but he knew the fight was far from over.[2]

That these two Federalists—one a congressman intimately involved in the debate, the other a college president miles removed from its center—could write with such a curious mixture of trepidation and confidence about the ultimate outcome suggests just how perilous and significant the House debate was. To fully understand the stakes of the debate—as well as its status when Foster and Appleton each wrote, one week before the final vote—we need to retrace the actions of the preceding months. If many Federalists had been so confident of triumph just a few months before, if public opinion, swayed by the towering epistolary work of Alexander Hamilton and others and manifested in petitions and memorials proclaiming support for George Washington and the constituted authorities, seemed so solidly on their side after the summer and fall 1795 campaigns, then why the sense of "anxiety" that Appleton spoke of? Why were Federalists anxiously scouring their newspapers for the latest intelligence on town meetings and petitions from around the nation? And, most significantly, why did Federalists—so long critical of Republican efforts to stimulate petitions to Congress the previous summer—feel the need to hit the streets to collect signatures and mobilize their own followers, all for the purpose of influencing the House of Representatives? Indeed, in order to ensure passage of the treaty, Federalists had to overcome whatever scruples they had—some of them considerable—about popular politics and mobilizing the citizens.

Before the final chapter in the story of the debate was closed, both sides would engage fully and bitterly in a titanic struggle not only in the halls of Congress, but, more importantly, in the streets. In the process, they helped to transform early American political culture. Understanding what happened between the tumultuous summer of 1795 and April of 1796, when the debate raged inside and outside of Congress, helps explain why the period of calm many detected after the initial period of engagement was misleading. Any Federalists who believed, that winter, that the battle was behind them, a triumph already won, were sorely mistaken. And Republicans who thought that their hopes of defeating the treaty were ended, a victim of Washington's unequaled prestige, were just as wrong—or at least quite premature in their conclusions. And what happened in the spring, as the treaty debate reached its climax, reveals another crucial layer of the political culture of the time.

As the two sides battled that spring, they largely revisited the leading arguments they had made for and against the document the previous summer. Federalists warned against the threat of war and damage to the nation's commerce if the treaty were not fulfilled. They stressed that the measure was far more beneficial than many had first thought, and claimed that mature reflection would reveal this to be true. Republicans railed against it as a sellout to Great Britain, a violation of the nation's honor and independence, and scarcely more than a ploy, as Thomas Jefferson put it bluntly, to unite "England & the Anglomen of this country against the legislature & people of the United States."[3]

But there were some important differences in the context and positioning of these renewed arguments. These subtle repositionings had everything to do with the vagaries of public opinion, particularly with the widespread sense that the nation had generally opposed the treaty in the summer of 1795, but now, in the spring of 1796, generally supported it. The shift in strategy, then, came in how the two sides framed their arguments, not about the merits of the instrument itself, but about its standing with the American people.

In 1795, Federalists ridiculed petitions—which were at the time overwhelmingly opposed to the treaty—and denounced them as the work of mobs and factions, not as valid expressions of public opinion.They stressed instead the importance of trusting the constituted authorities to decide what was right for the public good. Republicans, of course, held the reverse, that the petitions were clear indications of public sentiment and that the actions of the Senate and president in ignoring that sentiment constituted insensitivity and dereliction of duty, at best, and at worst something far more sinister.

By the spring of 1796, matters had shifted. Federalists now hailed petitions—which were lately running strongly in their favor—as an authentic voice of the people, urged citizens to continue collecting and sending petitions and memorials to Congress, and dared Congress to disavow these clear indicators of public sentiment. Republicans now denigrated the petitions, charging that they were coerced under questionable circumstances, or represented only the mercantile elite. Anomalously, *Republicans* were now urging the public to trust the constituted authorities in the House of Representatives—which was widely believed to be opposed to the treaty and inclined not to vote for the appropriations—and singing the praises of noninterference. In short, as public opinion shifted, so, too, did the views of the parties on the need to follow it, at least in part dictating how they positioned themselves for the spring debate.

On the whole, it left the Federalists in a considerably stronger position. They could still claim to be upholding the constituted authorities (who had made and ratified the treaty), but could now also claim the apparent voice of public approval for the measure. Thus, they had it both ways: they positioned themselves as being on the side of the public's demonstrated wishes at the same time as they upheld the actions of the administration. Republicans were in a bind. Their claim that the people should trust the constituted authorities in the House rang hollow, after months of denouncing that same deferential notion. And they appeared to be dismissing public opinion now that it seemed to be more clearly in favor of the treaty than against. They were left in the awkward position of arguing that the real voice of the people had been registered the previous summer, and that the outpouring of support now was somehow less authentic—or that the people had been "right" the past summer but were "wrong" now. Furthermore, as soon as they tried to argue that some petitions carried more weight than others, that some were more representative of true public opinion than others, Republicans started to sound as exclusionary as they had charged the Federalists with being. It was a trap the Republicans never quite got themselves out of, and it added to the rising difficulty of their situation as the spring debates unfolded.

As an issue of daily contention, the treaty largely receded from view during the winter months of December 1795 and January and February 1796. The heated demonstrations of the previous summer had long since given way to a more sober consideration. More significantly, there was no real forum for acting on the document, since George Washington had yet to formally declare it in effect and had sent nothing to Congress on which they might act. As a result, House Republicans, spurred on by

Benjamin Franklin Bache's editorials and John Beckley's activities around the nation, were almost giddy at the prospect of getting their hands on the hated treaty. But they could do nothing until they had Washington's declaration and the treaty in front of them; to act without these would be premature and unseemly.

That House Republicans found themselves so agitated was owed in large part to Washington's extraordinary sense of timing and use of delay. He knew as well as anyone that public opinion had calmed considerably. It could even be said—as many Federalists claimed—that the public, while still not wildly enthusiastic, now supported the measure, that calm reflection had supplanted the violent anger of the previous summer. Washington knew that the longer he withheld the treaty from the House, the greater the likelihood that public opinion would continue its drift towards the pro-treaty position. And so he waited. His ostensible reason for not sending it to the House was that Great Britain had yet to formally accept the measure. But he and other Federalists clearly understood the advantages of delay to their position and could not help but notice the frustration of Republicans who, ready to pounce, could not do so on a treaty they had yet to officially see.[4]

Finally, on February 29, 1796, Washington declared the Jay Treaty to be in effect by proclamation and a day later, on March 1, sent the treaty to the House at long last. Just a day after that, New York Republican Edward Livingston—in a move which upset James Madison on many grounds—proposed a resolution calling on Washington to put before Congress copies of Jay's instructions on negotiations plus all of the documents and correspondence pertaining to the treaty. It was an extraordinarily bold request. Its immediacy and peremptory nature suggested condemnation of the measure; moreover, it implied that the House had a constitutional right to pass judgment on the *merits* of the treaty, not merely the question of appropriations for it. That presumption troubled Madison, who, in a letter to Thomas Jefferson, noted that Livingston's resolution was "so questionable that he will probably let it sleep or withdraw it." However much Madison may have wished for this (and for a less directly confrontational stance generally), Livingston refused to give up. His call for papers signaled the resumption of partisan battles and the start of the final stage of the Jay Treaty debate.[5]

Despite Madison's discomfort—exacerbated by the fact that the Virginian did not yet have an alternative strategy in mind—and despite the fact that the resolution put the Republicans on shaky ground both constitutionally and politically, the House Republicans with some Federalist support passed Livingston's revised resolution 62–37 and sent it to Washington on March 25. Because this vote was a rough indicator of congressional support for (and opposition to) the treaty, it bears closer examination. In general, Federalist strength was concentrated in New England with some additional support from the middle states. The South was, however, overwhelmingly anti-treaty. As table 1 shows, New England lined up solidly against the Livingston resolution, providing 22 of the 37 votes against the measure. Only five New England congressmen voted in favor. In the middle states, 11 members voted against but 15 voted in favor of calling for the papers. The southern states provided 42 of the 62 votes in favor of the resolution, with only four southerners opposing. The anti-treaty coalition won this crucial early test of strength decisively, and demonstrated the power of a solid southern voting bloc.[6]

TABLE 1
House Vote on Livingston Resolution, by Region

REGION	NO VOTE ON CALL FOR PAPERS	YES VOTE ON CALL FOR PAPERS
NEW ENGLAND	22	5
MIDDLE STATES	11	15
SOUTH	4	42
TOTAL	37	62

The House vote, while it strongly augured ultimate rejection of funding for the treaty, also shifted the initiative back to the president. Washington had expected that the treaty would be censured "in several points," he told Gouverneur Morris earlier that month. But he expected that the "great change . . . in the public mind with respect to this Treaty within the last two months, is apparent to every one." He believed, furthermore, that "If the people of this country have not abundant cause to rejoice at the happiness they enjoy, I know of no country that has. We have settled all our disputes, and are at Peace with all Nations." To Washington the matter seemed straightforward, but the House resolution, passed by such a wide margin, gave him pause, even if it ultimately served to strengthen his resolve not to cede to the House ground which he fervently believed they should not hold.[7]

Once he received the House resolution, Washington considered his options, asked for advice on how best to respond, and then fired back on

March 30 a polite but firmly worded refusal to hand over the papers. His response at one and the same time invoked the prerogatives of the president and Senate in conducting foreign policy and asserted his own independence, while taking pains not to appear above the law by instead portraying the House as usurpers of constitutional authority, and the House request for papers as a blatantly partisan political act. First, he insisted that his conduct had never risen from a desire to withhold any information he should provide to Congress, and that it had always been his ardent wish "to harmonize with the other branches" of government. Above all, it was his duty, as the presidential oath went, to "'preserve, protect and defend the Constitution.'" Having pledged his faith, Washington proceeded to lecture Congress for overstepping its bounds. "The nature of foreign negotiations requires caution; and their success must often depend on secrecy: and even when brought to a conclusion, a full disclosure of all the measures, demands, or eventual concessions . . . would be extremely impolitic: for this might have a pernicious influence on future negotiations." This was why, he argued, the Constitution very clearly vested these powers in the executive and the Senate. "To admit then a right in the House of Representatives to demand, and to have as a matter of course, all the Papers respecting a negotiation with a foreign power, would be to establish a dangerous precedent." Then Washington went even further, exploring the possible motives of the House in calling for the papers. This call could serve no purpose "except that of an impeachment, which the resolution has not expressed." Washington went on to remind Congress—and, perhaps none too subtly, Madison especially—that he had been a member of the Constitutional Convention and that the journal of debates there would underscore the rectitude of his position. He closed, "A just regard to the Constitution and to the duty of my Office, under all the circumstances of this case, forbids a complyance with your request."[8]

It was a command performance. Washington's address galvanized treaty supporters and set the stage for the furious battles still to come. In a landmark address which summarized much of the Federalist campaign, brilliantly fusing appeals to both constitutionality and his own reputation, Washington had reframed the public contest almost as one of personalities, between the House and the president, so as to maximize the strength of his ascendent position. To share with the House such sensitive materials would be not only unwise but unconstitutional. It would abrogate the delegation of specific powers to the respective constituted authorities. Now, just as he had told the Boston selectmen to trust their duly chosen public leaders, Washington told the House to do the same with regard to the Senate and executive. The constitutional thinking behind Washington's refusal to hand over the papers to the House was consistent with the views expressed and implied in his widely read responses of the previous summer.[9]

Federalists poured out their support for the president. "Firm as a majestic rock in the ocean, he braves the tempest of popular clamour and the attacks of usurpations," praised one paper, while another restated Washington's main points and concluded that "The President's answer contains all that ought or could be said." Another paper delightedly noted the effect Washington's response was having on treaty opponents (his answer "greatly enrages our meek and mild democrats") and predicted what would follow. Treaty opponents "will flatter us, and tell us, that there is nothing . . . they adore so much as *the People,* if we will only be pleased, in return for this humble language, to let them pull down THE PRESIDENT." The president's message had confounded the Republicans: "The plain good sense of THE PRESIDENT's message sunk the hopes of the party." In their private correspondence, Federalist leaders made the same points. Peter Van Schaak told Theodore Sedgwick that "Never was there a more daring Usurpation" than that shown in the House call for papers. Van Schaak believed Washington's answer was exactly to the point and hugely effective, and could be even more so if Federalists spread his words more widely. "Pity his Message was not universally circulated. I do all in my Power. . . . I have always been of Opinion that the measures of a Government like ours should be supported by its friends, because they are actively assailed by its Enemies."[10]

As Congress reconvened, the unfinished Jay Treaty business cast an enormous shadow over all else. Vice President John Adams wrote to his wife that "We are wasting our time in the most insipid manner, waiting for the treaty. Nothing, of any consequence, will be done till that arrives and is mauled and abused, and then acquiesced in." A few days later he again wrote her, claiming "The House of Representatives will do no business with any spirit, before the treaty arrives."[11]

Republicans busied themselves outside of Congress to mobilize the public against the treaty and prepare it to play its important role during the House deliberations. It was especially important, many stressed, for citizens to get involved and make their displeasure with the treaty known to Congress. "Codrus" wrote, "*now or never* ought to be your watch word." If citizens sat back at this moment "pregnant with your dearest interests, you may bid adieu to a free Government, you may take your leave of liberty," he warned. The people must support their representatives as they fought against usurpation. He also noted that treaty supporters had shamelessly used sophistry, even turning the public's statements on the measure against them. "Verity" reminded the citizens of their preeminent role. The treaty had already damaged the French cause and fanned party spirit in the United States, and the president and Senate had already been "deceived," he asserted. Would the House be likewise fooled "into a voluntary sacrifice of their political importance?" Or would they "contend for their Rights, and in them for the greatest security the people can enjoy for the permanence of their own." Since the House "originates directly from the people," it was hoped they might see that citizens were clearly opposed to the treaty and thus uphold their interests.[12]

At the height of the spring demonstrations, another writer stressed the vital importance of citizens turning out for a town meeting in Boston on April 25. "You are to determine this day, whether you mean to influence the constituted authority of the people," referring to the House, which was then nearing its climactic vote. This writer decried the tactics of the Federalists, claiming that they were using the threat of war to intimidate the public into supporting a measure a great many had already condemned. "Shall a few interested men, in a clandestine manner, presume to counteract our doings, by basely, and falsely alarming your fears on the idea of war?" Such talk was ridiculous and "Impossible," he believed. Americans must now "act like freemen in vindicating our rights . . . never let it be said, that the citizens of the United States submitted to a Treaty not from choice, but from fear." Benjamin Franklin Bache, spearheading the anti-treaty effort as he had since the previous summer, tried to goad the House into defeating appropriations by making it clear that public censure would fall squarely on Congress if it voted to approve. Since the people looked to the House to defend their rights and protect the Constitution, "all their censure will fall upon the House." Should "timidity or too refined sensations for the President betray them into improper measures, the golden opportunity may be lost, and [the House] will be accomplices in the assassination of liberty. The true question," Bache stated, "is shall the PEOPLE or the PRESIDENT be the sovereign of the United States?"

By raising the stakes and threatening the House with the opprobrium they would face from their constituents by voting for the treaty, Bache tried a none too subtle form of intimidation in an effort to sway House members to his position.[13]

Just as they had done the previous summer, Republicans called on citizens to turn out for demonstrations and to sign petitions to persuade Congress not to pass the measure. The petitions of three such anti-treaty meetings reveal important themes and suggest the approach opponents used to influence the House. A meeting held in New York City on April 22 denounced the treaty as "disgraceful" and charged that it infringed on the rights of the House and the people. However, even this petition showed that the Federalists had largely succeeded in controlling the terms of the debate: its signers were anxious to preserve "the blessings of peace" and declared that they "deprecate unnecessary and unprovoked wars," both statements obviously in response to the Federalists' incessant chant about the probability of war if the treaty were not approved. But the petition then strongly asserted the right of the House to make appropriations for treaties and decried "all attempts to excite the apprehensions of the people, to intimidate," and called attempts to influence the House "unwarrantable and odious."[14]

A petition circulated at a Philadelphia meeting, reportedly signed by 1,500 people, began by noting that the subscribers placed "full reliance" in the wisdom and patriotism of the House, and hesitated to offer admonitions—a version of the Republicans' appropriation of the "trust the constituted authorities" argument. But, since others from the opposite side of the political spectrum failed to show a similar reticence, they believed it would be a dereliction of their duties if they abstained from expressing their views and supporting the House in the assertion of its constitutional prerogatives. The Philadelphia group denounced the treaty harshly. It was "unequal in its stipulations, derogatory to our national character, injurious to our national interests" and offered "insult instead of redress." Given this assessment, the petitioners believed they could no longer in good conscience remain silent. The petition offered full support for and confidence in the House, calling its members "the guardians of our independence and the avengers of [the nation's] wrongs." Another petition from residents of Norfolk and Portsmouth voiced similar themes. They had been following the deliberations closely and would have been content simply to trust the House to finish its deliberations, but, since others were attempting to induce Congress to take action on the treaty, the subscribers felt they could no longer refrain from making known their sentiments. These citizens indicated that they had long thought that the House had a constitutional role to play in the treaty process and condemned efforts to undermine that role. They concluded a carefully worded petition by stating that they were firmly convinced that "the honor, interest, and happiness of the people of the United States, will not be endangered by withholding the appropriations required to carry the treaty into effect."[15]

Anti-treaty forces made several concerted efforts to mobilize the public and influence the vote in Congress during the final weeks of the campaign. But the Republicans' most prominent leaders, Thomas Jefferson and James Madison, were nearly invisible and, at best, ineffectual. Jefferson remained at Monticello, receiving reports and correspondence but not exerting himself in the efforts. For his part, Madison was in an uncomfortable position. As a leading member of the House, he could hardly shrink from the scene, but he was deeply troubled by the imprudent actions of Edward Livingston and found himself compromised in a number of ways as the debate proceeded. Madison made a game effort to oppose the treaty but Federalists trapped him by citing some of his writings and statements on the Constitution which seemed to contradict the anti-treaty arguments about the proper role of the House. Madison knew, better than anyone, that the House could only properly (and constitutionally) be involved in those matters ceded it by the Constitution. Thus, his intellectual honesty got the better of his partisan commitment, and his speeches and resolutions offered in the House debate seemed inconsistent and were of little effect.[16]

Federalists pounced on Madison's apparent vacillations, taunting their rival for his inconsistency. Fisher Ames declared that "Madison is deeply implicated by the appeal of the President to the proceedings of the General Convention, and most serious persons think him irrevocably disgraced, as a man void of sincerity and fairness." A few weeks before, after Madison had finished speaking in the House, Ames wrote to one ally that "Madison spun cobweb yesterday—stated five constructions of the Constitution, and proceeded to suggest the difficulties in each, but was strangely wary in giving his opinion." Ames ascribed Madison's peregrinations to the workings of a guilty conscience. "Conscience made him a coward. He flinched from an explicit and bold creed of anarchy." Another Massachusetts Federalist, Henry Van Schaak, commented on the chaos among Republicans in the anti-treaty leadership, exclaiming with glee, "alas! Poor Madison! He seems to have dwindled into nothing—I cannot yet find out who is the leader of the faction—is it [Virginia congressman William Branch] Giles?"[17]

Part of the problem for Republicans was the tremendous activism of the Federalists that spring. Energized by Livingston's motion and call for papers, Hamilton and others took to mobilizing an imposing counterattack which built on many of the themes and arguments the Federalists had been using since the previous summer. This counterattack took place in the congressional debates, but, more importantly, out in the streets as well, and reveals much about the nature of popular politics in 1796 and the aptitude of the Federalists for engaging in them.

Federalists were plainly concerned in the weeks leading up to the House vote, as it became clear that Republicans meant to do all they could to block appropriations. They believed that the public now favored the treaty but that there was also a majority in Congress determined to defeat it. It was crucial for Federalists, then, to bring the pressure of public opinion to bear on the House. In a letter to Rufus King, his fellow "Camillus," dated April 15, Alexander Hamilton suggested a strategy for Federalists to pursue. He clearly grasped the seriousness of the situation. "Great evils may result unless good men play their card well & with promptitude and decision. For we must seize and carry along with us the public opinion," he noted, "& loss of time may be loss of everything." Hamilton believed Federalists should plan for the worst. If the House did vote to deny appropriations the president should issue "a solemn Protest" which challenged the constitutionality of the House's actions and testified to the likely damage to foreign relations and future treaty making. A copy should be sent to the Senate so that it might pass a resolution supporting the president's message. Copies of the president's message and the Senate's resolution should then be sent around to merchants in the various cities, who should be encouraged to draft addresses which could circulate among the public and be signed. "But in all this business," Hamilton cautioned, "celerity decision & an imposing attitude are indispensable. The Glory of the President, the safety of the Constitution, the greatest interests depend upon it. Nothing will be wanting here." This letter was Hamilton's call to arms and reflected both his concern for the measure's fate and his determination to mobilize every weapon at his disposal to avert rejection.[18]

With the fate of the treaty in the balance in the spring of 1796, Federalists put aside whatever scruples they may have had about mobilizing the people and actively courted public opinion. Federalists artfully but not illogically continued to claim that interfering with congressional decisions was wrong but, in this case, necessary and justified because of improper Republican efforts at manipulation. "It may be said," stated one Federalist editorial, nicely summarizing the party's position, "that we ought to trust our Representatives, and let them act for us. Perhaps we might safely do so, if such clamour had not been raised elsewhere against the Treaty, and our silence, in this critical state of the Treaty, could not be considered, as approving that clamour." The editorial went on to say that just as citizens had a duty to express themselves when they found acts of government harmful to them, "it is equally our duty, when the acts of government are advantageous to us, and while they are yet unfinished, to express our approbation." It closed with a call to citizens to "strengthen the hands" of their representatives by showing support for the treaty so as to secure its advantages.[19]

Pro-treaty advocates became increasingly emboldened about calling on the people to petition Congress—a reversal of their negative stance toward petitions the previous summer and a reflection of a perceived shift in public opinion in the interim. If citizens preferred the advantages of peace to war, they should "exercise a right which we undoubtedly have of instructing our Representative in Congress." Another Federalist urged citizens to make their wishes known, claiming "there never was a time which called more loudly for the interference of the people." So widespread was the public preference for the treaty, this writer believed, that he had no doubt that "a great majority will co operate in any plan that shall produce so desirable an effect." These treaty supporters and others plainly revealed the Federalists' willingness to engage the public and attempt to persuade it.[20]

But treaty backers realized they faced a crisis, and they did far more than simply urge the public to get involved: they organized forums and meetings to support not only the treaty but the administration and President Washington as well. These meetings were designed both to demonstrate visible public support for the measure and to provide a forum to circulate petitions and memorials, which would then be sent to Congress *and* reported in the newspapers, joining with other reports to create and further a sense of momentum. This practice of organizing and then publicizing meetings imitated closely the routinization of nationalist celebrations, and deserves closer examination since it formed a crucial part of the Federalists' strategy.[21]

Concerned that the House might fail to fund the treaty, a group of New York merchants and traders gathered at the Tontine Coffee House on April 19. The meeting, chaired by Gulian Verplank, chose a committee to correspond with traders in other towns. The committee was also charged with another critical task; they were to "appoint a suitable number of proper Characters to proceed through the different Wards of this city to obtain the signatures to the said address of all those of our Fellow Citizens who shall agree in opinion with this meeting." Federalists were now willing to go door to door, if necessary, to add signatures to their pro-treaty petitions to Congress. The petition they drafted and circulated talked of a broad consensus. "Whatever differences of sentiment may at any time have existed among us respecting particular public measures . . . on this occasion and at this time, we all unite in one opinion . . . that the above mentioned Treaty ought to be provided for, and executed." The petition denied any interest in entering the debate over which constitutional authorities had which prerogatives. "[H]owever these may stand, we are convinced after full and mature deliberation, that no existing considerations are of sufficient weight, to render it adviseable to refuse making provision" for the treaty. Any delay—or, worse still, failure—to execute the measure "must inevitably produce . . . the calamities of a war." Federalists then circulated the petition for three days, stressing, as they sought to persuade their fellow citizens to sign, the inevitability of war if the measure failed. They gathered 3,200 signatures, prompting Alexander Hamilton to point out gleefully that it fell "within about 300 of the highest poll we ever had in this City *on both sides,* at the most contro verted election. Nothing can more clearly demonstrate our unanimity & I feel no doubt of equal or greater unanimity throughout the state."[22]

Not content simply to support their own efforts, New York Federalists set out to undermine the anti-treaty meetings as well. Hamilton himself produced a broadside condemning a public meeting: a recent call for citizens to gather, ostensibly for a public discussion, was a veil for anti-treaty activity. He urged the public not to be misled by such strategems and to keep in mind the central question on which the entire matter pivoted: did citizens prefer peace or war? "The truth most assuredly is, Fellow Citizens, that the CONSTITUTION and PEACE are in one scale—the overthrow of the CONSTITUTION and WAR in the other. Which do you prefer?" Hamilton and the Federalists preferred to put the question just that starkly. He went on to ask if such proven patriots as Washington and Jay would sell out their country, as some charged. He urged the public to think carefully about what was at stake and not to be duped "by the ambition of an VIRGINIAN FACTION" into sacrificing essential interests. The proper response, as the *American Minerva* suggested, was for the real friends of the government and Constitution not to attend the meeting.[23]

New York's Federalists were hardly the only ones spurred to action. Treaty proponents in other towns organized meetings and circulated petitions in a similar fashion, engaging in popular politics on a scale not seen since the advent of the new government. In Boston a large crowd gathered at Faneuil Hall at ten o'clock on April 25. The meeting had been advertised and there were too many people for the hall to accommodate, so it adjourned to the Old South Meetinghouse. The principals on each side included some of the town's leading political lights. An account of the meeting in the *Massachusetts Mercury* stressed the superlative efforts on both sides. "Every exertion was used to dissipate the subjects of controversy. LANGUAGE displayed new powers, and ORATORY exhibited new beauties." Various motions were made, considered, and dismissed until finally, at two o'clock, the moderator asked the crowd whether it would assent to a pro-treaty memorial. The question "passed in the affirmative, with about 100 dissentients." The whole number present was moderately supposed to be two thousand.[24]

This meeting at Old South Meetinghouse was a climax to several days of strenuous activity. Boston publisher Jeremy Belknap on April 23 published a memorial to Congress urging passage; at the time, it had been signed by nine hundred citizens, a figure which increased to thirteen hundred upon further circulation. It was this memorial which was voted on at the April 25 meeting, and Belknap reported that "a majority of at least 5 to 1 in a very full meeting" approved the document. The memorial stated that citizens had waited to see the necessary measures adopted to secure the treaty, and were "now seriously alarmed, lest those measures should be further delayed or entirely omitted." The signers felt "an interest, in common with their fellow citizens of other descriptions, in the preservation of Peace, on which the prosperity of this country depends." They would consider themselves "wanting in that spirit and independence which ought ever to characterize freemen, if they forbear . . . to express their wishes and expectations."[25]

This memorial was intended for mass distribution. A note signed by Belknap, Thomas Dawes (the moderator of the Old South Meetinghouse gathering), and others, dated April 28, indicates that the memorials enclosed should be circulated "immediately in order that the Memorials contained therein may be ready for Subscription in the Several Parishes on Sunday after Service." This letter was sent "to influential Gentlemen in the several Counties." The memorials were accompanied by a circular also intended for distribution, addressed "To the FREE and INDEPENDENT CITIZENS of ________"—with space left open to fill in the appropriate town name. In far more unrestrained language than that found in the memorial, the circular made it clear that the nation faced a "CRISIS" threatening its very "HAPPINESS and SAFETY." Should the House refuse appropriations for the measure, "WAR! Horrid WAR! with all its varied and multiplied desolations" would occur. Given such a prospect, it is no surprise the circular proudly claimed, "We cannot hesitate to follow where WASHINGTON leads—we must prefer PEACE and PROSPERITY to *War* and *Distress*."[26]

In Hartford, Connecticut, citizens received "sundry communications" from residents of Philadelphia and New York, imploring them to join with them "*Constitutionally* to procure the necessary appropriations to be made" by the House. Wishing to add their voices to those already on record favoring the treaty, the Hartford citizens convened a town meeting on April 21 at the North Meeting House, which was "unusually full, and constituted of the most respectable inhabitants of the professional, Mercantile, Mechanic and Farming interests." The meeting, with only three dissenters, voted to address Congress "earnestly requesting that provision may be made without delay" for carrying the treaty into effect. The meeting also resolved to send a circular to various towns in Connecticut, requesting them to do the same. The petition passed by the Hartford meeting informed Congress that the citizens were writing "in order that the REAL wishes of the people may be fully known." It stressed the threat of war and what it might mean for prosperity. "War will sweep away our wealth, our prosperity, and our happiness," and any nation which weakly forfeited its blessings "will have little claim on posterity for reverence or gratitude."[27] Each of these meetings was reported in newspapers and the petitions were widely reprinted, thereby providing models for other towns to imitate and furthering a sense of broad-based momentum.

The town meeting held in Frederick-Town, Maryland, illustrates the manner in which treaty proponents went about extending their networks to produce favorable meetings and resolutions. Philadelphia merchants led by Thomas Fitzsimons, a former U.S. congressman defeated for re-election in 1794 by the Republican John Swanwick, wrote to Thomas Johnson and other merchants in Frederick-Town with news of the Philadelphia meetings. Fitzsimons asked them "to obtain the sentiments of your fellow-citizens, on this interesting subject, as early as possible." Frederick-Town convened on Saturday, April 23, with Johnson in the chair. The meeting resolved unanimously that the people felt "the warmest attachment to the President . . . for his wisdom, prudence, patriotic firmness, and indefatigable disinterested services." The citizens also resolved that nothing less than the "honour, tranquility, prosperity, and happiness" of the nation required the full execution of the treaty. The final resolution that day called for a memorial expressing the town's wishes to be drawn up and communicated to U.S. Representative Thomas Sprigg, a Republican, so that he might present it to the full House.

Chairman Johnson sent the memorial to Sprigg with a note which provides further evidence as to how the Federalists publicized and circulated such petitions. Johnson noted that since the meeting was held on a Saturday, "several of the neighborhood from the country, being as common, occasionally in town, attended. Their anxiety in the existing crisis, urged them to a similar expression of their wishes. They have therefore subscribed a like memorial, and desired me also to enclose it to you." Johnson's note indicated that others were circulating copies around the county. It was his opinion, he informed Sprigg, "that of the 30,000 people of this county, there is scarce a negative inclination." In other areas, similar modes of gathering signatures prevailed. The citizens of Washington and Prince George's counties in Maryland held a town meeting on April 22, drafting a memorial to send to Congress. "The memorial was immediately signed by several hundred of the citizens present. . . . It will be left at different hours; in various parts of the City and County until Tuesday next, for the convenience of those who wish to affix their names." In small towns as in large, then, Federalists called town meetings, drew up petitions and memorials, printed the accounts of the meetings and resolutions in the news papers, and then circulated those materials to other outlying areas, just as Fitzsimons and the Philadelphia Federalists had done with the Frederick-Town inhabitants.[28] By fanning out in this manner, Federalists actively influenced and mobilized the public to a degree scarcely seen before.

The various petitions and memorials from other towns—collected, reproduced in the newspapers, and sent to Congress—were mostly variations on the same themes and language developed in the aforementioned memorials. Many of the petitions reflected the *Columbian Centinel* editorial, "A PLAIN CASE!" which set the tone early for the final month of debate by stating directly, "Either the Constituted Authorities of the Union, as established by the Constitution of the PEOPLE, must be supported entire, or anarchy must ensue! The friends of the Constitution know this, and they will unite their efforts to support it, should it be assailed." The editorial also voiced great faith in Washington, stating that the people's "Anchor of Hope is in the long-tried firmness of the Man who has ever resisted oppression, and who has sworn to defend that Constitution." The grand jury of Allegheny County, Pennsylvania, sent to Congress a petition which declared that no matter what the merits of the treaty were, "it has acquired the sanction of the American Constitution" and, at the risk of losing national faith, should be carried into execution. To do otherwise would create the "dreadful spectacle . . . of a government at war with itself, one branch defeating the purposes and acts of another." The memorial of Salem, Massachusetts, stated concisely that when the treaty was "ratified by the Constituted Authorities" it became the "SUPREME LAW OF THE LAND." The citizens were "very seriously alarmed" at reports that it might be obstructed by withholding appropriations.[29]

Other petitions argued that to allow the treaty to die for want of appropriations would reflect terribly on national honor and would give other nations little reason to treat with the United States in the future, seeing the consequence of duly negotiated measures such as this one. The citizens of George-Town, Maryland, declared that "the national character for good faith, may be injured" in addition to the peace and happiness of the nation. Memorialists in Beverly, Massachusetts, declared that both "the interest and the honor" of the U.S. required that provisions be made for carrying the treaty into effect. Similar memorials were addressed from citizens of Newburyport, Marblehead, and Hingham, all in Massachusetts. Citizens of Washington and Prince George's counties in Maryland declared that they were "alarmed for the interest, reputation and tranquility of CONFEDERATED AMERICA." And residents of Haverhill, Massachusetts, urged the House to make appropriations so as "to preserve the honor, interest and tranquillity of the United States, and to prevent the calamities of war." From various points, then, the message of the petitions was the same: the treaty must be carried into effect to preserve the honor and pledged faith of the country and to uphold the constituted authorities. Failure to do so would undermine the U.S. government abroad and at home, a price too dear for the infant republic to pay.[30]

Some petitions reflected continuing themes of the Federalist campaign since the preceding summer. For example, one contended that if citizens gave the measure a careful review, they would see its advantages and reject its opponents' arguments. The electors of Albany and Lansingburgh, New York, declared their support "after full and mature deliberation" and urged the House to likewise give the document their "solemn and dispassionate consideration." One letter stated explicitly what was implicit in many of the pro-treaty petitions: that the public possessed the honesty and good sense to see matters as they were and not be misled by intriguers. "I am fully persuaded," wrote this Federalist, "that, although [anti-treaty writings] may cause some temporary evils; there is too much good sense and discernment in the great body of the people, to suffer them to be long misled by foreign *agents* or *political enthusiasts*."[31] Nearly all the petitions and memorials stressed the great themes of the earlier Federalist campaign (the threat of war and the danger to commerce if the measure were not enacted, the need to support the constituted authorities, particularly President Washington), with the addition, that spring, of the linkage of the Jay Treaty with the Pinckney Treaty with Spain, a significant twinning which allowed Federalists to argue that failure to fund one treaty could harm the chances of the second and render the nation devoid of the benefits of either.

No theme, however, was pursued more ardently than the threat of war with Great Britain. Federalists were not above explicitly threatening the public with dire warnings of the danger. "How can you sleep at this awful crisis of your affairs? The prospect every where blackens around you," declared "Brutus," writing on April 18. "Do you not hear the thunder roll? Do you not see the approaching storm?" he asked melodramatically.

After praising Washington's character and firmness he warned of the horrors of war and then gave a lengthy catalog of the ills that would befall agriculture, business, trade, and the national economy generally if the appropriations failed. "Every source of our national prosperity will be dried up. Let us therefore with an unanimous voice pronounce in favour of the Treaty being carried into effect." Other writers were as explicit about what would happen if the House usurped the constitutional authority of the Senate and president. "The voice of the people appears to be decidedly against a war. . . . And it can hardly be doubted, that, if [the House refuses to execute the treaty] and involve their country in a war, that they have not acted in conformity with the sentiments of the constituents, and will draw upon themselves almost universal execration."[32]

One of the other major themes of the Federalists that spring linked the Jay Treaty to the Pinckney Treaty with Spain. This connection had special resonance for those living on the western frontier.[33] Citizens gathered at Greensburgh, Pennsylvania, in Westmoreland County on March 14, 1796, and drafted a petition which stated that the surrender by the British of the western forts (accomplished by the Jay Treaty) and the free navigation of the Mississippi (due to the Pinckney Treaty) "are objects of the first importance to the inhabitants of the Western country." Another western paper noted that no section of the country "had so deep an interest in the fate of the treaty" as the western country. Since the "safety & prosperity" of the region was "connected to the execution of these treaties [it is] proper for us, to step forward, instantly and heartily, with petitions for their complete and immediate execution."[34]

Federalist leaders recognized, too, the strategic importance of linking the treaties in influencing both the public and, in turn, Congress. While Hamilton had expressed opposition to linking the treaties (preferring to argue for the Jay Treaty on its merits), Christopher Gore noted that "The coming of the Spanish Treaty about the same time may be a fortunate event." One of Theodore Sedgwick's correspondents observed that the Pinckney Treaty would arrive at about the time the House was to consider the Jay Treaty. The confluence "may save you and your Coadjutor, the federalists, in congress some Trouble." Newspaper publisher Loring Andrews noted that Congress would soon have "*an abundance of treaties* before them" and hoped that "our *democratic branch*" would treat them "in such a manner, as to conduce to the good of our country, and render the American name respectable."[35]

While Federalists went into overdrive with their newspaper and petition campaigns, Republican papers seemed spent, as if they had exhausted their store of anti-treaty energy the previous summer and now had little else in reserve. Bache and others tried. But, in general, the Republican newspaper war in spring 1796 lacked the fervor and power it had before, and failed to match the Federalists. Republican papers singled out for stinging criticism Washington's refusal to submit the papers to the House. Such high-handedness by the president threatened constitutional government and undermined the prerogatives of the House. Newspapers like the *Aurora* framed the debate as a contest between Washington's executive privilege and the rights of the majority. Bache's paper turned its full fury on Washington for attempting to strip the House—and the people it represented—of its rights. Correspondents to the paper speculated that the real reason for the president's refusal to hand over the papers was that doing so would "unmask" the administration's true aims and jeopardize the treaty. One newspaper asked readers point blank, "Will you support your representatives in Congress, or put all power in the hands of twenty Senators and the President?" Boston's *Independent Chronicle* was similarly blunt, asking, "shall the *people* or the PRESIDENT be the sovereign of the United States?"[36]

In the final days before the House vote, Bache's paper inveighed against some House members who talked about abstaining on the final vote although they were opposed to the treaty. To do so, Bache warned, would be deeply disloyal. Anyone who followed that course of action should "be branded with the same ignominy as those who vote against their country." The *Aurora* also reminded its readers of many of the points that Republican papers had been making all along: that funding the treaty would provoke a breach with the French, that the Federalists were being alarmist in raising the war cry, and that the administration was acting arrogantly in showing disregard for the Constitution. While Republican newspapers tried, they were not as effective during the spring debate as they had been the previous summer. Besides the usual denunciations and vituperative attacks on Jay, Washington, the treaty, and the administration, the Republican press seemingly had little new to offer. In the face of the resurgent Federalist newspaper campaigns, calls for public meetings, and aggressive petition drives, joined with the force of Washington's popularity and the continued shouts of "war" should the treaty not pass, the Republican press was comparatively tame in the final weeks of the debate, when even the staunchest anti-treaty critics sensed, along with many Federalists, that the battle was about to be lost.[37]

Meanwhile, as the petitions came cascading in from town meetings mostly held in the middle states and New England, Federalist editors took great delight. The *Massachusetts Mercury* noted, "Innumerable are the Memorials, which have already been drafted, signed by almost every Citizen to whom they have been presented, and presented to Congress in favor of the Treaty. A *few* of the towns memorializing we have mentioned to our Readers," but there was simply not room to print them all. The editors had heard of meetings held in Virginia, Maryland, New Jersey, Delaware, Pennsylvania, New York, Connecticut, Rhode Island, Massachusetts, and New Hampshire. "Meetings have also doubtless taken place in the other States of the Union, equally patriotic," the paper noted breathlessly. Benjamin Russell's *Columbian Centinel* reveled in the outpouring of public support for the treaty. "Accounts of the patriotic ardor of the citizens of Massachusetts . . . are hourly pouring in." The accompanying memorials "are signed by greater numbers than were ever known on any former political question." Such a vast outpouring showed that the "loud voice of Free Citizens will neither be unheard nor unregarded! . . . [T]his phalanx of patriotic sentiment—this mass of evidence of the unequivocal federalism of Massachusetts" was manifest for all to see. "TRUTH IS OMNIPOTENT," crowed the *Centinel*.[38]

Publicly, Federalists expressed optimism and confidence that they would prevail in the treaty vote. In doing so they were simultaneously pointing to what many truly believed to be a favorable current of public sentiment, *and,* by expressing their views publicly, hoping to build momentum and create a groundswell of public favor and a sense of inevitability about House passage. This effort was designed to persuade not only the public, but the House itself, of the state of public opinion on the measure.[39]

Treaty advocates believed, as they had hoped for some time would happen, that the public after a period of excitement and agitation had been persuaded by cool reason, close analysis, and the passage of time that the treaty was not lethal, as opponents charged. The petitions and memorials offered proof. "Now that the paroxism [*sic*] of intemperance, which fumed so admirably last summer, is spent, and reason has resumed her power, people begin to perceive that the good effects of the treaty have, as yet, exceeded its bad." Another writer noted that "since the first hot fever against the treaty has cooled off, the general sentiment has turned strongly." Federalists now made much of the discrepancy between the pro-treaty tone of public opinion and the anti-treaty posture of the House. "How is it," asked "Epistolary," "that a majority of one popular body is found so little in correspondence with the sense of the country?" Another writer ventured that "The public will, in regard to the treaty, is not represented in the popular branch of Congress. . . . A vast majority . . . are in favor of fulfilling the treaty, and this fact will soon appear."[40]

Reports reprinted in the *Gazette of the United States* from correspondents in various locations provided readers with an unambiguous sense of the public's position. Everywhere, it seemed, there was great concern lest the treaty not be funded. Writing from Baltimore, one author noted that people were "disquieted" by the congressional debates and feared for the passage of the treaty. No matter the tone in Congress, that of Baltimore was quite clear. People there were moving beyond partisanship. They "seem in some degree to have dropt their party spirit, and become more united in their wishes for appropriations." The writer hoped that the decision of the House "may be favorable to the wishes of the People." A few days later, another writer, reporting on a Richmond, Virginia, town meeting "more numerous than any I have ever seen at this place," saw a clear majority vote in favor of a resolution declaring that the "peace, happiness, and welfare . . . [and] national honor" depended on the fulfillment of the treaty.[41]

Correspondents writing from Newport, Rhode Island, and George-Town, Maryland, expressed the same conviction about the depth of public opinion in their areas. When word arrived in Newport that the House might not fund the measure, it seemed "so improbable that many will not yet believe it." If true, such news would produce alarm. Of particular concern was the prospect of war with the British and the renewal of violence and conflict with Indians. Given these concerns, the correspondent wrote, "You may rest assured that the great body of the people of this State are sensible of the interest they have, in the preservation of the constitution and peace of the country." In George-Town, citizens realized the necessity of making a public declaration of support for the treaty lest the House act on misleading information. The correspondent reported a town meeting where four hundred citizens signed a pro-treaty memorial to present to Congress as a gauge of public opinion. "If nothing else will make your House act right—and if the unequivocal sense of the people, will, I think it would be good policy to delay for a few weeks" the vote. "Even in Virginia," he observed, many were "becoming very friendly to the treaty." As to popular opinion on George Washington, the writer assured readers that "*The President's conduct is approved every where I believe where men can think.*"[42]

Toward the end of the debate, one Federalist offered his assessment of the state of public opinion by contrasting not only the numbers but the composition of the crowds mobilized for and against the treaty and the ways in which they were summoned. This account suggested not only that pro-treaty advocates were backed by public opinion but that the anti-treaty side was demoralized, bitter, and disorganized. The merchants, traders, and substantial mechanics of New York were in overwhelming agreement on the importance of fulfilling the treaty. When the petition went door to door, nearly the only persons who did not sign were those who were away from their houses, and "most who were absent when called upon, wish to subscribe." A meeting held in the Fields on April 22—the one for which Hamilton prepared a broadside urging citizens to stay away from—was desultory. Only eight hundred or so turned out, "almost totally of those who at 12 o'clock could be spared from their manual labours." A good third of these, the writer estimated, were, "as is usually the case, composed of negroes, sweeps, boys, apprentices, Frenchmen, and curious people opposed to the meeting." He called it the most "unimportant" meeting ever held on such a significant occasion, and noted that few of the opposition's leaders were on hand, "and those of them who did appear, the least distinguished for their consequence." He concluded with a concise explanation for the apparent triumph of the pro-treaty position: "The reason is obvious—In serious time, serious men are prudent."[43]

Despite these expressions of confidence and certainty, some Federalists in private showed a bit more caution and were not as ebullient as their public pronouncements made them seem. Henry Van Schaak wrote to Theodore Sedgwick on April 16 with great concern for the fate of the treaty. He noted that his intelligence told him things looked bad for the Federalists. "It is now two days since this disagreeable piece of intelligence reached me. And ever since my mind has been absorbed with the most gloomy apprehensions on this subject—God grant that those apprehensions may not be verified—They are serious indeed." The same day, in a second letter to Sedgwick, Van Schaak again expressed his distress over impending action in the House, claiming, "Upon the whole my hopes are by no means so equal as my fears." In Maine, Jesse Appleton wrote on the 23rd of reading the newspapers with anxiety over the treaty business. Generally, however, those Federalists in Philadelphia and involved in the House proceedings expressed more confidence in the situation; they certainly had more first-hand knowledge than those in the backcountry. Dwight Foster in his journal noted that the task ahead for Federalists was a difficult one, but expressed his firm belief that they would prevail and that the public was on their side.[44]

No matter whether they expressed confidence or foreboding, Federalists ratcheted up the pressure as the congressional vote neared. On April 18, 1796, a committee appointed by the New York and United States insurance companies resolved unanimously to cease underwriting American vessels traveling the high seas until the treaty matter was resolved. "[D]uring the present critical and alarming situation of Public Affairs, it will be inexpedient for the Insurance Companies and individual Underwriters in this city to insure American property against Capture or detention by any foreign Power." This had the effect of raising public anxiety even higher and bringing not inconsiderable pressure to bear on Congress.[45] As for the debates in the House itself, there was a considerable bit of speaking and maneuvering on both sides. All of this came against a backdrop of batches of petitions arriving daily, most announcing that the citizens of one or another town endorsed the treaty and wished the House to appropriate funds to fulfill it. Dwight Foster noted each day the arrival of petitions to the House, and also noted that "the Hall is constantly crowded with Spectators anxious for the Results" of the debate. As the process neared its conclusion, Foster continued to report the appearance of petitions and memorials to Congress from all parts of the country, "continually pouring in requesting that the Measures requisite for carrying the Treaty into Effect may be adopted." Foster observed the results of the petitions: "They visibly have an Effect upon the opposers of the Treaty."[46]

Undaunted by Washington's refusal to send the papers, House Republicans pushed hard against the treaty. They reiterated all of their earlier denunciations. In his speeches, James Madison largely recapitulated points he had made before. While his speeches represented, as Lance Banning has noted, a continuation of Madison's "elaborate and agonized attempts to understand the spirit and provisions of the Constitution," they seem to have had little effect on the debate itself. As his major speech did not come until April 15, just fifteen days before the final vote, perhaps it was too late to have any decided impact in the face of what was happening outside of Congress in the town meetings and petition campaigns.[47] Still, Federalists saw the Republicans' final efforts coming, and anticipated their substance. John Adams wrote to his wife on April 16 that the people "are about to be stirred up in every quarter of the union.The House of Representatives are determined to go all lengths. . . . The state parties will all be agitated, and party spirit will be carried to the highest pitch."[48]

Republicans began April 1796 still optimistic that they would defeat the treaty. By the end of the month, their cautious optimism gave way to disillusionment and bitterness about the way the Federalists had, to their minds, manipulated the public and induced a number of fence-sitters in Congress to desert the Republicans—even though Federalists were doing essentially what the Republicans had done the previous summer. Even early in April, Republican operative John Beckley had his doubts. "I *fear* the B. Treaty will be carried into effect; it will not, however, without some vote asserting the Constitutional power of the House," he wrote to James Monroe. "A meeting of the republicans will be had this evening to consider what is best to be done; there appears a disposition to make a firm stand, and I think that should the treaty take effect *at all,* it will be by a very small majority." Nonetheless, while Beckley wrote to DeWitt Clinton that things generally looked bright for the Republican cause, "we are not without fears that some of our republican friends may want the necessary stamina to carry them thro' and more particularly from your State. . . . I would suggest a doubt as to our friends [Theodorus] Bailey, [Philip] Van Cortlandt, and [Jonathan] Havens on the final question. . . . Elected by small majorities, and doubtful from the present circumstances of your state how the political scale will preponderate at another Election, they perhaps wish to steer that course which will best ensure their reelection. So often & so fatally my friend," Beckley lamented, "do personal, supersede public considerations." Beckley urged Clinton to act promptly. "You can best judge of, and will I am sure pursue *the most Earnest* means to keep our three friends in the true course. If they go right, the British treaty will infallibly be rejected. But remember," he warned, "whatever is done *must be done quickly.*"[49]

Beckley was right to worry about the firmness of these New Yorkers, for Federalists, even as they were playing an effective "outside" game to influence public opinion, were also pursuing an aggressive "inside" game by identifying and assiduously lobbying individual congressmen who they believed to be persuadable. One of their chief targets was Van Cortlandt. On April 17, Rufus King noted to Hamilton that Van Cortlandt would be leaving Philadelphia for New York in a couple of days. "Would it not be well to prepare a Reception for him which may return him in favor of the Treaty," he asked. "His Friends may be induced to act upon his Mind, so as to decide it." Other Federalists resorted to even more personal and forceful appeals. Pennsylvania Republican Frederick Muhlenberg received a vow from the father of the young woman his son was courting. Referring to the treaty, the father threatened Muhlenberg, "If you do not give us your vote, your son shall not have my Polly." Evidently, Muhlenberg's response reassured Polly's father, because he consented to the marriage even before the opening of the congressional session.[50]

Even as these events transpired, as late as April 18, Madison could confidently assert to James Monroe that the treaty would be defeated in the House. "If no defections take place the motion [to refuse appropriations] will succeed by a majority of about twenty." But, he warned Monroe, as if with a premonition of what might come, "vast exertions are on foot without and within doors. . . . The Country also is stirred up to join in petitions for carrying the Treaty into effect." Just a few days later, Madison admitted there was slippage. Writing April 23 to Thomas Jefferson, he noted that the "majority has melted, by changes and absence, to 8 or 9 votes." He did not know whether these votes would hold steady, for "Every possible exertion is made as usual on the other side." Madison noted, with a trace of bitterness and contempt, "A sort of appeal has been made to the people, with an expectation that the mercantile force would triumph over the popular sentiment." In short, as the climatic days neared, Madison and the Republicans were growing less optimistic.[51]

Federalist Fisher Ames, in an April 2, 1796, letter, also made an assessment of how the vote was shaping up. His count was considerably more accurate than the hopeful Republican measurements, and quite close to the final vote. Ames told George Richards Minot that the appropriation of funds for the treaty "will be vehemently contested, and it is hard to say how it will go. I think some will flinch. . . . More are doubtful, and should one or two leaders desert the terrorists, they will drop off rapidly. Such an event is probable." Ames then gave Minot a state-by-state assessment of how the congressmen might vote. He listed 49 likely "Nay" votes against the treaty, 47 "Yea" votes in favor, five doubtful votes, and 4 absences. His reading proved remarkably prescient. A full four weeks before the vote, he exactly forecast the New England votes and foresaw that the treaty would win six votes from the Maryland delegation. The only place Ames underestimated pro-treaty strength was in the middle states, particularly New York and Pennsylvania. Of course, those states were already seeing the results of intensive petitioning efforts and public campaigning designed to influence congressmen to vote for the treaty. Ames's forecast suggests that Federalists were better vote counters than were the Republicans, who seemed to be relying too much and with too little evidence on replicating the result of the Livingston resolution vote even as they regularly commented on that majority "melting" away. Ames's letter also suggests that the outcome of the treaty vote was in real doubt, and that the active pro-treaty campaign to gather petitions and shape public opinion may have been crucial in converting "No" or "doubtful" votes to favorable ones.[52]

As Republicans contemplated this "melting" of votes, they were frustrated by the demagogic way the Federalists treated the threat of war. New Hampshire senator John Langdon wrote to Madison from Portsmouth that "the British party are makeing every exertion to obtain their object." He told Madison, "The Cry is war, war, no Insurance to be had, Vessells hauled up, no employment for the people." Edmund Randolph noted, upon observing John Marshall's address at a Richmond town meeting, that Marshall's "argument was inconsistent, and shifting." But he similarly reported that Marshall "conclud[ed] every third sentence with the horrors of war." Benjamin Bache wrote scathingly, weeks earlier, that "*Before the President's signature was obtained,* the cry was *war*. . . . It is true we were not, at that time, precisely told who would declare war. . . . But still the thunder of *war, war,* rolled on our ear."[53] It was against this backdrop that Republicans began defecting, citing the influence of petitions, their sense of obligation to vote their constituents' wishes, and their belief that not fulfilling the treaty at this stage would cause serious harm to the nation's commerce or its chances of remaining at peace. On April 22, Samuel Smith of Baltimore announced that he would support the measure because it seemed now "to be the opinion of the great majority of the people of Maryland, who he had the honor to represent," that less harm would come from adopting the treaty than from rejecting it. On April 29, House Speaker Jonathan Dayton of New Jersey declared that while he had never liked the Jay Treaty, he now believed it would be better to bring it into effect than to reject it. Others joined these leaders in "melting" away.[54]

In the final days before the vote, Pennsylvania's Albert Gallatin made the most sustained and complete attack on the treaty yet, going through each of the articles individually, questioning what the true benefits would be, exposing the weaknesses he saw, and excoriating the Federalists for trying to confuse and inflame people by resorting to the cry of war. Gallatin had stepped into the leadership void created by Madison's hesitation and he took up the reins of the anti-treaty side in the House debate. For much of the month of April, Gallatin worked hard to scotch Federalist efforts in the House and led the opposition to the treaty during the floor debates. But Gallatin was swimming against the tide of popular opinion from his own district in western Pennsylvania. As Gallatin led the fight against the treaty he could not ignore the petitions pouring in from his frontier constituents, informing him of their support for the very document he was just then doing so much to defeat.[55]

As these events were occurring it was announced that Massachusetts congressman Fisher Ames, recognized as a master orator, would—despite the ailments that had kept him largely silent during the debate—rise and speak in favor of the treaty. What followed when Ames spoke on April 28 was, by nearly unanimous historical verdict, one of the truly great oratorical performances the House of Representatives had ever heard. To Ames's opponents, however, it would go down as a piece of sheer melodrama. Ames warned at length of the danger to a nation's honor in breaking a treaty, of the disruptions to commerce, and of the threat of war with all of its calamities. To Ames's mind, the prospect of war and Indian violence on the frontier was a certainty. The Jay Treaty provided for removal of the British from these frontier posts. Speculating that breaking the treaty would result in the loss of the posts, Ames played on this fear. Hostile Indians would run rampant and settlers on the frontier would be endangered. Ames spoke of "the reach of the tomahawk" and cautioned that the circumstances in the west from rejecting the treaty "will not be peace but a sword." He warned, with gripping intensity, of a "spectacle of horror which cannot be overdrawn." Ames concluded by speaking of the treaty as a last hope to preserve the peace so necessary to the young nation. By carrying the treaty into effect, Ames said, the United States would uphold its national faith, preserve peace, and set loose an enterprising spirit which would bolster prosperity. "If however the vote should pass to reject, and a spirit should rise, as it will, with the public disorders to make confusion worse confounded, even I, slender and almost broken as my hold upon life is, may outlive the government and constitution of my country."[56]

As soon as Ames finished speaking, the reaction and appraisals began. Among those who heard the speech, the response was nearly universal: it was a classic piece of oratory. Vice President John Adams listened to the speech with Supreme Court Justice James Iredell and noted that Ames "was attended to with a silence and interest never before known," making an impression which "will never be forgotten." Adams exclaimed to his wife, "Our feeling beat in unison. 'My God! how great he is,' says Iredell, 'how great he has been!'" Dr. Joseph Priestley, who had heard all the greats of contemporary British oratory, commented that the speech was "the most bewitching piece of parliamentary oratory he had ever listened to." And Ames's friend, Jeremiah Smith, told Ames "that he ought to have died in the fifth act; that he never will have an occasion so glorious, having lost this he will now be obliged to make his exit like other men."[57]

Federalist newspapers joined in the chorus of praise. In New York, the *American Minerva* ventured that the address "was held to be the finest display of eloquence ever exhibited in this country," while Boston's *Columbian Centinel* said, "He was a fine ship, on a summer sea, decorated with her colours, and bearing a rich cargo of spices before a fair wind."[58] Subsequent generations of historians have also underscored the emotional, dramatic nature of Ames's speech. Most scholars have retold the dramatic circumstances surrounding the speech, playing up Ames's weakened physical condition and emphasizing the emotional power and effect of the speech on listeners. Other scholars, in noting the impact of the speech, have ranked it with the best of the era. The performance gave Ames "a firm position in the ranks of great American orators and was remembered long after Federalism had passed on." Ames's biographer judged it "a display of oratory which remained unsurpassed in his generation."[59]

However, even those historians who discuss the content of the speech have not fully appreciated its relationship to the broader Federalist campaign for support of the Jay Treaty.[60] For all of its emotion and eloquence, Ames's speech was also the culmination of a ten-month campaign by Federalists to win public support. In this speech, Ames voiced positions and arguments Federalists had advanced throughout the course of the public debate. He raised many of the same issues that Federalist leaders had been raising since the previous summer. And he brilliantly encapsulated the thrust of Federalist positions by dramatizing the dangers and disasters which would occur if the treaty were not approved. In short, Ames's speech succeeded on both an emotional and an intellectual level and served as the final summation of the Federalist campaign to win ratification.[61] One of the reasons it made such an impression was because Federalist writers and speakers had so thoroughly prepared the groundwork for the preceding nine months that Ames was able to provide the peroration to a well-established campaign. Ames introduced no new arguments in favor of the treaty. He did not raise any fears of what might happen if the treaty were not enacted that had not already been stated. But Ames had no need to raise new themes. Rather, what he did was to articulate, draw together, and reinforce, more eloquently and forcefully than others, the main arguments the public had heard for the previous months. His rhetorical appeal served as the crowning achievement of the Federalists' campaign, providing a final emotional push that led to passage. But, just as important as the emotion, it was also an intellectual summation of what had been written and spoken earlier during the pro-treaty campaign.

How much of a direct effect Ames's speech had on the vote is debatable. It may well be that the matter was settled in the minds of most members before his powerful oration. And it seems likely, as a number of congressmen declared, that far more effective than speeches were the petitions supporting the treaty which poured in daily. Historians have provided some concrete evidence of the sense many on both sides of the debate had, about both the volume of petitions coming into Congress and their generally pro-treaty tone. Stephen Kurtz reviewed the petitions coming to the House that spring and found sixty-four favoring the treaty and forty opposed. The favorable petitions contained 10,200 signatures; the opposing petitions held the names of 7,200 persons. As another scholar has noted of the petition drive, the Federalists "seem to have been more effective organizers than their opponents." At least one of the targets of those fierce efforts—New York's Van Cortlandt—appears to have been persuaded not so much by speeches or arguments but by the volume of petitions. In a circular letter to his constituents in May 1796, he explained that his affirmative vote reflected what he believed to be public opinion:

"as it appeared during the course of the debates from memorials and other sources of information, to be the general wish of the people of the northern and eastern states, that it ought to be carried into effect; and taking into view all the existing circumstances, I upon the whole conceived it most advisable to give an affirmative vote on the occasion." Thus, the combined weight of the petitions—and the dramatic effect of reading them into the record of the House debates—provided some very firm reasons to justify congressmen voting for treaty appropriations on the ground of following public opinion.[62]

A day after Ames's speech, on April 29, the House, which had convened in a Committee of the Whole, split when the question was put to it—but Pennsylvania's Frederick Muhlenberg, who chaired the committee, broke the 49–49 tie in favor of the treaty. This desertion of the Republican position infuriated Madison and led to Muhlenberg's defeat at the next election. But it had a more immediate and painful effect for him as well: a few days after the vote he was stabbed by his brother-in-law, a fervent Republican. The next day came a final anti-treaty effort, a motion to fund the instrument but to add a preamble declaring it "highly objectionable." That motion, too, failed by a 50–49 vote, with Speaker Dayton this time casting the tiebreaker. Dayton now believed, he said, that it was necessary to put aside "every resentment, every prejudice, and every personal consideration" and do what was in the best interests of the country. He was bolstered in his opinion by a deluge of petitions from his constituents favoring the treaty, and by a warning from his own family of the violence the people of New Jersey might wreak on anyone voting against the measure. Finally, the question itself came before the full House, and the appropriations were finally passed 51–48. At long last, the contest was over.[63]

Why did the House vote to fund the treaty? How, exactly, just a month after the decisive 62–37 vote for the Livingston resolution, did the House come to shift its position to vote in favor of the treaty? After all, the anti-treaty majority seemed solidly in place by late March, yet that majority melted completely away by the end of April. A comparison of these two votes—on the Livingston resolution and on the treaty—reveals where the votes shifted. It also provides some insight into why.

TABLE 2
Change in Treaty Support of Representatives, by State and Region

	LIVINGSTON RESOLUTION MARCH 25 (*no = pro-treaty*)		JAY TREATY VOTE APRIL 30 (*yes = pro-treaty*)		
STATE	NO	YES	YES	NO	NET SHIFT
CONNECTICUT	7	0	7	0	
MASSACHUSETTS	9	3	10	3	+1
NEW HAMPSHIRE	3	1	3	0	
RHODE ISLAND	2	0	2	0	
VERMONT	1	1	1	1	
New England	22	5	23	4	+1
DELAWARE	0	1	0	0	
NEW JERSEY	2	1	4	2	+2
NEW YORK	5	5	7	3	+2
PENNSYLVANIA	4	8	7	5	+3
Middle States	11	15	18	8	+7
GEORGIA	0	2	0	2	
KENTUCKY	0	2	0	2	
MARYLAND	2	5	6	1	+4
NORTH CAROLINA	0	10	1	9	+1
SOUTH CAROLINA	2	4	2	4	
TENNESSEE	0	0	0	0	
VIRGINIA	0	19	1	18	+1
Southern States	4	42	10	36	+6
TOTAL	37	62	51	48	+14

As the table illustrates, the greatest movement of votes occurred in the middle states—which saw intensive use of petitions to Congress—and in the upper-South state of Maryland. The process that brought about a net change of 14 votes between these two pivotal votes is a fascinating one to explore, particularly so in regard to the 11 congressmen who changed their minds (that is, who voted with the anti-treaty side in favor of the Livingston resolution but then switched to cast a vote in favor of appropriations for the treaty). A brief discussion of the individuals involved and the process of voting will illuminate some crucial points about how the public debate on the treaty shaped the congressional votes.

In brief, the anti-treaty coalition of 62 votes did not hold, as 11 congressmen switched to vote for the treaty while four who had voted for the resolution were not present and did not cast a vote on the treaty. Madison's side gained one additional vote from a congressman who did not vote on the Livingston resolution. Put another way, the anti-treaty forces held only 47 of their 62 votes from the earlier resolution and gained only one new vote. The pro-treaty side showed remarkably firm support. Not a single congressman who voted against the Livingston resolution switched and voted against the treaty. And only one congressman (Massachusetts' Nathaniel Freeman, Jr.) from this coalition did not vote on the treaty, so 36 of the 37 "No" votes on the resolution formed the bedrock of the pro-treaty bloc. Added to the 36 solid votes were those of four congressmen who did not vote on the resolution but returned and voted in favor of the treaty, plus the 11 who changed their votes. From these additions, subtractions, and recombinations, the 37 became 51, and the 62 shrank to 48.

In the final vote, the Jay Treaty was carried by a margin of three, which exactly equaled the net pro-treaty margin of those congressmen who absented themselves from one vote or the other. Five congressmen who did not vote on the Livingston resolution returned to vote on the treaty; only one of those five (Daniel Hiester of Pennsylvania) cast a vote against the treaty. The other four (Fisher Ames and George Leonard of Massachusetts, Jeremiah Crabb of Maryland, and Thomas Henderson of New Jersey) voted in favor, a net swing of three. Another five congressmen voted on the Livingston resolution but did not vote on the treaty; all but one of them (Nathaniel Freeman, Jr., of Massachusetts) had voted with the anti-treaty side. The absence from the treaty vote of four likely "No" votes was devastating to the anti-treaty cause. Some absences were perhaps understandable. Delaware's John Patten was ill and Maryland's Gabriel Duvall had resigned. New Hampshire's John Sherburne (along with Freeman) was recorded as "on leave" in the House records. But the failure of William Findley to be present for the vote (more on this below) was inexcusable to Madison, Beckley, and the angry Republicans who learned the price of not turning out every possible vote.

But those handful of votes would not have made a difference if not for the 11 representatives who changed their votes from, effectively, "No" to "Yes" on the treaty (that is, from "Yes" on the Livingston resolution to "Yes" on the treaty). Without this massive shift, the absence or presence of a few representatives would not have affected the outcome of a vote Madison still expected to win just a matter of days before it took place. Who changed their minds and why? How did the public debate and, specifically, public opinion come into play?

Moving from south to north, North Carolina's William Barry Grove and Virginia's George Hancock were the only representatives south of Maryland to switch their votes. The anti-treaty coalition remained rock solid in the deep south. Grove was a Federalist who tended to support the administration and who came around on the treaty after voting in favor of the Livingston resolution. Hancock, while nominally a Federalist, had a fairly independent voting record in the House. Apparently influenced by Ames's speech, Hancock declared in favor of the treaty the day afterwards, along with New Jersey's Jonathan Dayton and Maryland's Gabriel Christie. He also seems to have been influenced by the provisions of the treaty removing the British from the western forts, which would open lands in the west to settlement by some in his district. All in all, the somewhat independent-minded Grove and Hancock were essentially Federalists and pro-administration. In a sense, their change in votes may be explained as simply a return to their party roots, which, though relatively weak, were strong enough to win their allegiance on the crucial treaty vote.[64]

If the deep South largely held, the border-South state of Maryland experienced a profound shift in sentiment, with a net pickup of four votes for the treaty, a deep and decisive blow to Madison and the anti-treaty forces. George Dent's vote on the treaty was perhaps a matter of falling back in line with his party, as he was generally regarded as a Federalist. His change of vote may also have reflected pressure felt from the constituents in his district, which was in the orbit of Baltimore's commercial activity. Gabriel Christie's defection could not have been predicted so easily, as he was considered a Republican. Christie was a late decider and was apparently influenced by the petitions and by Ames's speech. Along with George Hancock and Jonathan Dayton, he announced his intention to vote for the treaty the day after the speech. But even more influential in his decision was the sense that his constituents back home supported it. Although Christie announced that he thought the treaty was bad, he justified his vote in favor of appropriations by noting that "his constituents were desirous it should be carried into effect, and he found himself bound to lay aside his own opinion, and act according to their will." Samuel Smith's change of vote has already been mentioned earlier in this chapter and in the discussion of petitioning in chapter five above, but further analysis of his reasons for voting in favor of the treaty may be in order. Smith was under great public pressure and bombarded by petitions in favor of the treaty, which may well have been influential although not necessarily decisive in his vote. Smith's biographer is of the opinion that, despite his public statements against the treaty and his previous efforts to propose amendments to it, Smith was following his own judgment in voting for the measure, believing that it would pass and would be preferable to no treaty at all. Thus, the public pressure on Smith merely encouraged him to do what he was already inclined to do: switch his vote and cast it in favor of appropriations.[65]

Five of the changed votes thus came from Maryland and points south. The remaining six came from representatives of three middle states: New Jersey, New York, and Pennsylvania. It is no coincidence that the bulk of the petitioning efforts and the door-to-door efforts at persuasion were concentrated in this region, since both sides recognized the high number of swing votes among its congressmen. New Jersey's Aaron Kitchell was nominally a Republican and had voted in favor of the Livingston resolution. But his voting record was mixed; he often voted in favor of administration measures, as he would do on April 30. This has led scholars to categorize him both as a Republican and as a Federalist. In a speech of April 25, 1796, Kitchell told his House colleagues that he would vote in favor of appropriations for the Jay Treaty. He did not find the treaty "to be that box of Pandora, which was to scatter evils of every kind upon the land." In his speech Kitchell concentrated on the consequences of rejecting the treaty and specifically mentioned the threat of a possible war with Great Britain at a time when the nation was bitterly divided. Believing that passing appropriations for the treaty was the best course, Kitchell announced that "he had been impelled to give his vote for carrying the Treaty into effect. He hoped it would prove for the good of the Union; if not, he should acquit himself of having done what appeared to him the best at the time." But Kitchell likely knew that his decision would not be unpopular, either with his New Jersey congressional colleagues or, more importantly, with constituents back home. The New Jersey delegation voted 4–0 in favor of appropriations for the treaty. As congressional scholar Rudolph M. Bell writes of Kitchell, "His state strongly favored the treaty, and his vote reflected the will of his constituents."[66]

Two of the three New York congressmen whose firmness in opposition to the treaty had worried Republican operative John Beckley ultimately changed their votes, casting them in favor of the treaty and deeply frustrating Beckley and the Republicans. Theodorus Bailey and Philip Van Cortlandt each represented areas—Westchester County for Bailey, Dutchess

County for Van Cortlandt—with close ties to the New York merchant community, which was, obviously, heavily invested in the outcome of the vote. Both men, particularly Van Cortlandt, were targeted by Federalists and found themselves the recipients of tremendous pressure. No doubt, merchant Federalists reminded Van Cortlandt that he had been elected by an extremely small margin in 1794 (as he would be again in 1796). While he generally gravitated toward the Jeffersonian faction, he probably broke ranks over the treaty because of his narrow victory margin and because it was clear how the most outspoken of his constituents felt about the treaty. Virtually the same factors applied to Bailey, who was also a nominal Republican and a usually reliable vote (as he had been on the Livingston matter), but who here abandoned Madison's ranks to vote "Yes" on the treaty, apparently convinced—as pro-treaty forces endlessly argued—that a failure of the treaty meant war with England.[67]

Besides New York, the other key location for petition drives and efforts at persuasion was Pennsylvania. Here, Federalist efforts paid off handsomely, as three congressmen switched their votes from favoring the Livingston resolution to supporting the Jay Treaty appropriations measure—which, again, passed by exactly three votes. All three represented either the Philadelphia area or the Delaware river region, both of which served as commercial centers. The efforts of the merchants and Federalists in Philadelphia were especially intense. Of these three changed votes, at least one was perhaps no great surprise. John Richards was a Federalist who was disgusted enough with the treaty to vote "Yes" on the Livingston motion but whose antipathy was not so great as to derail the treaty altogether. His vote in favor of the treaty was another case—like those of Dent and Hancock—of party members siding with their colleagues on a crucial vote. In fact, as Rudolph Bell has written, "possibly his treaty vote needs less explanation than his earlier support of the Livingston resolution." But the loss of the other two votes devastated the anti-treaty cause. Frederick Muhlenberg was Speaker of the House and, thus, usually did not vote. While nominally a Republican, he was obviously acceptable to both parties and was at heart a compromiser who was habitually besieged by those on both sides. His vote in favor of appropriations satisfied some of his constituents, but he paid a heavy price in two ways. First, as noted earlier, on May 4, 1796, he was stabbed by his unstable brother-in-law, a devout Republican. Later that year, angry Republicans targeted Muhlenberg and he was beaten badly in his reelection campaign. The defection of the third Pennsylvania congressman, Andrew Gregg, earned him the undying enmity of John Beckley, who forever after referred to him as "the trimmer Gregg." While Gregg was nominally a Republican, his voting history was ambiguous and he was not a consistent anti-administration vote. Gregg rose to address the House on the day of the vote and announced that he would vote for the measure, "not because he thought the Treaty a good one, but because he believed the interest of the United States would be promoted by making the necessary appropriations." Gregg also believed that rejecting a treaty already approved by the president and ratified in the Senate would do more harm to the country than accepting it. Gregg's defection was "a severe blow," according to Rudolph Bell. But it should not have been altogether surprising. A year earlier, Gregg failed to join in support of Madison's bill to impose discriminatory reprisals against British shipping. In fact, to the Virginia leader's continuing frustration, Gregg's was neither a consistent anti-British nor anti-administration vote, for throughout his long House career (he served until 1807, when he went to the U.S. Senate), Gregg was often difficult to predict. On the Jay Treaty vote he could not have been unswayed by the torrent of petitions and the impact of public opinion urging support, especially when—despite his dislike of the measure itself—he seemed to be coming to a grudging acceptance of the treaty on his own.[68]

When it was finally over, Federalists celebrated a hard-won victory. Republicans seethed. Madison wrote to Jefferson that he had hoped until the very end that the treaty would still fail. "A few wrongheads however thought fit to separate, whereby the motion was lost by one vote." He observed that "The progress of this business throughout has to me been the most worrying & vexatious that I ever encountered; and the more so as the causes lay in the unsteadiness, the follies, the perverseness, & the defections among our friends, more than in the strength or dexterity, or malice of our opponents." Some of the "wrongheads" Madison had in mind were the New York Republicans Bailey and Van Cortlandt—two of the three men John Beckley had urged DeWitt Clinton to lobby lest they slip away—and Pennsylvania's Findley, who, incredibly and unsatisfactorily, explained that he had had to step out of the House at the time of the roll call to mail a trunk and had therefore missed the vote.[69]

Madison was not the only participant in or observer of the debates and the final vote who recorded his views. For weeks after the vote, Federalists and Republicans alike spent a considerable amount of time deciding what the vote, and, even more important, the campaigns for and against the treaty, meant—to the parties, the nation, the government, and the process of politics in the young nation. Those who had been involved as well as those who watched on the sidelines busied themselves in writing to friends or for the broader public, opining about the significance of the process. For, as Madison's letter to Jefferson a day after the vote suggests, the final House action may have capped the debate over the treaty, but it did nothing to resolve or tamp down the larger questions about foreign policy, partisanship, popular politics, public opinion, and, most broadly, the evolving political culture of the nation. The next and final chapter will analyze the interpretations offered by Madison and other contemporaries in 1796, as they tried to explain and make sense of the public debate, then nearly a year old, as well as the disparate and often ambiguous conclusions Americans were reaching about the larger meaning of the debate for the future of American politics.

7 | Reflections on the Debate

Citizens in Worcester, Massachusetts, gathered at three o'clock at Houghton's Inn on May 7 for dinner and toasts. Earlier, the local approval of the Jay Treaty vote a week before in the House of Representatives had been expressed by the ringing of bells and other "demonstrations of joy." A large group at Houghton's heard eight toasts that day. The first was to George Washington: "The Savior of America! May he stand secure amid the storms of faction; and long live to bless his country!" The vice president and Senate were toasted next, followed by a toast for the majority of the House who voted to fund appropriations for carrying the treaty into effect: "May the laurel of their country's approbation, never wither on their brow!" Next came toasts to John Jay, the United States of America, the Commonwealth of Massachusetts, "The Fair," and, finally, "All Mankind. May peace and harmony pervade the universe." This last toast, like the first to Washington, was met with three cheers. At six o'clock the company retired from the dinner. "It is but just to observe," a newspaper account of the proceedings noted with pride and a sense of triumph, "that true federalism brightened the countenance of each individual, and peace and harmony were the order of the day."[1]

The celebrants who gathered that day in Worcester were obviously pleased with the Jay Treaty's approval and, based on their toasts, saw it as tidings of good things for the nation's future. All across the country in the days, weeks, and months following the House vote on April 30, 1796, participants in as well as observers of the public debate on the treaty weighed in with their postmortems on the way the debate had proceeded and their observations on the short- and long-term implications of the debate for U.S. politics. As Americans of various stripes began to put the treaty debate in perspective, they reached a range of conclusions. Whether they had favored or opposed the measure, nearly all were convinced that not just the treaty itself, but the intense public debate over it, had somehow—in ways not yet fully discernable or even fully developed—been an important milestone which continued the transformation of the young nation's political culture.

Needless to say, the treaty opponents showed none of the glee exhibited by the Worcester, Massachusetts, diners. For those close to the scene in Philadelphia, it had seemed for the several weeks leading up to the climactic vote that the chances of defeating the measure were slipping away. The steady barrage of pro-treaty petitions arriving daily in Congress, and the effect they and other considerations were having on the representatives, led James Madison to note ruefully to Thomas Jefferson late in April that opposition to the treaty—which he thought just weeks before would be easily defeated—was "melting" away. Thus, the 51–48 vote on April 30 was less a shocking surprise than a bitter pill treaty opponents found themselves forced to swallow after months of unavailing protest. In the wake of the vote many Republicans looked about for targets worthy of blame. In their immediate postmortems, Republicans did not cast their nets very wide, aiming a torrent of criticism at the same targets they had attacked throughout the campaign—the administration, George Washington, and the tactics Federalists had used (resorted to, in Republican minds) to mobilize the public and, ultimately, persuade Congress to approve the measure. In newspaper pieces as well as private correspondence, Republicans launched assaults on these prime culprits as they struggled to make sense of the vote and the ramifications of the bitter campaign.

Some treaty opponents were critical of the American public itself, or at least that portion of it that had succumbed to Federalist pressure and signed pro-treaty petitions. "Corporal Trim" wondered "how the inhabitants of Boston can *consistently* do any thing more, respecting [the treaty] than they have already done." He noted that at first, in the summer of 1795, they had begged Washington not to sign the treaty, calling it "that fatal compact . . . that death warrant of our liberties." Then, in the spring of 1796, "they have as pathetically intreated our Representatives in Congress to put our death warrant in execution, and not suffer us to commit suicide." He questioned the judgment of citizens who could be so easily manipulated and suggested that a people ripe for being misled did not bode well for the nation's future. Other Republican critics turned their wrath on the clergy, who they believed, not without some justification, had openly and actively aligned themselves with Federalists in the treaty debate. "Sydney" reiterated the standard anti-treaty complaints about the secrecy of Jay's negotiation, the use of fear and threats of war to persuade citizens to support it, and the conduct of treaty supporters more generally. But his last paragraph zeroed in on the role of the clergy, noting harshly that "The CLERGY (a few excepted) have taken a conspicuous part in promoting the adoption of the treaty; let them abide the event." He warned that, once the treaty went into operation and harmed France, as he expected, provoking them to "retaliate for our ingratitude," Americans would look unfavorably on those who had backed the measure: "those who advocated its adoption will become RESPONSIBLE for the consequences." A few weeks later the same newspaper printed an open letter to the clergy wondering whether "it may not injure the CAUSE OF RELIGION, for the Clergy to become zealous partizans on either side." Particularly in such a contentious partisan environment as then existed, "A Friend to the Clergy" believed, the clergy should not engage in political disputes. If they became too active politically, he warned ministers, it might "injure *that cause,* which must be considered to be more peculiarly within your religious functions." Thus, at least some Republicans were now extending blame from merchants, the administration, insurance underwriters, and Washington himself, to include the clergy.[2]

Republican newspapers struck two main themes once it was clear that the treaty would go into effect. One was to argue that the French would be deeply resentful and that the nation might fairly expect French reprisals of some kind. The second was to emphasize the defects of the treaty itself and the ineffectual nature of the document in securing relief to Americans in the presence of documented British violations.[3] In most of their early assessments, treaty opponents concentrated their fire squarely on the administration and George Washington himself, believing that Washington was behind the pro-treaty activities and had sanctioned the range of actions undertaken to win backing for the measure. Leading the way were Republican newspaper editors, notably, Thomas Adams and Isaac Larkin of Boston's *Independent Chronicle,* and, especially, Washington's long-time foe, Benjamin Franklin Bache of Philadelphia's *Aurora*. Both newspapers devoted sizable chunks of their papers for May 1796 to bitter diatribes and acidic attacks. In one piece a correspondent wondered how Washington could make peace with his conscience in approving a treaty "even his most passionate admirers cannot justify," indeed, that "he confessed himself was bad." Washington had made an offering of America's rights and welfare to the British and turned his back on his nation's former ally, the French. It was almost, said the writer, as if the Revolution had been fought for Washington alone: "then indeed was the blood and treasure of a seven years conflict expended to minister to the ambition and gratify the lust for the power of *one man.*" Then this writer excoriated all the Federalists who had used "*design* and *fraud*" to force the measure through, accusing them of inventing hypothetical problems that would befall the country if the treaty were not approved. "We must provide for an instrument *confessedly bad,* to guard against a war *confessedly doubtful.*" Another writer argued a few days later that the recent assertion by Federalist editor Benjamin Russell in the *Columbian Centinel,* that "the voice of the *People* is the voice of God," was quite accurate. However, he charged, the authentic voice of the people "was more fairly, fully, and without *'Fear'* expressed . . . in the several town and other meetings last summer in condemnation of the treaty." Public opinion had seen its truest expression before the Federalist propagandists went to work. The public never would have changed its mind or been persuaded to petition for the treaty "but for the hue and cry of War! War! raised at the same moment from one end of the Continent to the other, by the Hamilton faction." This writer was thus echoing what fast became the leading explanation for how an unpopular treaty had been brought into effect. But he closed with a warning which stressed another theme Republicans fell back on after the vote: that the treaty *was* a bad measure and would bring disgrace and perhaps worse on the young nation. When that happened, "The *responsibility* will therefore fall upon those who have been so strenuous for carrying it into operation."[4]

By far the loudest voice of outrage and fury against the treaty and its supporters belonged to Bache. For him, the Jay Treaty debate represented a turning point and the circumstances of its narrow passage in the House confirmed his worst fears about Washington, his administration, and their supporters around the country. Bache turned his full fury on the president with whom he had been at war since Washington signed the document the previous August. Now, with the treaty a fact, approved by the president and Senate and funded by the House, Bache spared no vitriol in condemning everything and everyone connected to the hated measure. "If an artful war whoop had not been raised, and Bank influence had not been exerted," the treaty would have been defeated. Bache scoffed at a Noah Webster editorial which argued that it was improper for the people to petition their officials and try to interfere with the constituted authorities. "Who besides the Editor of the New York Minerva ever attempted to stigmatize the voice of the people, in a popular government as extraneous and improper." Bache did agree that the right of petitioning could be abused, "as in the late instance," referring to Federalist efforts. But to any suggestion that the people had played an "improper" role, Bache could only react with contempt. He believed that the nation had gone along with the treaty because of fear. Restating common Republican themes, he noted that, despite all the confessed shortcomings of the treaty, it had been acquiesced in because of pressure from the administration and its supporters, who were bent on using any tactic necessary to bring the measure into operation. As several other treaty critics had done, Bache called the Federalists accountable for their actions. "[W]hen our *children* feel the operation of the doings of their fathers" and the "destructive effects" of the treaty came to pass, they would surely look back and blame the Federalists for their present predicament.[5]

Finally, and fittingly, given the Republicans' conception of the ongoing nature of the American Revolution, Bache on July 4, 1796, wrote in elegiac terms of the end of American independence. He took dead aim at Washington and his administration. Noting that the nation was beginning its twenty-first year of independence, he lamented that so little ground had been traversed. "How far the lapse of a few years since that glorious period has brought us back towards the point whence we started" was plain to see, he implied. "Since the late treaty has become the law of the land it may be a doubt whether our independence be more than nominal," so bad were the terms of the measure. The treaty specifically and the administration more generally had gone a long way "towards re-colonizing us anew." Having begun by noting that there was an eclipse of the sun that day, Bache wondered sadly and melodramatically if perhaps American liberty was about to be eclipsed by the treaty.[6]

Another Republican writer, William Manning, began his *The Key of Liberty* shortly after the treaty debate subsided, and it is clear that recent events left him angered. Calling the treaty a "monster," Manning surveyed the public debate of the previous year. He castigated the Federalist campaign and accused supporters of spreading "the most horrid and frightful falsehoods that ever were invented by the devil in order to frighten the people to petition the House." Those attempting to counter such "cursed lies" risked being attacked as "Jacobins, Shaysites, disorganizers, and enemies to all government." Manning ruefully noted that this pro-treaty campaign had had its effect: "for want of information among the people, they were so frightened with these lies that they hastened to see which could get his name to the petition first." It was the petitions that emboldened some in the House to vote in favor of the treaty, Manning believed. "Thus," he concluded bitterly, "by the combinations and arts of the Few, with the order of Cincinnati at their head, a seal was put upon the worst instrument that ever was signed in America." Manning saw the treaty passage as only the latest in a long line of Federalist strong-arm tactics which overwhelmed opponents and foisted unpopular policies on the public.[7]

Republican political operative John Beckley, who had done so much to organize the anti-treaty efforts, was still upset about the business as late as the fall of 1796. Writing to Pennsylvania Republican William Irvine, Beckley took great delight in the fall election results then already rolling in. Reflecting from his Philadelphia home on electoral returns from Pennsylvania, Beckley exclaimed, "The great victory obtained here, over the united & combined force of the British & Aristocrats, gives us great confidence. . . . [T]o rule out [Frederick] Muhlenberg, who gave the casting vote for the British treaty, and elect Blair McClanahan [*sic*], in his room, who recommended to kick the treaty to hell, and to reelect [John] Swanwick against the most violent exertions ever made in this City, are sufficient to Shew that republicanism remains firm here." Beckley positively gloated over what he and other Republicans must have considered the just deserts of those who voted the "wrong" way on the treaty. Since their stray votes cost Republicans victory on the issue, Beckley and others could at least take pleasure in vindication.[8]

But if some Republican newspapers, writers, and operatives adopted an unremittingly bitter and hostile tone regarding the final approval of the treaty, other Republicans were more measured in their assessment of the matter, and attempted to take a longer view of the measure and the public debate that had just ended. Republican congressmen who opposed the treaty, realizing the need to continue to deal with their Federalist rivals on other matters and rejecting the kind of scorched earth policy Bache and some others advocated, took the time to explain their reasoning on the vote and to map out a future course of action. Virginia congressman Thomas Claiborne, a Republican who voted against the treaty, wrote an open letter to his constituents, explaining how he had arrived at his decision and that he believed it corresponded with their wishes on the matter, and looking ahead to how the nation should proceed now that the matter was settled. This letter is striking for the absence of the rancor and bitterness of Bache's writings and for its conciliatory tone, despite having been written just a few weeks after the acrimonious debate ended.

Claiborne was from Brunswick County in the southeastern part of the state. He had served as a member of the state house of delegates in the 1780s and as county sheriff before being elected to the Third Congress in 1792. He was reelected twice, then, after two years out of the office, elected again to Congress in 1800 and 1802. Shortly after voting against the Jay Treaty, Claiborne wrote a letter to his constituents. He told them that when he had been at home he found them to be opposed to the measure and had heard nothing from them to convince him that they now thought otherwise. He assured them that he had not approached the treaty with a prejudiced mind. He did not enter into the House debate, "lest having taken a part my mind might be biassed," but instead studied the compact thoroughly. He considered the measure to be a poor one, yielding more than it should. He was disturbed by the charges by some that the House had no right to debate the treaty because it had already passed through the other constituted authorities. Claiborne mentioned the horrors promised by Federalists if the instrument were refused: wars abroad, war with the Indians, civil unrest, and even revolution. "But these bugbears I did not believe," Claiborne said, as he reported that he had voted with the minority to withhold appropriations. Now, however, since the treaty had passed, it would no longer be right to oppose it. "I hope in conformity to the President's proclamation, we shall as good citizens, observe and keep the treaty." It was important now for opponents to "lay all heart burnings aside" and "let the government go on smoothly." Looking beyond the immediate vote, Claiborne reminded his constituents, "We have opposed it then, as long as we could consistently, and farther resistance may now produce all those evil consequences and cal[a]mities above mentioned."[9]

But the party's leaders showed little of Claiborne's equanimity. The loss of the House vote found James Madison seething and disillusioned. It sealed his decision to retire from Congress and left him furious, not only at Federalists for their tactics, but also at the Republicans who deserted and gave the Federalists their majority. In letters written shortly after the vote Madison attacked both groups. Writing to Jefferson, as noted above, he mentioned "A few wrongheads" who had turned against the party line. Furthermore, he announced that the entire business had been "the most worrying & vexatious that I ever encountered; and the more so as the causes lay in the unsteadiness, the follies, the perverseness, & the defection among our friends, more than in the strength or dexterity, or malice of our opponents." Later, to James Monroe, Madison observed severely that the majority that once existed against the treaty "was not entirely composed of materials firm enough for the crisis." Of the attempt by Henry Dearborn to add a condemnatory preamble to the appropriations bill, a measure which lost by a single vote, he observed incredulously that "seven or eight of the stiffest antitreaty men taking a wrongheaded course" had caused the defeat.[10]

But if Madison was disappointed and frustrated at Republican shortcomings, he was positively livid at the methods Federalists had employed to influence the public. He complained bitterly about the means used "for stirring up petitions &c." supporting the treaty. The plan was laid in Philadelphia, he said, and spread by correspondence to other towns. "In the mean time the Banks, the British Merchts. the insurance Comp[anie]s were at work in influencing individuals, beating down the prices of produce, & sounding the tocksin of foreign war & domestic convulsions." Such tactics had the desired effect, he admitted; in some districts "the people have been so deluded" as to enjoin their congressmen not to withhold appropriations. Madison closed ominously: "An appeal to the people on any pending measure, can never be more than an appeal to those in the neighborhood of the Govt. & to the Banks, the Merchts. & the dependents & expectants of the Govt. at a distance."[11] Madison never shook this feeling and returned to these very thoughts at several points later in the decade, since they represented his very real frustration with Federalist governance and the sources of their power.

Nine days later Madison was just as upset. While noting that things were calm, he referred to the continued arrival of petitions, most supporting the treaty, and indicated that New England had been "ready to rise in mass agst. the H. of Reps. Such have been the exertions & influence of Aristocracy, Anglicism, & mercantilism in that quarter, that Republicanism is perfectly overwhelmed, even in the Town of Boston." Everywhere, he claimed, Federalists led the public to believe that the House's purpose in initially resisting the treaty was to bring about war, and thus, quoting from a Boston pro-treaty circular, people chose "'to follow where Washington leads.'"[12] To other correspondents he made much the same points. At no time had "more extraordinary means been used, or with more success, to accomplish a party object." Federalists had succeeded in provoking "a perfect delirium" in New England. Under the delusion that refusing the treaty meant a declaration of war, the people everywhere were cajoled to sign the petitions which continued to pour into Congress. He ascribed the House vote primarily to "an appeal to petitions under the mercantile influence and the alarm of war." He noted that the people "were everywhere called on to chuse between peace and war and to side with the treaty if they preferred the former." Looking ahead to the 1796 elections, Madison was glum as he offered a final postmortem on the treaty vote. "The name of the President & the alarm of war, have had a greater effect, than were apprehended on one side, or expected on the other," he told Jefferson. "A crisis which ought to have been so managed as to fortify the Republican cause, has left it in a very crippled condition." And the immediate prospects did not look good in a number of states where things had "taken a wrong turn under the impressions of the moment. Nothing but auspicious contingencies abroad or at home, can regain the lost ground," he wrote dejectedly.[13]

But some Republicans viewed the methods undertaken to win the treaty debate—if not the final vote itself—in a different, much more favorable light. While Madison's responses to events conveyed the inner workings of the treaty debate as only a participant could, they could hardly be dispassionate or objective since he was caught up in the intensity of the partisan conflict in Philadelphia. By turns angry, frustrated, dispirited, and disillusioned by the proceedings, Madison lacked the distance—in both space and time—to assess the larger consequences of the debate and to see past the recriminations which dominated his letters immediately afterward. His great friend back in Virginia, however, had both distance from the immediacy of the debate and time for reflection. Consequently, the conclusions which Thomas Jefferson reached about what the treaty business held for the Republicans' future were a good bit more optimistic and accurate, as we shall see shortly.

Before turning to Jefferson's reflections, we should first examine those on the victorious side in the debate. What did pro-treaty people think? Surprisingly, Alexander Hamilton, one of the major architects of the Federalist campaign, said next to nothing in his writings after the vote. Turning his attention swiftly to electoral matters and the 1796 elections, Hamilton noted in a classic understatement, "The late turn of the Treaty question makes us all very happy." He added briefly, "I hope no future embarrassment will arise," before turning to a consideration of candidates for the presidential election. Fisher Ames, whose powerful speech was the capstone of the Federalist exertions, said little also, noting that in the weeks since the vote he found himself "indifferent" to the remaining business of the session. "I attend Congress daily, but crack jokes instead of problems," he wrote.[14]

Many Federalists, like those in Worcester, wanted to celebrate their hard-won triumph first. Residents of Walpole, New Hampshire, showed "the highest exultation" on the news of the House vote. While they did not "manifest their political joy like the mobs of France," they were clearly happy. "It was delightful to overhear the honest husbandmen congratulating each other upon the good news, and remarking that the plough would be again prospered, and the wheat of our vallies sold for a price." In New York, the *American Minerva* appreciatively noted "the joy expressed since the vote of the house for executing" the treaty. "Every where friends, when they meet, take each other by the hand, and mutually congratulate each other . . . as they do on the most festive occasions." The celebrations were said to be unequaled since the establishment of the Constitution. Indeed, Noah Webster's paper explicitly compared treaty opponents to the anti-Federalists. Just as they had in 1787–88 "foretold all imaginary evils . . . [and] painted tyranny and despotism in a thousand hideous forms," so, too, had treaty opponents forecast the worst. Webster predicted that just as the anti-Federalists had been wrong, treaty critics would be as well, and he proclaimed freedom and prosperity ahead as a result of the document.[15]

Other Federalist editors chimed in with the same theme. John Fenno's *Gazette of the United States* was filled with self-congratulation. When the vote was declared, he wrote, the "friends of order and good government" took the news with "a *tranquility* highly honorable to them." The vote had proved to be, Fenno said, the product of exactly what the Federalists had called for all along: it was "the triumph of reason—the conduct of the majority, the triumph of temper." Benjamin Russell's *Columbian Centinel* celebrated the vote by proclaiming "ALL'S WELL!" in bold type. He declared that phrase as the "watchword" of the paper "notwithstanding all the croakings and abuse of the Ravens of the Chronicle." He announced that "ALL IS WELL" with the president, the constituted authorities, the states, the yeomanry, merchants, mechanics, seamen, and, most generally, the "*Great Body of the People of the United States.*" Russell declared that nine-tenths of them "have given their Voice for Peace," and peace was theirs to enjoy and prosper under.[16]

Some Federalist congressmen, returning to their homes from Philadelphia, were feted with dinners and toasts and praised in newspapers. Vermont congressman Daniel Buck, it was declared, deserved public acknowledgment of his work for constituents in voting to fund the treaty. Buck would have "a good conscience, [and] has the pleasing satisfaction of having spoken the unanimous voice of his constituents." On his return, the *Rutland Herald* predicted, "he will meet a most cordial reception from every patriot and friend of the union." The paper was correct. As Buck passed through Hanover, New Hampshire, he was met with a celebration to honor him. The town's citizens presented Buck with an address which noted that, although he was not their representative or even from their state, they saluted him "as a neighbor, a patriot, and friend," and declared, "we bid you a most cordial welcome." Buck, a Revolutionary War veteran who lost an arm in the conflict, was praised as "our war-worn soldier" who was now "appointed to guard the acquisition" of peace. In response, Buck thanked them and assured them that he joined in their devotion to the Constitution, attachment "to the constituted authorities, love to the President, and veneration for the public faith," all comments which echoed those expressed in the citizens' address to him. When Buck left Hanover he was escorted to the river by a military company in full regalia, "the members of college, and the principal gentlemen of this vicinity." He was met by friends and neighbors on the other side of the river and taken to his seat. "Such a reception," crowed the paper, "the partisans of faction may look for in vain."[17]

Buck proved to be very popular. On his way home he was also given a reception near Walpole, Vermont. As he passed through Greenfield, "the inhabitants vied with each other in exhibitions of gratitude to this genuine

Republican." Some of those in Walpole regretted that his route would not take him directly through their town since the "Sober and good men wished to demonstrate their respect for one, who in battle was a valiant soldier and in d[e]bate an inflexible patriot, to whom without flattery, might be applied Pope's praise of the Duke of Argyl, 'His Country's thunder born to wield, And shake alike the Senate and the field.'" When Buck, not surprisingly, was overwhelmingly reelected that fall, the *Rutland Herald* observed, "We are happy to find that Mr. Bucks's exertions, and federalism, have met with the universal approbation of his constituents."[18]

Still other Federalists returning from the legislative wars found themselves celebrated. New Hampshire congressman Jeremiah Smith—who had so lavishly praised Fisher Ames's speech on the treaty—was honored at Amherst on June 18, with judges and members of the bar, along with "a number of respectable citizens," presenting him with an address. Afterwards, "an entertainment was provided," which ended with a set of toasts to the confidence of the citizens in their representative and in the Federalism of the state.[19] In Cooperstown, New York, when representative William Cooper returned home, word of his arrival preceded him and he was met by an escort. Upon his entrance into town, "16 cannon were fired, and every appearance of pleasure and satisfaction was exhibited." He was welcomed by "a double row of citizens, who testified their joy on his arrival by three cheers." That evening, Cooper obliged his neighbors by joining them at Huntington's Inn and describing the leading events of the past congressional session. There were addresses to and from Cooper, with the townspeople praising him for his conduct during the treaty debate and Cooper thanking them for their approbation.[20]

But Federalists did more than simply celebrate their triumph. Amidst their effusions of joy, some offered assessments of the contest and its implications both for the upcoming elections and for political culture more generally. Noah Webster saw it as proof of the national government's sound administration: "*all public measures, when well explained and understood by the people at large, have given general satisfaction.*" The problem, Webster believed, was the opposition's newspapers, which had fomented discontent. However, the Jay Treaty debate was but another example of first impressions being set right. "[W]henever the public mind has been inflamed to discontent by means of false charges against the officers of government, or by false representations of facts; time, further information and cool reflection have invariably allayed the ferment, and defeated the effect of the first impressions." Of course, this process—time, further information, and cool reflection—was exactly what Federalists had been urging since the previous summer.[21]

Other papers took the opportunity to praise the people and lambast their opponents. "The *voice of the People, is the Voice of God,*" cried Benjamin Russell's *Columbian Centinel.* "Its omnipotence has recently been demonstrated. Had they been silent, our country was *ruined.*—FACTION has fallen! fallen, like LUCIFER, never more to rise." The people were now convinced, the paper maintained, "that all the noise *about* and *about* the Treaty, was mere *rant.* They have had reliance on the constituted authorities of their country, and ninety-nine of every hundred of the virtuous yeomanry of *Massachusetts* are ready to follow where GEORGE WASHINGTON leads."[22]

Several papers carried accounts of town meetings and petitions which exactly articulated the Federalists' positions on the proper role for citizens to play in public debates. A letter accompanying a memorial from Sheffield, Massachusetts, stated that at times it might appear that citizens lacked an enlightened knowledge of the situation and the best interests of the nation, and that they wavered in their support for the Constitution. Yet this writer was pleased to see that, as the treaty controversy had demonstrated, should a vitally serious matter arise, the people "will rouse from their quiescent state—and with the force and velocity of lightning, confound and pervade the darkest recesses of ignorance, faction and corruption." Another memorial, from Leeds in Prince William County, Virginia, read like a recapitulation of Federalist writings for the past months. Stating their "deep regret and distress" at the tactics used by the treaty opponents, the memorialists had been hesitant, having chosen their duly elected leaders, to instruct them in how to act. They "have hitherto been always disposed to rely rather on the good sense, the caution, the wisdom, and integrity of their delegates . . . than attempt to prescribe rules for their guidance." However, since the opposition did not evince a similar restraint, they had felt compelled "to the exercise of a power which is inherent in them, but which prudence requires never to be called into action but in cases of extreme necessity, when the public good must and ought to supercede every other consideration." The Jay Treaty debate was just such an occasion; indeed, it marked a time "when silence in the constituent body would be a crime." These citizens, then, nicely reflected the notions of the role of citizens that Federalists had been articulating throughout the debate.[23]

Some Federalists expressed, even before the debate had ended, a wish that treaty supporters had become involved in the public contest sooner, believing that much of the turmoil could have been avoided. William Willcocks noted, just a few days before the House vote, that the American people had been too long deceived, in part because government supporters had been reticent. "A mistaken confidence, and unaccountable apathy in the friends to peace and good order, have given a sanction to licentiousness—Whilst they have been asleep, the demons of discord, have been busily, and too successfully employed—the truth must be told," he warned. A few weeks after the vote another writer lamented that Federalists had not been more active earlier. While the "anti-treaty mobs" were fomenting opposition, the administration's supporters, "who hate brawling and disputation," appeared intimidated and shrank from public confrontations. But this had been an unfortunate reaction. "Let such men learn from the event that a bolder course of plain dealing will better comport with manly principles and the public good." The outcome of the treaty debate should be a lesson to the friends of order: "let our over-prudent shy good men be induced when another violent party clamor is raised (and party will raise fifty such) to take their ground with sincerity and decision. Let them tell the multitude of credulous well designing clamorers that they are misled, that facts and principles are not as they have been represented to them by party." Had this been done sooner in the treaty debate, "the clamor would not have been so loud, nor would it have been in the power of party to keep it up so long." Such were the lessons for the future Federalists should take away from this episode.[24]

But if some Federalists concluded that the appeal to the people should have come sooner and been bolder and less apologetic, several other leaders were less convinced. These men were deeply troubled by the implications of the public meetings, the petitions to Congress, and the appeals to the public generally. It seemed to a number of Federalists that such activities ran counter to the Federalists' assertions about the primacy of the constituted authorities. Appealing to the people, even in behalf of administration policies, seemed to open the doors to an entirely different political world. The Federalists directly involved in the treaty debate were uniquely ambivalent about the enterprises they had taken part in, especially in the spring of 1796. That ambivalence—voiced by some of the most active leaders of such appeals—shows Federalists, circa 1796, to have been repelled by popular politics even as they successfully engaged in it. This merits closer examination, since it cuts right to the heart of the evolving political culture in which both Federalists and Republicans plied their trade.

These reflections by Federalists were primarily based on the experiences of the treaty debate, but they drew as well on the broad sweep of political events of the decade. George Cabot believed that the people were "well satisfied" with the government, but he also warned that in the future "we ought to think before we decide on public measures, or *reflection may come too late*." Making the point even more forcefully, Treasury Secretary Oliver Wolcott, Jr., rejoiced that "truth has at this time prevailed over cunning," but feared that "faction, calumny and opposition will continue with as much violence as ever." Wolcott was even blunter about the future prospects for government. "It is folly to suppose that this government can be long administered against the opposition which now exists. . . . Light and darkness can as well exist together, as the hostile principles in our government with a regular administration." Anyone who had observed the preceding three years would have to be concerned at the growth of opposition. Had anyone, Wolcott asked, except for the president, not been attacked and harmed? "Is not malice now attempting to destroy his fame by perfidiously creating misfortunes for our country, with which to excite discontents?" The future looked bleak, Wolcott thought, especially since there could be no guarantee that the opposition could be perpetually turned back.[25]

George Washington also reflected on the treaty debate as he prepared to issue his May 15, 1796, Farewell Address, a document surely influenced in part by his dismay over the proceedings of the previous year. In letters to Charles Carroll and Edward Carrington, both dated May 1, Washington expressed his belief that anyone following the House debate would see that "the *real* question" was not whether the treaty "was a *good* or *bad* one; but whether there should be a *Treaty at all* without the concurrence of that House." As to the motives that led some to bring the country's peace, happiness, and prosperity "to the brink of a precipice . . . I shall say nothing," Washington remarked. "[C]harity tells us they ought to be good; but suspicions say they must be bad. At Present my tongue shall be silent." In the letter to Carrington, he accused the House of "striking at once, and boldly too, at the fundamental principles of the Constitution." Had the

House had its way, it would have rendered the treaty-making power "not only a nullity, but such an absolute absurdity as to reflect disgrace on the framers of it."[26]

But in writing to the man whose name was attached to the treaty, Washington voiced some even broader concerns. In articulating them, Washington gave voice to the fears many Federalists had of the nature of political disputation in the mid-1790s, which Washington and others thought had troubling ramifications and revealed the transformations already reshaping early national political culture. "I am *Sure,*" he told John Jay, "the Mass of Citizens . . . *mean well,* and I firmly believe they will always *act well,* whenever they can obtain a right understanding of matters." But in some parts of the nation where the political leaders were opposed to the government "great pains are taken to inculcate a belief that their rights are assailed, and their liberties endangered." These circumstances made it difficult to communicate that "right understanding" Washington referred to. Matters were worsened when "the Inventers, and abettors of pernicious measures use infinitely more industry in dissiminating the poison, than the well disposed part of the Community to furnish the antidote. To this source," the president continued, "all our discontents may be traced and from it our embarrassments proceed. Hence serious misfortunes originating in misrepresentation frequently flow and spread before they can be dissipated by truth." These were among the several reasons Washington, embittered and disillusioned by the partisan wrangling, ultimately decided to stand down and not seek a third term. They were also themes other Federalists would echo in the weeks following the climactic House vote as they reflected on the current political state.[27]

Other Federalists lamented not merely the exertions of opponents to rally opposition to the government, but the very substance and fact of such direct popular politicking. Some, like New York newspaper editor Loring Andrews, argued that Federalists had needed to mobilize the public because their opponents had done so, leaving them little choice. Writing to Theodore Sedgwick, he reported that "a vast majority in the Country have exhibited the most unequivocal attachment to government, and the measures of [the] administration." Despite the positive outcome, his opinion was that "popular interference on such occasions is generally to be reprobated, yet as faction began it—it was the best method undoubtedly, to 'fight the devil with his own weapons.'" In the same letter Andrews told Sedgwick of a number of well-subscribed pro-treaty petitions coming to Congress, and advised that "it would not be amiss to have the petitions made publick." Such comments reflect the ambivalence among Federalists: they "reprobated" the tactics and effect of popularizing politics through direct appeals, yet engaged in them anyway because they recognized the importance of such methods to their cause.[28]

Perhaps the Federalist most troubled by the evolving political practices evinced in the treaty debate was New York's Noah Webster. Editor of both the *American Minerva* and the *Herald,* author of the "Curtius" essays in support of the treaty, Webster had been as consistently active as any participant in the debate. But, in several postmortems, he voiced grave concerns about the progress of the controversy. If many Federalists were overjoyed by the Jay Treaty victory and eager to bask in the triumph, Webster was less sanguine; the success of the measure was for him only a qualified one, if that. In the victory over the treaty were sown the seeds of future Federalist defeats. He recognized, perhaps better than anyone else, whether participant or observer, that something vital, something fundamental in U.S. politics, had changed. In his newspapers during the weeks after the vote, Webster addressed the broader implications of the politics of public opinion as practiced in 1796 and as projected into the future. It was, for Webster, a disturbing vision, and his writings constitute a threnody for an older political culture which was dying before his very eyes.[29]

On May 3, 1796—less than a week after the House vote—Webster published a long editorial which reviewed the progression of the treaty debate and offered some conclusions. He began, more in a spirit of weariness than of triumph, by observing that the majority of the House had resisted voting for appropriations until "the sense of the people compelled them to abandon their opposition." It was certainly to be lamented, Webster wrote, "that party spirit should make men blind and obstinate; for nothing but obstinate blindness could have prevented any man from admitting the propriety of executing the treaty" from the start. But acceptance had been gradual at every turn. Jay as negotiator had "hesitated whether to sign," as had the Senate and the president. So, too, with the American people, who "after deliberating almost a year . . . have decided that on the whole view of circumstances, it is best to accept the treaty and carry it into effect. The friends of our government have uniformly viewed this business in the same light; and its enemies have been compelled to conform to this reasoning."[30]

But for Webster there could be no celebration, no reveling in a hard-won triumph, as there was for some other Federalists. Something worried Webster, even in the aftermath of a great triumph achieved barely days before, and after a year-long effort during which he had done as much as nearly anyone. Too much ink and too much sheer hard work had been expended in pursuit of that final 51–48 vote. And it was the *nature* of the effort, the very *orchestration* of public opinion, the descent into popular politics during that year-long campaign, that troubled him so. His remarks deserve quoting at length:

> [T]he progress of the business has been marked with improper conduct. The appeal to the people by the disorganizers the last summer, was a gross violation offered to Freedom of Deliberation, in the constituted authorities. The recent appeal to the people by the friends of the Constitution, tho' less improper, because in favor of an acknowledged law of the land, yet has been irregular; *it is all improper* [emphasis added]; it is an extraneous influence, unknown to the regular governmental proceedings; one that is liable to be misused and perverted to dangerous purposes. Besides, such a resort to the people, weakens the operations of law and constitution; diminishes the confidence that foreign nations and our own citizens ought to place in government, and in short exhibits our system of government in a ludicrous light.[31]

"[I]t is all improper." This, from one of the leaders of the effort to transform public opinion and bring that opinion to bear on Congress. Webster's writings had been in large part "an appeal to the people" of the kind he now found "dangerous," "weaken[ing]," "ludicrous." It is important not to miss the larger point here, for Webster's words suggest not hypocrisy so much as ambivalence—a characteristic that marked the Federalists' campaign on the Jay Treaty specifically and their forays into popular politics during the 1790s more generally.

The treaty "business," as he called it, was a milestone for Webster's political thought. The process forced him to reconsider his most cherished beliefs about government, the political system, and his own role in them as newspaper editor and shaper of public opinion. The next day, May 4, Webster published in his *Herald* a long, signed editorial, "To the Public," which spelled out his reflections on the treaty debate and, specifically, the role of newspapers in the shaping of opinion. Webster stated up front that he had consistently defended the administration "because I believe it to have been incorrupt and according to the spirit of the constitution. . . . I have vindicated neutrality," he continued, reviewing the political history of the preceding years, "because there has appeared no occasion for war, but great advantages in peace. . . . I have reprobated Democratic Clubs, because I foresaw the mischief they would produce and which they *have produced*. . . . I hold it proper for us to attach ourselves to no foreign nation whatever, but to respect ourselves, and be in spirit and truth, *Americans*."

As for the role of newpapers in the political wars, Webster had reached some troubling conclusions. "I am persuaded that these channels of information may be the instruments of great good or extensive evil. . . . It is obvious that the falsehoods and calumny propagated by means of public papers, have been the direct and principal means of all the civil dissensions which distract this country and have threatened it with civil war." It was only *despite* the efforts of some newspapers to inflame the public with lies, misrepresentations, and distortions that, when the administration's measures were explained and people had time to consider them, they met with strong support. The pattern he detected in the political conflicts of the 1790s—strong opposition to government measures, fomented by papers but turned aside with "time, further information, and cool reflection"—led him to a bold conclusion. "This is to my mind a decisive proof that there must be something wrong in *principle* in opposition—*Forever* to mistake truth and the public sentiment, cannot be the effect of ignorance or want of information," he wrote, implying far darker and more sinister forces at work. Webster then served notice that as long he superintended his paper it would be devoted to countering all attempts to "weaken or subvert our constitution." He had uncovered something dangerous and would be eternally vigilant in heading it off.[32]

A month later, his mind still troubled by such thoughts, Webster underscored his earlier worries. He wrote this time with a tone not of brave vigilance but of dismay and disillusionment not only with administration opponents in Congress and the papers, but, more fundamentally, with the very constituents who chose those representatives and subscribed to and read those papers—that is, with the sovereign people themselves. Commenting on the close of the congressional sessions, Webster told his readers that "reflections naturally occur to a man who has attended to the progress of public measures." One point Webster noted was that public servants, no matter how honest, found themselves and their actions scrutinized at every turn. There was always "some foe watching, with eagles eyes, to detect him in errors, to expose him to censure and charge upon his *intentions* all the inconveniences that result, perhaps *necessarily,* from his measures." As soon as an opportunity arose, "these calumniators . . . charge them to the account of wicked designs and corruptions." This was all bad enough, perhaps even to be expected, but the next step deeply troubled Webster. Once charges were made, "The people, jealous of their rights and very credulous, give ear to these suggestions—They say the officer of government could certainly have done better—he is a bad man or a weak one—he must be sacrificed," and his challenger is elected in his stead. But then the pattern repeated itself: soon, inevitably, the new officer committed some alleged indiscretion. "The same tricks are played over with him; he is ousted to give place to some intriguer, probably more worthless than himself."

All of this led to tremendous instability in the government, and the sacrifice, Webster believed, of many honorable men for daring to take unpopular positions or risking the ire of irresponsible newspapers. But now Webster began to spread the blame beyond the "calumniators" to the citizens themselves. "Will not facts of this kind open the eyes of an honest, but discerning people? Will they still listen to the stale abuse perpetually retailed from opposition presses? Do they choose to be deceived. . . . Will they persist in trying to believe and to propagate falsehoods, for the mere sake of being uniform in error? It is hardly possible," Webster concluded, "to believe all this. A people capable of being thus hood-winked, times without number, may be deemed honest, but they must forfeit all claim to discernment." In the same issue, Webster also displayed his growing sense of foreboding. Discussing *Columbian Centinel* editor Benjamin Russell's "All's Well" editorial, Webster could not bring himself to share the Bostonian's enthusiasm. Where Russell wrote that "the voice of the people is the voice of god," that factions had fallen and would never again rise, Webster wrote, "There you are wrong, Mr. Centinel. Faction has fallen indeed; but it *will* rise again." "Popular governments," he continued, "want continual weeding. There is no alternative. You must either make the ground barren with despotism, or make it rich with freedom. In a barren soil, you will destroy fruit as well as weeds; in a rich one, weeds always grow first. These in government, are the ambitious demagogues, who preach their own patriotism in popular meetings—like rank weeds they push their heads higher than others, until they fall and wither before the scythe of justice."[33]

Webster's conclusions point to a central irony. While Webster was on the winning side of the debate—was in fact a primary architect of the victorious campaign—his reflections and words lacked the ecstatic ring of victory that might be expected. Instead, at the moment of triumph, Webster was despondent. He saw the seeds of future Federalist setbacks in the exertion and practices that had been necessary in the treaty debate. Beyond the ambivalence with which Webster and other Federalists practiced popular politics, there was a revulsion of those tactics and their implications which left him incapable of enjoying the triumph. The "improper" conduct exhibited by both sides had led the friends of the administration to victory this time. In the long run, however, those same tactics, along with the factors he addressed in his May 4 and June 1 *Herald* editorials, left Webster—and many of his fellow Federalists—feeling worried and dejected about the democratized future of American politics.

Another irony can be found in the writings of a Republican leader, Thomas Jefferson. If Webster seemed gloomy and pessimistic despite winning the debate, Jefferson, while ostensibly on the losing side, found in the debate's aftermath much encouragement and hope for the future. Indeed, Jefferson saw in the means used by Federalists to involve the public a countermanding force which, while used against Republicans this time, would explicitly favor them in the future. That force was the rapid democratization of politics and society. Thus, Jefferson's postmortems showed none of the gloom and dismay of the victorious Webster's, nor, for that matter, any of the anger and bitterness of James Madison's reflections. Indeed, Jefferson, unlike Madison and Webster, had the broader perspective of one who had observed but not participated in the debate. This critical distance allowed him to take in all the news of the contest without being as invested in it as the other two. True, his absence undoubtedly harmed the anti-treaty efforts during the contest—but afterwards, that sense of distance and lack of personal involvement led the opposition leader to find in defeat the seeds of future Republican victories. Jefferson's perspective on the debate thus stands in marked contrast to Webster's, on the opposing side, and to Madison's, on his own.

That summer at Monticello, Jefferson looked both back to the debate and forward to the Republicans' electoral prospects in 1796 and beyond. Writing to James Monroe, he offered an interpretation that was much more optimistic than one might expect. The Federalist triumph on the treaty was owed, as were all their others, to Washington's enormous and,

Jefferson believed, inappropriate prestige. As Monroe read reports of the House debate he would see, Jefferson argued, "the truth of what I always observed to you, that one man outweighs them all in influence over the people, who have supported his judgment against their own and that of the representatives. Republicanism must lie on its oars, resign the vessel to its pilot, and themselves to the course he thinks best for them."[34] Republicans should bide their time, Jefferson counseled, and trust in a better future.

A month later he wrote again to Monroe, still hopeful. The Federalists' victories were temporary, and would persist only as long as Washington remained president. His unequaled prestige could not be transferred to others, and once Washington's stature—which had done so much for Federalists—was no longer a political factor, the party would be exposed. "The Anglomen have in the end got their treaty through," Jefferson observed, "and so far have triumphed over the cause of republicanism. Yet it has been to them a dear bought victory. . . . They see that nothing can support them but the Colossus of the President's merits with the people, and the moment he retires, that his successor, if a Monocrat, will be overborne by the republican sense of his constituents, if a republican he will of course give fair play to that sense, and lead things into the channel of harmony between the governors and the governed." So, he concluded, "In the meantime, patience." In short, Jefferson was disappointed, but believed—as he and Madison always had, deep down—that the people would see through the Federalist artifices and side with the Republicans. The short-term victory belonged to the Federalists, but there was no way that the Republicans would not be triumphant eventually. Public opinion had been shaped artfully by the Federalists but it could be remade by the Republicans in the future. And the techniques Federalists used to shape and mobilize public opinion in the Jay Treaty debate were the sorts of measures with which Republicans were much more comfortable.[35]

If the participants themselves drew a wide range of conclusions about the nature of the Jay Treaty debate, the reasons for the approval of the treaty, and the ramifications for the future, what of historians? The most careful students of the treaty—notably, Samuel Flagg Bemis and Jerald A. Combs—have largely reached the judgment that the treaty was necessary to preserve peace and to maintain the trading relationship with Great Britain that was so vital to U.S. economic growth. In other words, scholars have tended to validate Federalist claims on behalf of the treaty. While historians have not hesitated to point out the shortcomings of the treaty, they have generally stressed the weak U.S. negotiating position and judged that the treaty was probably the best the nation could have obtained from its stronger adversary. Historians have thus generally concluded that the treaty—imperfect as it was—was still preferable to no treaty and the possibility of war.

My examination of the treaty debate largely aligns with the impressive and valuable work of Bemis and Combs. But I have also sought to understand more fully the political culture of the treaty debate—its ebb and flow, the tactics and arguments employed, and, especially, the crucial role played by public opinion and the recognition of its power as a legitimate object of both sides' efforts. It is clear from this study that a huge part of the Federalists' success lay in their skillful use of Washington's prestige to sway the public, as well as in Washington's own practiced sense of timing in his dealings with the public and Congress. Washington brilliantly managed the debate in such a way as to render Republican opposition extremely problematic. How could they oppose a treaty which had the blessing of Washington? As they had earlier in the decade in regard to the Neutrality Crisis, the Whiskey Rebellion, and the Democratic Societies, Republicans found themselves in an impossible situation, their political hopes run aground on the shoals of Washington's immense popularity and prestige.

But, more broadly, I see the debate as both a catalyst for and a reflection of the emerging, evolving democratization of political culture in early America. The contest over the treaty—carried out extensively in newspapers, pamphlets, and broadsides—both relied on and furthered the growth of print culture. The focus on town meetings as forums for public discussion of the merits or demerits of the treaty went a long way toward furthering popular politics. So, too, did the use of those meetings to circulate petitions and memorials as devices for informing representatives of citizens' views. Once set in motion, these newer methods of practicing popular politics took on a life of their own. Never again would an older, more restricted, or less open means of politics be possible. A line had been crossed in regard to both the scale and the spread of political activity, and going backwards, putting the genie back in the bottle, as it were, was impossible. This was the truth that Noah Webster realized to his great dismay, and it was one of the greatest transforming features of the treaty debate. Jefferson, for his part, grasped this point immediately, and soon others on both ends of the spectrum would recognize this new reality. The public debate over the treaty took place during a time which witnessed a gradual, uneven, evolutionary reshaping of American politics. This debate proved to be the culmination of forces developing during the previous contests of the first administration. Because *both* sides had appealed directly to the people in an open effort to shape and mobilize public opinion, it helped to legitimize popular politics. Both sides now realized, as Webster and Jefferson had, more quickly than most, that success in future policy measures, no less than in elections themselves, would depend on appeals to public opinion. And this realization—with the corollary that, once started down this new path, there was no going back—truly transformed the political landscape to a degree not before seen. Of course—again, as Webster and Jefferson had perceived, with wildly differing reactions—this newer political culture favored the Republicans and militated against the Federalists with their more conservative emphasis on constituted authorities and deferential politics. Their victory in the Jay Treaty debate was a Pyrrhic one, a classic case of winning a tactical victory at the expense of a larger strategic setback.[36]

A final consideration concerning the debate and the 1796 elections. Many scholars have seen the elections as being directly tied to the debate.[37] In this, they have echoed the views of many contemporaries in both parties. But there was another way in which the two events were linked, one which largely escaped the notice of both scholars and participants. It was not simply that the treaty controversy became an issue in the 1796 elections. Rather, it was that the forms of *political activity* for and against the treaty—the newspaper wars, the full blooming of the partisan press, the politicking, the behind-the-scenes organizing by John Beckley and Benjamin Franklin Bache, the town meetings, the conspicuous appeals to the public, the petitions and memorials from citizens to their representatives—all became part of the political culture of 1796 and beyond. Thus, the treaty debate was more than a simple prelude to the elections of 1796. It was the launching ground for a new means of practicing politics, for what Simon P. Newman calls the "regularization of popular politics."[38] Long after the concluding House vote, and growing apace after the 1796 elections, there was a transformation of the entire political culture as experienced by candidates, elected officials, voters, and other citizens. The Jay Treaty debate, long recognized as a watershed in the growth of party warfare, did more than solidify partisan divisions and rivalries: it altered the entire political system within which the nascent parties operated. An examination of the nearly year-long dispute reveals the ongoing nature of that transformation, and sheds light on the ambiguous culture of the early national politics it both furthered and reflected.

Abbreviations Used in the Notes

Certain frequently cited collected papers have been identified by the following short titles:

Corr. of Jay	*The Correspondence and Public Papers of John Jay.* Edited by Henry Johnston. 4 vols. New York, 1890–91.
Papers of Hamilton	*The Papers of Alexander Hamilton.* Edited by Harold C. Syrett. 27 vols. New York, 1961–87.
Life of King	*The Life and Correspondence of Rufus King.* Edited by Charles R. King. 6 vols. New York, 1894–1900.
Papers of Madison	*The Papers of James Madison.* Edited by Thomas A. Mason et al. 17 vols. Chicago, Ill., and Charlottesville, Va., 1962–91.
Papers of Jefferson	*The Papers of Thomas Jefferson.* Edited by Julian P. Boyd, John Catanzariti, et al. 28 vols. to date. Princeton, 1950–.
Papers of Wolcott	*Memoirs of the Administrations of Washington and John Adams, Edited from the Papers of Oliver Wolcott, Secretary of the Treasury.* Edited by George Gibbs. 2 vols. New York, 1846.
Works of Ames	*Works of Fisher Ames: As Published by Seth Ames.* Edited by W. B. Allen. 2 vols. Indianapolis, 1983.
Writings of Washington	*The Writings of George Washington.* Edited by John C. Fitzpatrick. 39 vols. Washington, D.C., 1931–44.

Contemporary newspapers have been identified by the following short titles:

Albany Gazette	*Albany Gazette.* Albany, N.Y.
American Mercury	*American Mercury.* Hartford, Conn.

American Minerva	*American Minerva, an Evening Advertiser.* New York, N.Y.
Argus	*The Argus, or Greenleaf's New Daily Advertiser.* New York, N.Y.
Aurora	*Aurora. General Advertiser.* Philadelphia, Penn.
Baltimore Telegraphe	*The Baltimore Telegraphe.* Baltimore, Md.
Boston Gazette	*The Boston Gazette, and Weekly Republican Journal.* Boston, Mass.
Claypoole's	*Claypoole's American Daily Advertiser.* Philadelphia, Penn.
Columbian Centinel	*Columbian Centinel.* Boston, Mass.
Connecticut Courant	*The Connecticut Courant.* Hartford, Conn.
Connecticut Gazette	*Connecticut Gazette.* New London, Conn.
Connecticut Journal	*Connecticut Journal.* New Haven, Conn.
Daily Advertiser	*The Daily Advertiser.* New York, N.Y.
Daily Gazette	*New-York Daily Gazette.* New York, N.Y.
Dunlap and Claypoole's	*Dunlap and Claypoole's American Daily Advertiser.* Philadelphia, Penn.
Federal Gazette County, Weekly Advertiser.	*Bartgis's Federal Gazette, or the Frederick-Town and* Frederick, Md.
General Advertiser	*General Advertiser.* Philadelphia, Penn.
Georgia Gazette	*Georgia Gazette.* Savannah, Ga.
GUS	*Gazette of the United States.* Philadelphia, Penn.
Herald	*The Herald, a Gazette for the Country.* New York, N.Y.
Ind. Gaz., Agric.	*The Independent Gazetteer, and Agricultural Repository.* Philadelphia, Penn.
Independent Chronicle	*The Independent Chronicle. And the Universal Advertiser.* Boston, Mass.
Independent Gazetteer	*The Independent Gazetteer.* Philadelphia, Penn.
Jersey Chronicle	*Jersey Chronicle.* Mt. Pleasant, N.J.
Massachusetts Mercury	*The Massachusetts Mercury.* Boston, Mass.
Massachusetts Spy	*Thomas's Massachusetts Spy, or Worcester Gazette.* Worcester, Mass.
National Gazette	*National Gazette.* Philadelphia, Penn.
New York Journal	*Greenleaf's New York Journal, and Patriotic Register.* New York, N.Y.

Pittsburgh Gazette	*Pittsburgh Gazette.* Pittsburgh, Penn.
Potomack Guardian	*Potomack Guardian, and Berkeley Advertiser.* Shepherdstown, Va.
Rutland Herald	*The Rutland Herald.* Rutland, Vt.
State-Gazette	*South-Carolina State-Gazette.* Charleston, S.C.
Western Telegraphe	*Western Telegraphe and Washington Advertiser.* Washington, Penn.

Notes

INTRODUCTION

1 *Rutland Herald,* July 6, 1795. For Fourth of July celebrations generally see Len Travers, *Celebrating the Fourth: Independence Day and the Rites of Nationalism in the Early Republic* (Amherst, 1997); David Waldstreicher, *In the Midst of Perpetual Fetes: The Making of American Nationalism, 1776–1820* (Chapel Hill, 1997); and Simon P. Newman, *Parades and the Politics of the Street: Festive Culture in the Early American Republic* (Philadelphia, 1997), esp. chap. 3.

2 See Stanley Elkins and Eric McKitrick, *The Age of Federalism: The Early American Republic, 1788–1800* (New York, 1993); James Roger Sharp, *American Politics in the Early Republic: The New Nation in Crisis* (New Haven, 1993); and Lance Banning, *The Jeffersonian Persuasion: Evolution of a Party Ideology* (Ithaca, 1978). For the debate over whether or not a party "system" was in place at the time of the first party conflicts see Sharp and also Ronald P. Formisano, "Federalists and Republicans: Parties, Yes–System, No," in Paul Kleppner et al. (eds.), *The Evolution of American Electoral Systems* (Westport, Conn., 1981), pp. 33–76.

3 Nathan O. Hatch, *The Democratization of American Christianity* (New Haven, 1989), and Gordon S. Wood, *The Radicalism of the American Revolution* (New York, 1992), are the principal works here.

4 Waldstreicher, *In the Midst of Perpetual Fetes,* p. 136.

5 Richard Hofstadter, *The Idea of a Party System: The Rise of Legitimate Opposition in the United States, 1780–1840* (Berkeley, 1970), remains the classic statement on the acceptance of the concept of an opposition party as a regular feature of government.

6 See Joanne B. Freeman, *Affairs of Honor: National Politics in the New Republic* (New Haven, 2001), pp. 98–99. Freeman notes further: "As the Republicans eventually understood more fully than Federalists, the game of govern-

ment could be won by the party that best orchestrated these conversations" (p. 99). For a similar and related point see the discussion in Waldstreicher, *In the Midst of Perpetual Fetes,* pp. 113–14. Although I agree in general with these formulations about the eventual lines of development, I emphasize the point developed in this book, that early in the 1790s the Federalists, too, could be extremely proficient and successful at the "seeding" of public opinion. My understanding of the workings of public opinion in the early republic has been further influenced by conversations and correspondence with Joanne Freeman, Albrecht Koschnik, and David Waldstreicher, to all of whom I owe a great debt. Needless to say, they would not necessarily agree with everything I have written. Although it appeared too late for inclusion in this study, Christopher J. Young's recent dissertation, "Contests of Opinion: The Public Sphere in Post-Revolutionary America" (University of Illinois at Chicago, 2001), examines some of the same larger questions I do.

7 For an example of the collection of public opinion gone awry because it revealed support for the other side, see James Madison to Thomas Jefferson, July 30, 1793, in *Papers of Madison,* 15:49. In this letter, written during the Citizen Genet affair and Neutrality Crisis, Madison laments that a recent sounding of public opinion in Virginia was disappointing. "I can only account for it by supposing the public sentiment to have been collected from tainted sources wch. ought to have suggested to a cautious & unbiassed mind the danger of confiding in them." Republicans presumably encountered the "wrong" public, since those canvassed did not return the desired opinion.

8 James Madison, "Public Opinion," December 19, 1791, in *Papers of Madison,* 14:170.

9 Colleen A. Sheehan, "The Politics of Public Opinion: James Madison's 'Notes on Government,'" *William and Mary Quarterly,* 3d ser., 49, no. 4 (Oct. 1992), 609–27, quotation at 620.

10 The classic works on Federalism which have done so much to shape historians' understanding of the party are David Hackett Fischer, *The Revolution of American Conservatism: The Federalist Party in the Era of Jeffersonian Democracy* (New York, 1965); Linda K. Kerber, *Federalists in Dissent: Imagery and Ideology in Jeffersonian America* (Ithaca, 1970); James M. Banner, Jr., *To the Hartford Convention: The Federalists and the Origins of Party Politics in Massachusetts, 1789–1815* (New York, 1970); Shaw Livermore, *The Twilight of Federalism: The Disintegration of the Federalist Party, 1815–1830* (Princeton, 1962); and James Broussard, *The Southern Federalists, 1800–1816* (Baton Rouge, 1978).

11 My reconsideration of Federalism joins other works. The argument of this book was anticipated in two of my articles: "Shaping the Politics of Public Opinion: Federalists and the Jay Treaty Debate," *Journal of the Early Republic* 20 (2000), 393–422; and "The Art of Presidential Leadership: George Washington and the Jay Treaty," *Virginia Magazine of History and Biography* 109 (2001), 127–58. See Doron Ben-Atar and Barbara Oberg (eds.), *Federalists Reconsidered* (Charlottesville, Va., 1998), for a collection of essays which joust with the conventional wisdom about Federalists. For considerations of

Federalist efforts at popular politicking before 1801 see my work cited above and Alfred F. Young, "Conservatives, the Constitution, and the 'Spirit of Accommodation,'" in Robert A. Goldwin and William A. Schambra (eds.), *How Democratic Is the Constitution?* (Washington, D.C., 1980), pp. 117–47. Particularly influential to my thinking on this score is Owen Ireland, "The Invention of American Democracy: The Pennsylvania Federalists and the New Republic," *Pennsylvania History* 67 (2000), 161–71. For other perspectives see Lisle A. Rose, *Prologue to Democracy: The Federalists in the South, 1789–1800* (Lexington, Ky., 1968). For a related argument see Jack N. Rakove, "The Structure of Politics at the Accession of George Washington," in Richard Beeman et al. (eds), *Beyond Confederation: Origins of the Constitution and American National Identity* (Chapel Hill, 1987), pp. 261–94.

12 My major quarrel with Newman's excellent and important *Parades and the Politics of the Street* (n. 1 above) is that he assumes fixed categories of partisanship as early as 1789, as well as an advanced state of a democratized popular politics, which oversimplifies the complexities of the political culture of the decade—and, if true, would make impossible the Federalists' undeniable political successes early in the decade. Others, even while appreciating the book's obvious strengths, have made this same point: see Joanne B. Freeman's review in *Journal of the Early Republic* 18 (1998), 315–17.

13 See the previously cited works by Newman, Waldstreicher, and Freeman. Pasley's book is *"The Tyranny of Printers": Newspaper Politics in the Early American Republic* (Charlottesville, Va., 2001).

14 I have also been influenced by the diverse and wide-ranging body of recent scholarship on political culture and the new political history. See, for example, Ronald P. Formisano, "The Concept of Political Culture," *Journal of Interdisciplinary History* 31 (2001), 393–426; Glen Gendzel, "Political Culture: Genealogy of a Concept," *Journal of Interdisciplinary History* 28 (1997), 225–50; T. J. Jackson Lears, "The Concept of Cultural Hegemony: Problems and Possibilities," *American Historical Review* 90 (1985), 567–93; William E. Leuchtenburg, "The Pertinence of Political History: Reflections on the Significance of the State in America," *Journal of American History* 73 (1986), 585–600; Mark H. Leff, "Revisioning U.S. Political History," *American Historical Review* 100 (1995), 829–53; Steven M. Gillon, "The Future of Political History," *Journal of Policy History* 9 (1997), 240–55; Joel H. Silbey, "The State of American Political History at the Millennium: The Nineteenth Century as a Test Case," *Journal of Policy History* 11 (1999), 1–30. See also the forum on "Limits of Political Engagement in Antebellum America: A New Look at the Golden Age of Participatory Democracy" in *Journal of American History* 84 (1997), 855–909. Also see three essay collections: Byron Shafer and Anthony Badger (eds.), *Contesting Democracy: Substance and Structure in American Political History* (Lawrence, Kans., 2001); Meg Jacobs, William J. Novak, and Julian E. Zelizer (eds.), *The Democratic Experiment: New Directions in American Political History* (Princeton, 2003); and Jeffrey L. Pasley, Andrew W. Robertson, and David Waldstreicher (eds.), *Beyond the Founders: New Approaches to the Political History of the Early American Republic* (Chapel Hill, 2004).

15 The literature is fast becoming unmanageable but among the key works—and the most influential in forming my conception of the public sphere—are three by Jurgen Habermas: *Structural Transformation of the Public Sphere* (1962; Cambridge, Mass., 1989); "The Public Sphere: An Encyclopedia Article," *New German Critique* 3 (1974), 45–55; and "Further Reflections on the Public Sphere," in Craig Calhoun (ed.), *Habermas and the Public Sphere* (Cambridge, Mass., 1992), pp. 421–61. This last piece anticipated and has since been supplemented by his *Between Facts and Norms: Contributions to a Discourse Theory of Law and Democracy* (Cambridge, Mass., 1996); see esp. chaps. 7 and 8. I have been particularly influenced, in considering the applicability of the term to early U.S. life, by John L. Brooke's "Ancient Lodges and Self-Created Societies: Voluntary Association and the Public Sphere in the Early Republic," in Ronald Hoffman and Peter J. Albert (eds.), *Launching the "Extended Republic": The Federalist Era* (Charlottesville, Va., 1996), pp. 273–377. For extended discussions see the essays in Calhoun, *Habermas and the Public Sphere,* especially Geoff Eley, "Nations, Publics, and Political Cultures: Placing Habermas in the Nineteenth Century," pp. 289–339; Nancy Fraser, "Rethinking the Public Sphere: A Contribution to the Critique of Actually Existing Democracy," pp. 109–42; and Mary P. Ryan, "Gender and Public Access: Women's Politics in Nineteenth-Century America," pp. 259–88. See also the related discussion in the important work of Bernard Manin, "On Legitimacy and Political Deliberation," *Political Theory* 15 (1987), 338–68.

16 John L. Brooke has led the way both in encouraging scholars to utilize public sphere theory and in demonstrating how it might be applied to thinking about early American politics. His "Ancient Lodges and Self-Created Societies" (n. 15 above) is the best extended treatment, but see also his valuable essay, "Reason and Passion in the Public Sphere: Habermas and the Cultural Historians," *Journal of Interdisciplinary History* 29 (1998), 43–67. For a more skeptical consideration of the utility of the public sphere concept see Robert A. Gross, "Print and the Public Sphere in Early America," in Melvyn Stokes (ed.), *The State of U.S. History* (Oxford, UK, 2002), pp. 245–64. Other extremely useful sources are Waldstreicher, *In the Midst of Perpetual Fetes,* pp. 216–45; and Newman, *Parades and the Politics of the Street,* pp. 1–10 and 186–92. For a variety of other applications and considerations see also Michael Warner, *The Letters of the Republic: Publication and the Public Sphere in Eighteenth-Century America* (Cambridge, Mass., 1990); Richard R. John, *Spreading the News: The American Postal System from Franklin to Morse* (Cambridge, Mass., 1995); and, more broadly, Benedict Anderson, *Imagined Communities: Reflections on the Origin and Spread of Nationalism* (New York, 1991).

17 Waldstreicher, *In the Midst of Perpetual Fetes,* p. 54. Waldstreicher is referring to the Great National Discussion over the Constitution as an effort at inventing a national political culture and a process of defining the nature of what was political. For important recent work on the role of women in early national political culture see Susan Branson, *These Fiery Frenchified Dames: Women and Political Culture in Early National Philadelphia* (Philadelphia, 2001); and Catherine Allgor, *Parlor Politics: In Which the Ladies of Washington Help Build a City and a Government* (Charlottesville, Va., 2000).

18 See Cayton's review essay, "We are All Nationalists, We are All Localists," *Journal of the Early Republic* 18 (1998), 521–28, quotation at p. 526.

19 For the notion of the public sphere and political culture and its use by European historians in a wide array of contexts see Arlette Farge, *Subversive Words: Public Opinion in Eighteenth-Century France* (University Park, Penn., 1995); Sarah Maza, *Private Lives and Public Affairs: The Causes Célèbres of Prerevolutionary France* (Berkeley, 1993); Roger Chartier, *The Cultural Origins of the French Revolution* (Durham, N.C., 1991); Lynn Hunt, *Politics, Culture, and Class in the French Revolution* (Berkeley, 1984); Keith Michael Baker, *Inventing the French Revolution: Essays on French Political Culture in the Eighteenth Century* (Cambridge, UK, 1990); Jay M. Smith, *The Culture of Merit: Nobility, Royal Service, and the Making of Absolute Monarchy in France, 1600–1789* (Ann Arbor, 1996), and "No More Language Games: Words, Beliefs, and the Political Culture of Early Modern France," *American Historical Review* 102 (1997), 1413–40; and Sarah Hanley, "Social Sites of Political Practice in France: Lawsuits, Civil Rights, and the Separation of Powers in Domestic and State Government, 1500–1800," *American Historical Review* 102 (1997), 27–52. I am indebted to my colleague Sara Chapman for directing me to some of these works.

20 Samuel Flagg Bemis, *Jay's Treaty: A Study in Commerce and Diplomacy* (1923; 2d ed. New Haven, 1962); Jerald A. Combs, *The Jay Treaty: Political Battleground of the Founding Fathers* (Berkeley, 1970).

21 See, for example, Richard Buel, *Securing the Revolution: Ideology in American Politics* (Ithaca, 1970); Joseph Charles, *The Origins of the American Party System: Three Essays* (Williamsburg, Va., 1956); and Stephen G. Kurtz, *The Presidency of John Adams: The Collapse of Federalism, 1795–1800* (Philadelphia, 1957).

22 For excellent accounts of the congressional debates see Combs, *Jay Treaty,* chap. 11; Elkins and McKitrick, *Age of Federalism,* pp. 444–49. See also Todd Estes, "'The Most Bewitching Piece of Parliamentary Oratory': Fisher Ames's Jay Treaty Speech Revisited," *Historical Journal of Massachusetts* 28 (Winter 2000), 1–22, for an analysis of the best known and most cited speech from the House debate over the Treaty.

23 See Irving Brant, "Edmund Randolph, Not Guilty!," *William and Mary Quarterly,* 3d ser., 7 (1950), 179–98; Combs, *Jay Treaty,* App. 2, pp. 193–96; and Mary K. Bonsteel Tachau, "George Washington and the Reputation of Edmund Randolph," *Journal of American History* 73 (1986), 15–34.

CHAPTER ONE

1 See Jerald A. Combs, *The Jay Treaty: Political Battleground of the Founding Fathers* (Berkeley, 1970), pp. 3–14; Reginald Horsman, *The Diplomacy of the New Republic, 1776–1815* (Arlington Heights, Ill., 1985), pp. 28–41; and Jerald A. Combs with Arthur G. Combs, *The History of American Foreign Policy,* 2d ed. (New York, 1997), pp. 18–22. For the terms of the Anglo-American treaty that ended the Revolution see Jonathan R. Dull, *A Diplomatic*

History of the American Revolution (New Haven, 1985), pp. 170–74; and Samuel Flagg Bemis, *Jay's Treaty: A Study in Commerce and Diplomacy,* 2d ed. (New Haven, 1962), pp. 442–52.

2 See the sources cited in note 1 above and also Richard B. Morris, *The Forging of the Union, 1781–1789* (New York, 1987), esp. pp. 194–219, for U.S. diplomacy during the 1780s. For a more comprehensive view of U.S. diplomacy during the post-Revolution years, particularly the relationship with Britain, see Charles R. Ritcheson, *Aftermath of Revolution: British Policy toward the United States, 1783–1795* (Dallas, 1969). The man charged by the Confederation Congress with overseeing these diplomatic challenges was John Jay, appointed secretary for foreign affairs in 1784. On this period of Jay's career see Frank Monaghan, *John Jay: Defender of Liberty* (New York, 1935), pp. 244–77.

3 Quoted in Combs, *History of American Foreign Policy,* p. 27. For fuller discussion see Combs, *Jay Treaty,* pp. 15–28; Horsman, *Diplomacy of the New Republic,* pp. 42–57; and Stanley Elkins and Eric McKitrick, *The Age of Federalism: The Early American Republic, 1788–1800* (New York, 1993), pp. 303–73.

4 The discussion of the Neutrality Crisis in this paragraph and the next is drawn from Combs, *Jay Treaty,* pp. 107–15; Elkins and McKitrick, *Age of Federalism,* pp. 336–41; James Roger Sharp, *American Politics in the Early Republic: The New Nation in Crisis* (New Haven, 1993), pp. 75–78; Horsman, *Diplomacy of the New Republic,* pp. 48–50; and John C. Miller, *The Federalist Era* (New York, 1960), pp. 140–54.

5 See the detailed discussion in Elkins and McKitrick, *Age of Federalism,* pp. 341–65; and Sharp, *American Politics,* pp. 78–91.

6 For an excellent discussion of Federalist foreign policy thinking, particularly attitudes toward England and France, see Combs, *Jay Treaty,* pp. 47–64. Also see Gilbert Lycan, *Alexander Hamilton and American Foreign Policy* (Norman, Okla., 1970).

7 For the ideological orientation of the Republicans in the 1790s see Lance Banning, *The Jeffersonian Persuasion: Evolution of a Party Ideology* (Ithaca, 1978); for the influence of the French Revolution on their thinking see esp. pp. 208–45. For an excellent discussion of the Republican view of "foreignness" in American politics in the 1790s see Peter S. Onuf, *Jefferson's Empire: The Language of American Nationhood* (Charlottesville, Va., 2000), pp. 80–108.

8 See Jefferson to Madison, April 28, 1793, in *Papers of Madison,* 15:10–11; Jefferson to Madison, May 13, 1793, ibid., 15:15–17; and Madison to Jefferson, June 19, 1793, ibid., 15:33–34. This paragraph and the next several draw upon the excellent discussions in James Morton Smith (ed.), *The Republic of Letters: The Correspondence between Jefferson and Madison, 1776–1826,* 3 vols. (New York, 1995), 2:744–60 and 2:821–27; Combs, *Jay Treaty,* pp. 65–85; Ralph Ketcham, *James Madison: A Biography* (Charlottesville, Va., 1971), pp. 337–68; Lance Banning, *The Sacred Fire of Liberty: James Madison & the Founding of the Federal Republic* (Ithaca, 1995), pp. 357–58 and 375–84; and Jack Rakove, *James Madison and the Creation of the American Republic* (Glenview, Ill., 1990), pp. 105–23.

9 Elkins and McKitrick, *Age of Federalism,* p. 381; and Smith, *Republic of Letters,* 2:821–27.

10 On Manning see Michael Merrill and Sean Wilentz (eds.), *The Key of Liberty: The Life and Democratic Writings of William Manning, "A Laborer," 1747–1814* (Cambridge, Mass., 1993), quotations at pp. 152, 150, 151, 152, 185, and 189.

11 *General Advertiser,* March 28, 1794, and April 11, 1794. The *General Advertiser* was the previous incarnation of the *Aurora: General Advertiser*, which began publication in November of 1794. For an excellent, detailed discussion of Bache's life and career see James Tagg, *Benjamin Franklin Bache and the Philadelphia Aurora* (Philadelphia, 1991), esp. pp. 239–74 on the treaty.

12 John Beckley to James Madison, September 10, 1795, in *Papers of Madison,* 16:85–86. My understanding of Beckley has been shaped by Jeffrey L. Pasley's fine article, "'A Journeyman, Either in Law or Politics': John Beckley and the Social Origins of Political Campaigning," *Journal of the Early Republic* 16 (1996), 531–69. See also Edmund Berkeley and Dorothy Smith Berkeley, *John Beckley: Zealous Partisan in a Nation Divided* (Philadelphia, 1973).

13 Combs, *Jay Treaty,* p. 116.

14 The preceding paragraphs draw on Combs, *Jay Treaty,* pp. 116–33; Elkins and McKitrick, *Age of Federalism,* pp. 388–93; Combs, *History of American Foreign Policy,* pp. 28–30; and Horsman, *The Diplomacy of the New Republic,* pp. 52–57.

15 See Combs, *Jay Treaty,* pp. 133–36; Monaghan, *John Jay,* pp. 364–68; and the editorial note in *Papers of Hamilton,* 16:261–65, for Jay's appointment.

16 Jay to Mrs. Jay, April 15, 1794, and April 19, 1794, in *Corr. of Jay,* 4:3–5.

17 For Jay's negotiating instructions see Combs, *Jay Treaty,* pp. 133–36; Elkins and McKitrick, *Age of Federalism,* pp. 396–401; Bemis, *Jay's Treaty,* pp. 289–98; Monaghan, *John Jay,* pp. 368–69; and *Papers of Hamilton,* 16:319–28. The full text of Randolph's instructions is found in *Papers of Hamilton,* 16:323–28 n. 13, and in *Corr. of Jay,* 4:10ff. See also the discussion in Lycan, *Alexander Hamilton,* esp. pp. 219–29.

18 Combs, *Jay Treaty,* p. 134; Hamilton to George Washington, April 14, 1794, in *Papers of Hamilton,* 16:266–79, quotations at pp. 276 and 271.

19 See Elkins and McKitrick, *Age of Federalism,* p. 406; and Monaghan, *John Jay,* pp. 370–74.

20 Elkins and McKitrick, *Age of Federalism,* pp. 407–08; Monaghan, *John Jay,* pp. 375–80; Bemis, *Jay's Treaty,* pp. 323–28; and Combs, *Jay Treaty,* pp. 148–50.

21 Elkins and McKitrick, *Age of Federalism,* p. 412. Discussion of the Hamilton-Hammond exchange and any effect it may have had on the mission may be followed in ibid., pp. 411–12; Bemis, *Jay's Treaty,* 337–40; Monaghan, *John Jay,* pp. 379–80 (whose interpretation follows Bemis's); and Combs, *Jay Treaty,* p. 157 (who disputes Bemis's contention that the revelation had serious detrimental impact). For Hamilton's conversation with Hammond see *Papers of Hamilton,* 16:548–50.

22 Elkins and McKitrick, *Age of Federalism,* p. 414, stress this point in a discussion of U.S. hopes to bind its interests with those of Great Britain over the long term. "Jay had put his whole mind to the effort; they [the British] had put barely half of theirs. . . . How could John Jay, or any other American . . . bear to face the real truth about Great Britain? Here were the British at the very center of our universe, and they did not really care about us, not half enough!"

23 See Jay to Alexander Hamilton, September 11, 1794, in *Papers of Hamilton,* 17:221–22; Jay to Edmund Randolph, September 13, 1794, quoted in Elkins and McKitrick, *Age of Federalism,* p. 407. Elkins and McKitrick observe that this approach characterized Jay's entire modus operandi for the negotiations. Jerald Combs notes that Jay's assessment of America's comparative strength meant that he "was on the defensive throughout the negotiations," but also that his diplomatic experience and philosophy had convinced him that successful diplomacy depended on "grasping opportunities as soon as they appeared and taking advantage of temporary circumstances" (*Jay Treaty,* p. 149). Fearful that extensive delay or hard bargaining, not to mention any actions taken by American citizens or the government that the British perceived to be unfriendly, might diminish their amicable feelings toward the U.S., Combs contends that Jay was willing to settle for less than might be gotten rather than risk missing the opportunity and coming away with less than he believed was truly necessary.

24 Monaghan, *John Jay,* p. 379; Elkins and McKitrick, *Age of Federalism,* p. 410.

25 The complete article-by-article terms of the treaty are found in Bemis, *Jay's Treaty,* pp. 453–82.

26 For the text of Article 12 see Bemis, *Jay's Treaty,* pp. 467–69. For discussion of other prohibitions in the treaty terms see Combs, *Jay Treaty,* pp. 152–53.

27 Jay to Oliver Ellsworth, November 19, 1794; Jay to President Washington, November 19, 1794; Jay to Alexander Hamilton, November 1794; Jay to Edmund Randolph, November 19, 1794; all in *Corr. of Jay,* 4:132–44. For more detailed discussion of Jay's relative lack of involvement in the Jay Treaty debate see Todd Estes, "John Jay, the Concept of Deference, and the Transformation of Early American Political Culture," *The Historian* 65 (2002), 293–317.

28 For excellent discussions and assessments of the Jay mission and the terms he obtained see Combs, *Jay Treaty,* pp. 151–58 (quotation at p. 158); and Elkins and McKitrick, *Age of Federalism,* pp. 410–14 (quotation at p. 410). Both accounts stress the relative weakness of Jay's bargaining position and the preoccupation of Britain with the war and other matters, and suggest that it is not likely that Jay, even had he pushed more insistently, could have achieved much more than he did. In his more recent textbook on foreign policy, Combs notes that "Historians with access to the British archives have generally agreed, however, that Jay obtained about as much as the British had been willing to give. The English could hardly undermine their war against France by bowing to the American view of neutral rights." Combs also observes, "Some figures high in the British cabinet were adamantly opposed even to those concessions Jay did win." See Combs, *History of American Foreign Policy,* p. 31.

29 James Madison to Thomas Jefferson, January 11, 1795, and February 15, 1795, in *Papers of Madison,* 15:441, 473; Robert Livingston to Madison, January 30, 1795, ibid., 15:460. See also James Monroe to Madison, February 25, 1795, ibid., 15:481.

30 For Bache's activity during the Treaty's prepublication period see James Tagg, *Benjamin Franklin Bache and the Philadelphia Aurora* (Philadelphia, 1991), chap. 9. The "Franklin" essays were originally published in the *Independent Gazetteer* between March 11 and June 10, 1795, and widely reprinted in other newspapers and in pamphlet form. Their authorship is still unknown, although speculation at the time centered on the French minister Joseph Fauchet and Pennsylvania Republican Alexander J. Dallas.

31 See Elkins and McKitrick, *Age of Federalism,* pp. 415–18. On Monroe's letter see ibid., pp. 415–16. Fisher Ames to Thomas Dwight, February 3, 1795, in *Works of Ames*, 2:1101–02.

32 Elkins and McKitrick, *Age of Federalism,* pp. 417–18; James Madison to James Madison, Sr., February 8, 1795, in *Papers of Madison,* 15:469; and Madison to Jefferson, February 15, 1795, ibid., 15:473.

33 Tagg, *Bache,* pp. 246–48.

CHAPTER TWO

1 For recent statements about the growth of parties which also address the voluminous literature on this subject see Stanley Elkins and Eric McKitrick, *The Age of Federalism: The Early American Republic, 1788–1800* (New York, 1993); and James Roger Sharp, *American Politics in the Early Republic: The New Nation in Crisis* (New Haven, 1993).

2 For background on the Neutrality Proclamation and the Citizen Genet episode see, among others, Harry Ammon, *The Genet Mission* (New York, 1973); Albert Hall Bowman, *The Struggle for Neutrality: Franco-American Diplomacy during the Federalist Era* (Knoxville, Tenn., 1974); Alexander DeConde, *Entangling Alliance: Politics and Diplomacy under George Washington* (Durham, N.C., 1958); Reginald Horsman, *The Diplomacy of the New Republic, 1776–1815* (Arlington Heights, Ill., 1985); Richard Kohn, *Eagle and Sword: The Federalists and the Creation of the Military Establishment in America, 1783–1802* (New York, 1975); and Paul A. Varg, *Foreign Policies of the Founding Fathers* (East Lansing, Mich., 1963).

3 *GUS*, July 13, 1793.

4 "The Charter of Absurdities," *GUS,* August 10, 1793; "Nestor," ibid., August 21, 1793. Explaining why some might stir up opposition, "Nestor" raised an even darker specter: "It should be considered that in every city there are men who are pleased with a conflagration; on every coast there are men who are pleased with a shipwreck, and in every State there are men who are pleased with wars and revolutions, because they may by those means have an opportunity of plundering."

5 *Ind. Gaz., Agric.*, August 10, 1793.

6 "Wilcocks," *Daily Advertiser,* August 6, 1793; also *GUS,* August 21, 1793.

7 *GUS,* August 14, 1793.

8 *GUS,* August 17, 1793; *Ind. Gaz., Agric.,* August 17, 1793.

9 The "Pacificus" essays are found in *Papers of Hamilton,* 15:33–43 (June 29), 55–63 (July 3), 65–69 (July 6), 82–86 (July 10), 90–95 (July 13–17), 100–06 (July 17), and 130–35 (July 27). For discussion and summaries of the essays see Forrest McDonald, *Alexander Hamilton: A Biography* (New York, 1979), pp. 278–79; Sharp, *American Politics in the Early Republic,* pp. 77–78; and Elkins and McKitrick, *Age of Federalism,* pp. 360–61. Elkins and McKitrick summarize the historians' verdict on the effectiveness of the essays when they write, "'Pacificus' was a strong performance, and seems to have been generally so recognized" (p. 361).

10 For an insightful discussion of the Federalists' use of "political gossip" to discredit Genet see Joanne B. Freeman, "Slanders, Poison, Whispers, and Fame: Jefferson's 'Anas' and Political Gossip in the Early Republic," *Journal of the Early Republic* 15 (1996), 45–50.

11 Thomas Jefferson to James Madison, July 7, 1793, in *Papers of Madison,* 15:43; Jefferson to Madison, August 3, 1793, ibid., 15:50–51. Jefferson was increasingly troubled in the fall of 1793 by Genet's activities and the difficult position in which the French minister placed his American friends. See Jefferson to Genet, September 7, 1793, in *Papers of Jefferson,* 27:52–53; and Jefferson to Madison, November 17, 1793, ibid., 27:395–96.

12 Madison to Jefferson, July 30, 1793, in *Papers of Madison,* 15:48. For the text of the "Helvidius" essays see ibid., 15:66–73, 80–87, 95–103, 106–10, and 113–20. See especially the excellent editorial note, pp. 64–66.

13 Madison to Jefferson, July 22, 1790, in *Papers of Madison,* 15:47. See also the editorial note, pp. 64–66.

14 "Helvidius" no. 4 (September 14, 1793), in *Papers of Madison,* 15:106–07. See also the discussion in Lance Banning, *The Sacred Fire of Liberty: James Madison and the Founding of the Federal Republic* (Ithaca, 1995), pp. 376–77.

15 For the efforts of the Republican press during the Neutrality Crisis see Jeffrey L. Pasley, *"The Tyranny of Printers": Newspaper Politics in the Early American Republic* (Charlottesville, Va., 2001), chaps. 3 and 4; and James Tagg, *Benjamin Franklin Bache and the Philadelphia Aurora* (Philadelphia, 1991), chap. 7.

16 Oliver Wolcott, Jr., to Noah Webster, August 10, 1793, in *Papers of Wolcott,* 1:103–4; Peter Van Schaak to Loring Andrews, August 1, 1793, Henry Van Schaak Papers, Massachusetts Historical Society.

17 Christopher Gore to Rufus King, August 4, 1793, in *Life of King,* 1:490; George Cabot to Rufus King, *ibid.,* 1:489; Fisher Ames to Alexander Hamilton, August 31, 1793, in *Works of Ames,* 2:964–65.

18 Stephen Higginson to Alexander Hamilton, July 26, 1793, in *Papers of Hamilton,* 15:127–28. For an account of the July 22 Boston town meeting at which Citizen Genet was denounced, see *Independent Chronicle,* July 25, 1793. Higginson also told Hamilton that "Pacificus is operating here without interruption."

19 Robert Troup to Alexander Hamilton, August 8, 1793, in *Papers of Hamilton,* 15:208–09. For accounts of the New York meeting of August 8, 1793, and the resolutions adopted see *Daily Advertiser,* August 9, 1793; and *GUS,* August 14, 1793.

20 For the Richmond meeting see Harry Ammon, "The Genet Mission and the Development of American Political Parties," *Journal of American History* 52 (1966), 732; and Ammon, *James Monroe: The Quest for National Identity* (Charlottesville, Va., 1971), p. 102.

21 See Madison to Jefferson, September 2, 1793 (second letter), in *Papers of Madison,* 15:93. For descriptions of the meetings and text of the resolutions see the editorial note, ibid., 15:76–80. See also Ammon, *James Monroe,* pp. 104–05.

22 Samuel Smith to Alexander Hamilton, June 16, 1793, in *Papers of Hamilton,* 15:1; George Cabot to Rufus King, August 2, 1793, in *Life of King,* 1:489–90. Cabot believed that a public debate would expose the true motivations of the two sides and clearly place the Federalists in the best light. Most of the "propagators of falsehood" were, he wrote, "stimulated by the strongest personal motives, while their opponents are actuated chiefly by a love of the public. Who can doubt on which side victory will be in such a contest?"

23 Samuel Smith to Alexander Hamilton, August 20, 1793, in *Papers of Hamilton,* 15:255; William Loughton Smith to Hamilton, August 22, 1793, ibid., 15:262.

24 David Ross to Alexander Hamilton, August 30, 1793, in *Papers of Hamilton,* 15:309–10. During the Jay Treaty debate, Fisher Ames wrote that Hamilton's "Camillus" essays were a form of overkill. "[S]o much answer to so little weight of objection is odds. He holds up the aegis against a wooden sword. Jove's eagle holds his bolts in his talons, and hurls them, not at the Titans, but at sparrows and mice." See Ames to Jeremiah Smith, January 18, 1796, in *Works of Ames,* 2:1130.

25 Jefferson to Madison, August 11, 1793, in *Papers of Madison,* 15:56–59; Madison to Jefferson, August 27, 1793, and September 2, 1793, ibid., 15:75, 92–93. Madison recognized, as well as the Federalists had, the need to appeal to the public. Despite his disappointment in the drift of opinion, he observed to Jefferson that "It is of such infinite importance . . . that the real sentiments of the people here should be understood, that something ought to be attempted on that head."

26 The "Address of the Philadelphia Merchants and Traders" is reprinted in *Ind. Gaz., Agric.,* May 25, 1793. Washington's reply is in *Writings of Washington,* 32:460–61.

27 See *Ind. Gaz., Agric.,* June 8, 1793; and *Writings of Washington,* 32:477.

28 *GUS,* July 27, 1793. For more reports of public meetings and resolutions on the Neutrality Proclamation see Ammon, "Genet Mission." But, as Stanley Elkins and Eric McKitrick rightly note, "a careful study of public opinion on the Proclamation would be useful. To our knowledge, none has been attempted" (*Age of Federalism,* p. 821 n. 154).

29 *GUS,* August 10, 1793. The contrast between "orderly" and "disorderly" citizens was a distinction Federalists would continue to make in this as well as later controversies. The prevalence of such accusations also helps to explain why, during the Jay Treaty debates, Republican newspapers went out of their way to describe anti-treaty crowds or protest meetings as orderly, proper, and peaceful assemblies.

30 *GUS,* August 28, 1793. The addresses were from Exeter, New Hampshire (which held a town meeting on August 12), Charlestown, Massachusetts (July 22), Pownalborough, District of Maine (August 9), Malden, Massachusetts (August 16), Springfield, Massachusetts (August 14), New Bedford, Massachusetts (no date given), New Haven, Connecticut (August 19), Newark, New Jersey (August 17), and Richmond, Virginia (August 17). See also *GUS,* August 21, 1793, for addresses from Newburyport and Marblehead, Massachusetts. For responses to such addresses typical of the kind sent by Washington see, among several examples, *Writings of Washington,* 33:489–90. Even as late as January 1794, citizens gathered in Savannah, Georgia, to draft an address to Washington which declared that, although publicly expressing disapprobation of government measures was "one of the greatest privileges of free citizens," so, too, was it a "duty to express our approbation of great and extraordinary acts, which have been the result of constant vigilance, and prudent precautions for national safety." With that they went on to praise "the great and good acts of our first magistrate" and condemn Genet's double dealings, calling it America's true interest to remain at peace. See *GUS,* February 13, 1794. For Republican reaction to these pro-administration petitions see James Monroe to Thomas Jefferson, October 14, 1793, in *Papers of Jefferson,* 27:236–37 and the accompanying editorial note.

31 Jefferson to Madison, August 11, 1793, in *Papers of Madison,* 15:57.

32 On the mixed results for the two parties see Elkins and McKitrick, *Age of Federalism,* pp. 362–65; Ammon, "Genet Mission," 737–41; and Ammon, *James Monroe,* pp. 106–07.

33 Fisher Ames to Thomas Dwight, August 1793, in *Works of Ames,* 2:964; Ames to Hamilton, August 31, 1793, ibid., 2:964–65.

34 Rufus King to Alexander Hamilton, August 3, 1793, in *Life of King,* 1:492–93. This letter is also found in *Papers of Hamilton,* 15:172–74.

35 See Donald Stewart, *The Opposition Press of the Federalist Period* (Albany, 1969), p. 166. Stewart writes, "Jefferson had always been acutely aware of the importance of newspapers, but very possibly the Hamiltonian propaganda success on this issue convinced him of the absolute necessity for an unswervingly Republican press." See also Ammon, "Genet Mission," 741, and Ammon, *James Monroe,* p. 107, for the Republican realization of the need to organize and shape public opinion through a reliable press, public meetings, and a better developed party network. Michael Lienesch has noted that by the time Jefferson left office as secretary of state at the end of 1793, he was well aware of the power of public opinion, and that appeals to the public could work against the Republican interest as well as for it. Lienesch notes the "irony" that, "in opening American politics to the power of public opinion, Jefferson had seen that power turned against him, against his party, and against the republican cause."

See Lienesch, "Thomas Jefferson and the American Democratic Experience: The Origins of the Partisan Press, Popular Political Parties, and Public Opinion," in Peter Onuf (ed.), *Jeffersonian Legacies* (Charlottesville, Va., 1993), pp. 316–39, quotation at p. 336.

36 Philip S. Foner (ed.), *The Democratic-Republican Societies, 1790–1800: A Documentary Sourcebook of Constitutions, Declarations, Addresses, Resolutions, and Toasts* (Westport, Conn., 1976), p. 320. For the Democratic Societies see Eugene Link, *Democratic-Republican Societies, 1790–1800* (New York, 1942); Elkins and McKitrick, *Age of Federalism,* pp. 451–61, quotation at p. 457; and John L. Brooke, "Ancient Lodges and Self-Created Societies: Voluntary Association and the Public Sphere in the Early Republic," in Ronald Hoffman and Peter J. Albert (eds.), *Launching the "Extended Republic": The Federalist Era* (Charlottesville, Va., 1996), esp. pp. 309–16. See also Thomas P. Slaughter, *The Whiskey Rebellion: Frontier Epilogue to the American Revolution* (New York, 1986). An excellent recent examination of the societies that locates their emergence in the ideological battles of the 1790s is Matthew Schoenbachler, "Republicanism in the Age of Democratic Revolutions: The Democratic-Republican Societies of the 1790s," *Journal of the Early Republic* 18 (1998), 237–61.

37 George Washington to Henry Lee, August 26, 1794, in *Writings of Washington,* 33:475.

38 *GUS,* March 10, 1794. This theme is treated at length in chap. 5 below.

39 Banning, *Sacred Fire of Liberty,* pp. 378–80.

40 "[Untitled] Against Jacobins" [1794?], in *Works of Ames,* 2:977–78, 983. For Ames's direct criticisms of the Democratic Societies see also Ames to Thomas Dwight, August 8, 1794, and September 11, 1794, ibid., 2:1045–46, 1048–50. In the September 11 letter Ames articulated a common perception many Federalists had of the clubs when he wrote that they "were born in sin, the impure offspring of Genet. They are the few against the many; the sons of darkness (for their meetings are in secret) against those of the light; and above all, it is a *town* cabal, attempting to rule the *country.*" He further characterized their continued existence as being "like the root of an extracted cancer, which will soon eat again and destroy." Ames elaborated publicly on many of his private critiques of the societies in his speech in the House of Representatives, defending Washington's use of the term "self-created" societies, on November 26, 1794. See ibid., 2:1053–71.

41 Ames to Thomas Dwight, September 3, 1794, in *Works of Ames,* 2:1047–48; and November 29, 1794, ibid., 2:1083.

42 See Joanne B. Freeman, *Affairs of Honor: National Politics in the New Republic* (New Haven, 2001), pp. 113–14, for a discussion of the different audiences reached by different forms of communication.

43 Nathaniel Chipman to Alexander Hamilton, June 9, 1794, in *Papers of Hamilton,* 16:465–70. This letter was also printed in the *Daily Advertiser,* June 12, 1794.

44 Edward Carrington to Alexander Hamilton, July 9, 1794, in *Papers of Hamilton,* 16:580–81. Several weeks later, Carrington again wrote to Hamilton,

voicing the same theme and assuring him that the true sentiment of Virginians was quite different than the Democratic Societies professed. As always, however, it was necessary for the Federalists to put information in their hands. The "people of Virginia mean to be right when they can be in possession of the truth. The Insurgency is a case in which the truth cannot be veiled." Carrington to Hamilton, August 25, 1794, ibid., 17:139.

45 Alexander Hamilton to Isaac Craig, August 25, 1794, in *Papers of Hamilton,* 17:140.

46 "Tully" no. 1, *Dunlap and Claypoole's,* August 23, 1794. The other three "Tully" essays appeared in *Dunlap and Claypoole's* for August 26, August 28, and September 2, 1794. They are also in *Papers of Hamilton,* 17:132–35, 148–50, 159–61, and 175–80.

47 *GUS,* March 17, 1794; ibid., February 6, 1794.

48 *GUS,* May 21, 1794; *Daily Gazette* (February 1794), quoted in Foner, *Democratic-Republican Societies,* p. 154. Another correspondent suggested appropriate symbols for the two sides: "The *olive branch and the sword*—these comprize the politics of the real friends of this country. A *nettle, and an empty scabbard*—the politics of the disorganizers."

49 *GUS,* June 10, 1794; ibid., June 23, 1794.

50 See Madison's speech in *Papers of Madison,* 15:390–92. See also Elkins and McKitrick, *Age of Federalism,* pp. 485–88, for a fuller discussion.

51 Madison to James Monroe, December 4, 1794, in *Papers of Madison,* 15:405–08; Jefferson to Madison, December 28, 1794, ibid., 15:426–28.

52 For Bache's role see Tagg, *Benjamin Franklin Bache,* pp. 205–38, quotations at p. 216; Pasley, *"Tyranny of Printers,"* pp. 88–91, quotation at p. 91.

53 *GUS,* February 17, 1794. The same issue also contains a piece lambasting the clubs for their hypocrisy and double standards. "The same wranglers who dread the corrupting influence of birth-day celebrations, behave as if they could not toast and celebrate Genet enough. The meaning is plain in both instances—they wish to bring one man within the reach of contempt, and to raise the other above it."

54 *GUS,* June 10, 1794. In contrast to the "real friends," the "partizans of discord on the other hand, have uniformly shouted hosannas to the triumphing faction in France . . . and have justified the measures of men who have destroyed EACH OTHER—Can this be right?"

55 "A Federal Republican," *GUS,* June 18, 1794.

56 Madison to Thomas Jefferson, November 30, 1794, and Madison to Monroe, December 4, 1794, in *Papers of Madison,* 15:396–98, 405–08. For an insightful treatment of the contest over the Democratic Societies and the broader contours of political culture see Albrecht Koschnik, "The Democratic Societies of Philadelphia and the Limits of the American Public Sphere, circa 1793–1795," *William and Mary Quarterly,* 3d ser., 58, no. 3 (2001), 615–36.

57 "Order," *GUS,* September 10, 1794. For a sarcastic Federalist effort to mock the "General Creed" of the societies see "Democratic Lessons," ibid., which

begins, "To be a modern democrat, To this you must agree, Sir, That *we the people are,* and yet, The people are not we, Sir."

58 *GUS,* October 4, 1794.

59 "A Federalist," *GUS,* September 6, 1794; ibid., September 24, 1794. For more on the role and content of opposition newspapers during this period see Stewart, *The Opposition Press of the Federalist Period,* and Tagg, *Benjamin Franklin Bache.*

60 For the Baltimore Society comments see "To the Government and People of the United States," in Foner, *Democratic-Republican Societies,* pp. 339–43; also see *Aurora,* December 17, 1794. See Madison to Jefferson, December 21, 1794, in *Papers of Madison,* 15:419–21.

61 *GUS,* October 18, 1794. For the story of the Whiskey Rebellion's anticlimactic ending see Slaughter, *Whiskey Rebellion,* pp. 175–228.

62 *GUS,* October 18, 1794.

63 *GUS,* September 26, 1794. See also Elkins and McKitrick, *Age of Federalism,* pp. 474–88.

64 Jefferson to Madison, December 28, 1794, in *Papers of Madison,* 15:426–29.

65 Fisher Ames to Christopher Gore, December 17, 1794, in *Works of Ames,* 2:1087.

66 Fisher Ames to Thomas Dwight, December 12, 1794, in *Works of Ames,* 2:1083–85.

67 Jesse Appleton to Ebenezer Adams, May 4, 1795, Jesse Appleton Letters, American Antiquarian Society. Adams was a professor at Dartmouth.

68 Alexander Hamilton to Rufus King, October 30, 1794, in *Papers of Hamilton,* 17:348–49.

CHAPTER THREE

1 *GUS,* July 24, 1795.

2 *Dunlap and Claypoole's,* July 25, 1795. The committee appointed to draft the resolution consisted of Philadelphia's leading Republicans, including Thomas McKean, William Shippen, Alexander J. Dallas, and John Swanwick, among others.

3 See Richard G. Miller, *Philadelphia—The Federalist City: A Study of Urban Politics, 1789–1801* (Port Washington, N.Y., 1976), pp. 71–72, for a description of the meetings. For the text of the memorial see *Dunlap and Claypoole's,* July 28, 1795.

4 For accounts of the July 10 Boston meeting see *Independent Chronicle,* July 13, 1795; *American Minerva,* July 17, 1795; and *Dunlap and Claypoole's,* July 18, 1795. The question debated by Hall and Jarvis, as to whether it was proper for citizens to act on the measure, is explored in much greater detail in chap. 3 below.

5 See the accounts cited in the previous note. The committee consisted of Charles Jarvis, Thomas Dawes, William Tudor, Benjamin Austin, Jr., William Little,

Thomas Walley, William Cooper, Nathaniel Fellows, Samuel Brown, Stephen Gorham, John Sweetser, Perez Morton, William Eustin, George Blake, and Joseph Blake, Jr.

6 Details of the Boston meeting and its anti-treaty resolutions were spread quickly to other towns by newspapers which reprinted descriptions of the rallies and the text of the resolutions. The transmission through newspapers, and the subsequent imitation of events in Boston by those who read the newspaper accounts, underscore the argument of David Waldstreicher for the primacy of newspapers in the development of a national political culture. See his "Rites of Rebellion, Rites of Assent: Celebrations, Print Culture, and the Origins of American Nationalism," *Journal of American History* 82 (1995), 37–61; and, for a fuller discussion, his *In the Midst of Perpetual Fetes: The Making of American Nationalism, 1776–1820* (Chapel Hill, 1997).

7 See *Independent Chronicle,* July 16, 1795, for the text of the Boston resolutions opposing the treaty.

8 Charles Warren (ed.), *Jacobin and Junto, or Early American Politics as Viewed in the Diary of Dr. Nathaniel Ames, 1758–1822* (Cambridge, Mass., 1931), pp. 58–60.

9 *Columbian Centinel,* July 25, 1795; *American Minerva,* July 25, 1795; *Independent Chronicle,* July 27, 1795. My account of the New York meeting draws on these newspaper accounts and the excellent discussion of the New York protests found in Alfred F. Young, *The Democratic Republicans of New York: The Origins, 1763–1797* (Chapel Hill, 1967), pp. 445–67.

10 For newspaper accounts of the New York meeting see *Herald,* July 22, 1795; *American Minerva,* July 25, 1795; *Columbian Centinel,* July 25, 1795; and *Independent Chronicle,* July 27, 1795. Young, *Democratic Republicans,* pp. 449–54, has a detailed account of the New York proceedings. See also Paul A. Gilje, *The Road to Mobocracy: Popular Disorder in New York City, 1763–1834* (Chapel Hill, 1987), pp. 102–04; and Graham Russell Hodges, *New York City Cartmen, 1687–1850* (New York, 1986), pp. 95–96. On Hamilton and the duel challenges see Joanne B. Freeman, "Dueling as Politics: Reinterpreting the Burr-Hamilton Duel," *William and Mary Quarterly,* 3d ser., 53, no. 2 (1996), 307.

11 See *American Minerva,* July 25, 1795, for the text of the resolutions, which were widely reprinted.

12 Accounts of the Portsmouth, New Hampshire, demonstrations are found in *Dunlap and Claypoole's,* September 22, 1795, and *Independent Chronicle,* October 8, 1795.

13 Jeffrey L. Pasley, *"The Tyranny of Printers": Newspaper Politics in the Early American Republic* (Charlottesville, 2001), pp. 91–94, quotation at p. 91. For additional discussion of the role of newspapers and printers in Philadelphia see Rosalind Remer, *Printers and Men of Capital: Philadelphia Book Publishers in the New Republic* (Philadelphia, 1996), esp. chap. 2.

14 John Beckley to James Madison, September 10, 1795, in *Papers of Madison,* 16:85–88. See also Edmund Berkeley and Dorothy Smith Berkeley, *John Beckley: Zealous Partisan in a Nation Divided* (Philadelphia, 1973), pp. 110–13; and Jeffrey Pasley, "'A Journeyman, Either in Law or Politics': John Beckley

and the Social Origins of Political Campaigning," *Journal of the Early Republic* 16 (1996), 550–53.

15 Fisher Ames to Oliver Wolcott, Jr., July 9, 1795, in *Papers of Wolcott,* 1:210.

16 George Cabot to Rufus King, July 25, 1795, and July 27, 1795, in *Life of King,* 2:17–20. See also Cabot to King, August 4, 1795, in ibid., 20–21.

17 Henry Van Schaak to Theodore Sedgwick, December 6, 1795, Sedgwick Papers I, Box B, Folder 2.15, Massachusetts Historical Society.

18 This feeling that they should take the pro-treaty message to the people in a vigorous campaign extended throughout the fall. One Federalist wrote, "Whatever may be the Fate of the Question, yet every Friend of our happy Government would wish that the Discussion should be full and explicit, and that the Public may see that if the Issue should be unfavorable, it has been in the Face of Truth and Propriety." See Peter Van Schaak to Theodore Sedgwick, November 19, 1795, Sedgwick Papers I, Box B, Folder 2.14, Massachusetts Historical Society. For a fuller discussion of Federalists and popular political activity see Simon P. Newman, *Parades and the Politics of the Street: Festive Culture in the Early American Republic* (Philadelphia, 1997), esp. chaps. 2 and 5.

19 "Fair Play," *Daily Advertiser,* July 3, 1795; reprinted in the *Jersey Chronicle,* July 11, 1795. This piece shows unmistakably how Federalists—at the outset of the public debate—expressed confidence in the "good sense of the people," a phrase that would reappear often in their writings. Interestingly, the *Jersey Chronicle* was Phillip Freneau's second newspaper (after the *National Gazette*). The paper was short-lived; its last issue came out on April 30, 1796—ironically, the very day that the House of Representatives ultimately voted to fund the treaty.

20 *GUS,* July 28, 1795; *American Minerva,* July 30, 1795. The *Minerva* piece concluded, "Let the people of America be on their guard and not fall a prey to false patriots." Of course, this is not to deny that some Federalists lashed out bitterly at those who demonstrated against the treaty. Jesse Appleton, president of Bowdoin College, wrote to Dartmouth professor Ebenezer Adams, asking, incredulously, "Do not ten thousand people take it upon themselves to judge of the merits of the treaty, who are intirely ignorant of [the commercial implications]? Is a man sufficiently cool & candid to decide on important political questions, when he sends brickbats at a very respectable fellow citizen [a reference to the stoning of Hamilton]? Can that be called a free discussion of a question, when one party is hissed & stoned & the other is clapped and applauded." Appleton then concluded acidly, "Who gave the common farmers, blacksmiths, and taylors sufficient knowledge to prove that two-thirds of the Senate are knaves or fools?" Jesse Appleton to Ebenezer Adams, August 4, 1795, Jesse Appleton Letters, American Antiquarian Society.

21 "Perseverando," *Columbian Centinel,* August 5, 1795.

22 Peter Van Schaak to Theodore Sedgwick, August 15, 1795, Sedgwick Papers I, Box B, Folder 2.14, Nos. 196–205, Massachusetts Historical Society.

23 For an early statement questioning the haste of treaty critics, particularly those in the cities, while praising the reserve of those in the countryside and calling for careful study of the document, see "A Middlesex Yeoman," *Columbian*

Centinel, August 5, 1795. See also four letters in *Columbian Centinel,* August 15, 1795, on the theme of the ability of those in the countryside to see the treaty issue clearly. Some also believed that the furor over the treaty was not likely to spread to "the great body of the people. The farmer returns from market, and [the] labourer attend to their daily avocations, without giving this momentous subject more than a transient thought. They seem generally content with their own prosperity, and to think others as happy as themselves." See *GUS,* August 15, 1795.

24 Oliver Wolcott, Jr., to Mrs. Wolcott, July 26, 1795, and William [Loughton] Smith to Wolcott, September 8, 1795, *Papers of Wolcott* 1:218, 230–31.

25 "Quiet," *American Minerva,* July 28, 1795. This piece, while calling upon treaty supporters to mobilize the public, nicely illustrates the older, paternal conception of politics to which many Federalists still clung. It speaks of the President as one "who loves you and watches over your political interests, as a father," and concludes that treaty opponents are raising a malicious false alarm. "Whenever your rights are *really* invaded; the firm band of patriots, who now support our administration, will be the first to sound the alarm."

26 Fisher Ames to Oliver Wolcott, Jr., July 9, 1795, *Papers of Wolcott,* 1:210. Ames went on to remark that he was perhaps "more provoked and discouraged than I should be. . . . It seemed as if the shining and prosperous period of our government would be safe and popular. But our federal ship is near foundering in a millpond. The pillars of the temple of liberty need holding up by the hand when the storm does not blow."

27 Rufus King to Christopher Gore, July 24, 1795, in *Life of King,* 2:17; George Cabot to King, August 4, 1795, ibid., 2:21. It should be noted, however, that not all Federalist leaders believed an immediate response to the treaty critics was needed. William Loughton Smith of South Carolina believed that only when tempers had cooled and men could discuss the treaty dispassionately would a reasoned defense of the measure have an impact. See Smith to Jedediah Morse, July 17, 1795, quoted in George C. Rogers, Jr., *Evolution of a Federalist: William Loughton Smith of Charleston, 1758–1812* (Columbia, S.C., 1962), p. 278.

28 Wolcott to Noah Webster, August 1, 1795, in *Papers of Wolcott,* 1:222.

29 William Vans Murray to Oliver Wolcott, Jr., August 7, 1795, in *Papers of Wolcott,* p. 223. Each of the vehicles—newspapers, pamphlets, broadsides—that Federalists discussed using to take their case to the public would reach a different audience. Newspapers had the broadest circulation, while pamphlets would likely be read by a smaller but more elite audience of opinion shapers. For a superb discussion see Joanne B. Freeman, *Affairs of Honor: National Politics in the New Republic* (New Haven, 2001), chap. 3.

30 Alexander Hamilton to William Bradford, June 13, 1795, in *Papers of Hamilton,* 18:374.

31 Hamilton wrote to Rufus King: "The common opinion among men of business . . . is that a disagreement to the Treaty would greatly shock and stagnate pecuniary plans and operations in general. This is not a small source of disquietude. Others who are not likely to be affected in that sense (and among these myself) look forward to the result with great soclicitude [*sic*] as fixing or

indangering the stability of our present beneficial desireable situation." Hamilton to King, June 20, 1795, in *Papers of Hamilton,* 18:383.

32 Hamilton to Oliver Wolcott, Jr., June 26, 1795, and June 30, 1795, in *Papers of Hamilton,* 18:388–89, 393.

33 Elizabeth Meredith to David Meredith, July 12, 1795, Meredith Family Papers, Box 3, Folder 5, Historical Society of Pennsylvania. Meredith's letter describes the burning of Jay in effigy on the evening of July 4th and the criticisms in opposition newspapers of the treaty and Federalist leaders.

34 See the excellent "Introductory Note" on the "Defence" essays in *Papers of Hamilton,* 18:475–79. See also John C. Miller, *Alexander Hamilton and the Growth of the New Nation* (New York, 1959), pp. 427–30; and Forrest McDonald, *Alexander Hamilton: A Biography* (New York, 1979), pp. 314–19. The pseudonym "Camillus," like most of Hamilton's others, came from Plutarch, after the figure who, against great opposition and enmity, articulated to the Roman public correct long-term policies "which, in their shortsighted greed and ignorance, they wished to reject." Plutarch's Marcus Furius Camillus (c. 446–365 BCE) was rejected by the very people he wished to help and guide, for their own and for their nation's good. No doubt, Hamilton saw himself as facing the prospect of similar treatment in 1795. See the discussion in Douglass Adair's essay, "A Note on Certain of Hamilton's Pseudonyms," in Trevor Colbourn (ed.), *Fame and the Founding Fathers: Essays by Douglass Adair* (1974; Indianapolis, 1998).

35 George Washington to Hamilton, July 3, 1795, in *Writings of Washington,* 34:226–28. Hamilton's response to Washington's request, "Remarks on the Treaty of Amity Commerce and Navigation," dated July 9–11, 1795, is found in *Papers of Hamilton,* 18:404–54.

36 *Papers of Hamilton,* 18:451–52.

37 "The Defence No. 2" (July 25, 1795), in *Papers of Hamilton,* 18:498; and "The Defence No. 3" (July 29, 1795), ibid., 18:516–17. Hamilton was emphatic here—as he would be in other writings—on the need to keep the U.S. out of war until it was stronger. "If we can avoid war for ten or twelve years more we shall then have acquired a maturity, which will make it no more than a common calamity and will authorise us on our national discussions to take a higher & more imposing tone. . . . [We must] exert all our prudence and address to keep out of War as long as it shall be possible to defer to a state of manhood a struggle to which infancy is ill-adapted. . . . We ought to be wise enough to see that this is not the time for trying our strength." See ibid., 18:499.

38 "The Defence No. 16" (September 18, 1795), in *Papers of Hamilton,* 19:277; "The Defence No. 12" (September 2–3, 1795), ibid., 19:231.

39 "The Defence No. 1" (July 22, 1795), in *Papers of Hamilton,* 18:480, 481, 483.

40 *Papers of Hamilton,* 18:484. Hamilton only slightly exaggerated the timing of the Boston meeting. Boston's *Independent Chronicle* published the first eight articles of the treaty on July 9. On July 13 the meeting opposed to the treaty was held at Faneuil Hall. See ibid., 18:484 n. 30.

41 *Papers of Hamilton,* 18:485–86.

42 "Philo Camillus No. 3," in *Papers of Hamilton,* 19:125. The four "Philo Camillus" essays were a rebuttal to an attack on "Camillus" by "Cinna," who was Brockholst Livingston. See ibid., 18:508 n. 1; and Stanley Elkins and Eric McKitrick, *The Age of Federalism: The Early American Republic, 1788–1800* (New York, 1993), p. 840 n. 177.

43 Noah Webster, "Vindication of the Treaty," *American Minerva,* July 18, 1795. For an editorial note concerning Webster's "Curtius" essays and their reprintings see Edwin Carpenter (ed.), *A Bibliography of the Writings of Noah Webster* (New York, 1958), p. 493. In addition to the newspapers, these essays were reprinted in Mathew Carey's *American Remembrancer* volumes on the Jay Treaty dispute.

44 See "An Address from Robert Goodloe Harper of South-Carolina, to his Constituents; Containing his Reasons for Approving of the Treaty of Amity, Commerce and Navigation with Great-Britain" (Boston, 1796); William Loughton Smith, "A Candid Examination of the Objections to the Treaty of Amity, Commerce, and Navigation" (Charleston, 1795); and "To the Citizens of New York," *GUS,* July 20, 1795. The public meeting to which Watson referred was the one Hamilton attempted to address before being struck with a stone and driven from the platform.

45 *American Minerva,* July 29, 1795. This editorial was in response to the *Baltimore Telegraphe,* which stated that "the Minerva and some other papers, hitherto the warm panegyrists of Mr. Jay and his Treaty, appear to have surrendered it up as a thing *indefensible.*" For the "three more gloomy weeks" quotation see Christopher Gore to Theodore Sedgwick, December 27, 1795, Sedgwick Papers I, Box B, Folder 2.15, Nos. 206–17, Massachusetts Historical Society.

46 *Columbian Centinel,* July 4, 1795. See also *American Minerva,* July 3, 1795; and "Candid Remarks on the Treaty," *GUS,* July 7, 1795, which offered an article-by-article defense of the treaty, following a preface which condemned the "spirit of party" and noted that, as regards the measure, for "those who are animated by a pure, and exclusive love of our country, truth will be acceptable."

47 *GUS,* July 13, 1795; "Americanus," *American Minerva,* July 22, 1795, and July 29, 1795. On the same theme from a slightly different perspective see "Nestor," who wrote that the treaty, "whatever are its merits, is the best that could be obtained, and as good a one as ought to have been expected," yet noted in his conclusion that he was a Revolutionary patriot, "sincerly [*sic*] attached to the cause of the French nation; I am a democrat . . . but I am at the same time, a friend to peace, good order, and effective government." See *American Minerva,* August 8, 1795.

48 This account of the New York pro-treaty meeting is drawn from Young, *Democratic Republicans,* esp. pp. 454–55; *New York Journal,* July 29, 1795; and *Dunlap and Claypoole's,* July 28, 1795. While this pro-treaty resolution claimed to speak for the whole of the Chamber of Commerce, one scholar has argued that Federalists exaggerated their support among merchants, since only one-third of the total membership was actually present for the meeting. See

Arthur Irving Bernstein, "The Rise of the Democratic-Republican Party in New York City, 1789–1800" (Ph.D. dissertation, Columbia University, 1964), esp. pp. 138–88. Still, Bernstein argues that whatever the numbers may have been, the Chamber resolution had great impact and encouraged Federalists in other cities to organize petition drives of their own. "The extensive space given in Republican papers in New York to the action of the Chamber of Commerce also is an indication that Federalists had scored their opponents. Moreover, the vicious nature of the Republican reaction showed that they had been deeply stung" (p. 160). It is precisely this point—on the effectiveness of the petition as a political device, which effectiveness Bernstein stresses—that I wish to emphasize as the most significant for my study of the public campaign for the treaty.

49 *GUS,* August 24, 1795.

50 Descriptions and the resolutions of the Boston Chamber of Commerce meeting of August 11, 1795, are found in *Dunlap and Claypoole's,* August 24, 1795; *American Minerva,* August 21, 1795; and *GUS,* August 21, 1795.

51 "Address of the Merchants and Traders of Philadelphia to the President," *GUS,* August 22, 1795; Washington's reply is found in "To the Citizens of Philadelphia," in *Writings of Washington,* 34:278–79. The Philadelphia pro-treaty resolution was the product of a concerted effort on the part of Philadelphia merchants and Federalist leaders working to organize support, and was signed by 412 merchants. For more on these efforts see Miller, *Philadelphia—The Federalist City,* p. 73. Also see Harry M. Tinkcom, *The Republicans and Federalists in Pennsylvania, 1790–1801* (Harrisburg, Pa., 1950), pp. 87–90, 142–44. Federalists also organized counter-resolutions in Boston, the scene of violent anti-treaty protests. One such stated that while the Boston anti-treaty resolution had been construcd as representing "the unanimous sentiments of the merchants and other inhabitants," the subscribers to the pro-treaty petition, "unwilling to be implicated in the number of those who approve of the doings of that meeting . . . do hereby declare our disapprobation of and dissent from the votes of said meeting." *GUS,* August 24, 1795. Petitions from York, Pennsylvania, Portsmouth, New Hampshire, and Plymouth, Massachusetts, among others, stated some of the advantages of the treaty, argued for supporting the constituted authorities, and often mentioned their opposition to earlier town meetings condemning the treaty along with their reasons for disassociating themselves from the "disorganizing antifederalists" of earlier in the summer. See *Dunlap and Claypoole's,* August 22, 1795; *Independent Chronicle,* October 8, 1795; and *GUS,* November 24, 1795.

52 *Writings of Washington,* 34:252–53. This letter was also reprinted in Mathew Carey (ed.), *The American Remembrancer, or, an Impartial Collection of Essays, Resolves, Speeches, &c. Relative, or Having Affinity, to the Treaty with Great Britain,* 3 vols. (Philadelphia, 1795), 1:39. For Washington's conception of the president's role and his thinking on other constitutional matters see Glenn A. Phelps, *George Washington and American Constitutionalism* (Lawrence, Kans., 1993).

53 Robert R. Livingston to James Madison, July 6, 1795, in *Papers of Madison,* 16:34–35; Madison to Livingston, August 10, 1795, ibid., 16:46–48.

54 See James Madison, "To an Unidentified Correspondent," August 23, 1795, in *Papers of Madison,* 16:55–58; and "Draft of the Petition to the General Assembly of the Commonwealth of Virginia" (ca. September 1795), ibid., 16:62–77, especially the excellent discussion in the editorial note.

55 Thomas Jefferson to Mann Page, August 30, 1795, in *Papers of Jefferson,* 28:440–41. Only after concluding this metaphorical discussion did Jefferson make clear what he was referring to: "But metaphor apart, there is much dissatisfaction with Mr. Jay and his treaty."

56 Jefferson to James Monroe, September 6, 1795, in *Papers of Jefferson,* 28:448–49; Jefferson to Philip Mazzei, September 8, 1795, ibid., 28:456–57. For his part, James Monroe, who was serving in Paris as minister to France and dealing with a considerable time lag in receiving information from the United States, weighed in to Madison and Jefferson with assessments which echoed theirs about the domestic political implications, namely that the Federalists were now irretrievably in the open as an Anglophilic party. Monroe told Madison that he considered the treaty "as forming an important epoch. . . . It fully explains the views of its author and his political associates; views which were long known to many & charged upon him & them but denied . . . but this is an act which speaks for itself, & fortunately it is one in which not he alone is compromitted." Several weeks later Monroe considered the effects of the treaty on France: "If it is ratified, it may be deemed one of the most afflicting events that ever befell our country. Our connection here will certainly be weakened by it. . . . To bear the British aggressions & spoliations without resentment was one thing, but to make this treaty is another. . . . It is impossible for me to describe the mortification I daily undergo in this respect." See Monroe to James Madison, September 8, 1795, and October 23, 1795, in *Papers of Madison,* 16:81 and 16:106, respectively. For further elaboration see the discussion in Harry Ammon, *James Monroe: The Quest for National Identity* (Charlottesville, 1971), chap. 8.

57 Jefferson to Madison, September 21, 1795, in *Papers of Jefferson,* 28:475–77.

58 Jefferson to Madison, September 21, 1795, in *Papers of Jefferson,* 28:475–77. In October 1795, Jefferson wrote at greater length and elaborated on his understanding of the early history of the nation in his "Notes on the Letter of Christoph Daniel Ebeling," dated after October 15, 1795, by the *Papers of Jefferson* editors. Professor Ebeling, a German historian, had written Jefferson on July 30. Jefferson's sketches for a reply mention that, since Ebeling listed the American sources he consulted for information, "it may be useful for him to know how far he may rely on their authority." Jefferson proceeded to delineate a history of the young nation which had as its story line the steadily encroaching efforts of "Monocrats" to introduce British-style monarchy to the nation. Once made aware of these undertakings, the people became aroused and were still in the process of restoring true republican principles to the government. Jefferson also listed the newspapers which could (and could not) be trusted and discussed the composition of the two parties. See ibid., 28:506–10.

59 Tench Coxe to Jefferson, July 30, 1795, in *Papers of Jefferson,* 28:421–23; Henry Tazewell to Jefferson, July 1, 1795, ibid., 28:399–400.

60 Jefferson to Philip Mazzei, September 8, 1795, in *Papers of Jefferson,* 28:456–57; Jefferson to James Monroe, September 6, 1795, ibid., 28:448–449; Jefferson to Tench Coxe, September 10, 1795, ibid., 28:460–61; Jefferson to Madison, September 21, 1795, ibid., 28:475–77.

61 For the Randolph affair see Jerald A. Combs, *The Jay Treaty: Political Battleground of the Founding Fathers* (Berkeley, 1970), pp. 165–70 and 190–93; Alexander DeConde, *Entangling Alliance: Politics & Diplomacy Under George Washington* (Durham, N.C., 1958), pp. 119–27; Stanley Elkins and Eric McKitrick, *The Age of Federalism: The Early American Republic, 1788–1800* (New York, 1993), pp. 422–31; John E. Ferling, *The First of Men: A Life of George Washington* (Knoxville, 1988), pp. 458–62; and James T. Flexner, *Washington: The Indispensable Man* (Boston, 1974), pp. 332–37. For the most recent detailed consideration, see Mary K. Bonsteel Tachau, "George Washington and the Reputation of Edmund Randolph," *Journal of American History* 73 (1986), 15–34.

62 See Ferling, *First of Men,* p. 460.

63 Washington to Hamilton, July 29, 1795, in *Writings of Washington,* 34:262–64. The ten "Camillus" or "Defence" essays not written by Hamilton were penned by his friend and ally, Rufus King. The essays appeared in newspapers from July 1795 to January 1796, with the first appearing in New York on July 22 in the *Argus, or Greenleaf's New Daily Advertiser.* They were widely reprinted. See also Washington to Edmund Randolph, August 3, 1795, which discusses Washington's wish that answers to public resolutions on the treaty appearing in the papers, pro and con, be disseminated immediately so that there would be no time lag before a response. See ibid., 34:268–69. For a fuller consideration of Washington's role in shaping the pro-treaty campaign see Todd Estes, "The Art of Presidential Leadership: George Washington and the Jay Treaty," *The Virginia Magazine of History and Biography* 109 (2001), 127–58.

64 For the contrasting reactions of Bache and Dallas see James Tagg, *Benjamin Franklin Bache and the Philadelphia Aurora* (Philadelphia, 1991), pp. 251–54; and Raymond Walters, Jr., *Alexander James Dallas: Lawyer–Politician–Financier, 1759–1817* (Philadelphia, 1943), pp. 66 and 72–73.

65 Warren, *Jacobin and Junto,* p. 63.

66 See Tagg, *Benjamin Franklin Bache,* pp. 252ff.

67 Cabot to Oliver Wolcott, Jr., August 13, 1795, in *Papers of Wolcott,* 1:225.

68 Ames to Oliver Wolcott, Jr., September 2, 1795, in *Papers of Wolcott,* 1:229–30. See also William [Loughton] Smith to Oliver Wolcott, Jr., September 8, 1795, ibid., 1:230–31, in which Smith notes that his own pamphlet provided a check to anti-treaty feeling in Charleston, South Carolina, and "induced a considerable change of sentiment among the moderate, and prepared their minds to read with attention and candour *Camillus* and *Curtius.*" Comments such as these suggest the ways in which Federalist pro-treaty writings worked in an interlocking and mutually reinforcing way.

69 Gore to Rufus King, September 13, 1795, in *Life of King,* 2:31; Murray to Oliver Wolcott, Jr., October 2, 1795, in *Papers of Wolcott,* 1:249. Gore ex-

pressed similar sentiments in a later letter to King. "The politics of our country are really good, unless I am much deceiv'd. Every information from the interior has convinced me, that no evil is to be apprehended from the violent proceedings of the Seaports. The outrages of this town [Boston] have produced a belief among the husbandmen, that very different motives than a regard for the public good have occasion'd the opposition to the Treaty." Gore to King, November 19, 1795, in *Life of King,* 2:32. See also Peter Van Schaak to Theodore Sedgwick, December 14, 1795, Sedgwick Papers I, Box B, Folder 2.15, Nos. 206–17, Massachusetts Historical Society.

70 Washington to Samuel Hopkins, Jr., quoted in *GUS,* October 13, 1795; *GUS,* October 20, 1795.

71 *American Minerva,* December 7, 1795; Christopher Gore to Theodore Sedgwick, December 6, 1795, and December 27, 1795, both in Sedgwick Papers I, Box B, Folder 2.15, Massachusetts Historical Society. See also Henry Van Schaak to Theodore Sedgwick, January 15, 1796, Sedgwick Papers I, Box C, Folder 3.1, Massachusetts Historical Society; and Van Schaak to Sedgwick, February 20, 1796, Folder 3.2, for intelligence from towns in Vermont which, after the furor of the previous summer, were now reportedly calm and in support of the treaty and the administration.

72 Thomas Jefferson to James Madison, September 21, 1795, in *Papers of Jefferson,* 28:475–76.

73 Madison to Jefferson, December 13, 1795, and December 27, 1795, in James Morton Smith (ed.), *The Republic of Letters: The Correspondence between Jefferson and Madison, 1776–1826,* 3 vols. (New York, 1995), 2:903, 904–905. For Virginia's opposition to the Treaty and Madison's role see Thomas J. Farnham, "The Virginia Amendments of 1795: An Episode in the Opposition to Jay's Treaty," *The Virginia Magazine of History and Biography* 75 (1967), 75–88.

74 Washington to John Jay, December 21, 1795, in *Writings of Washington,* 34:397. For a report on Jay's letter to Washington see Combs, *Jay Treaty,* p. 170 and p. 223 n. 84. Hamilton to Washington, December 24, 1795, in *Papers of Hamilton,* 19:515; Ames to Theodore Sedgwick, December 31, 1795, in Sedgwick Papers I, Box B, Folder 2.15, Massachusetts Historical Society; Ames to Oliver Wolcott, Jr., December 31, 1795, in *Papers of Wolcott,* 1:295–96; Ames to Jeremiah Smith, January 18, 1796, in *Works of Ames,* 2:1130.

75 *American Minerva,* January 14, 1796 (the letter, from Charleston, South Carolina, is misdated December 1796); *American Minerva,* February 4, 1796. See also "Caroliniensis" in *GUS,* February 6, 1796, who argues, based on the writer's travels through the eastern states, that "a very great majority . . . perhaps I might say seven eighths, are perfectly well satisfied with the treaty, and with the administration," and suggests the effects of the Federalist campaign. "Many of them, no doubt, wish that the treaty could have been more advantageous, but they are persuaded that, under all circumstances, it was a wise and useful measure."

76 *GUS,* March 1, 1796.

CHAPTER FOUR

1 Quoted in William Bruce Wheeler, "Urban Politics in Nature's Republic: The Development of Political Parties in the Seaport Cities in the Federalist Era" (Ph.D. dissertation, University of Virginia, 1967), p. 269.

2 Accounts of the McClenachan incident are drawn from Edward C. Carter II, "The Political Activities of Mathew Carey, Nationalist" (Ph.D. dissertation, Bryn Mawr, 1962), p. 218; Richard G. Miller, *Philadelphia—The Federalist City: A Study of Urban Politics, 1789–1801* (Port Washington, N.Y., 1976), p. 72; and James Tagg, *Benjamin Franklin Bache and the Philadelphia Aurora* (Philadelphia, 1991), p. 249.

3 "Atticus," *Independent Gazetteer,* July 8, 1795.

4 John R. Howe, Jr., in his "Republican Thought and the Political Violence of the 1790s," *American Quarterly* 19 (1967), 147–65, rightly notes that "American political life during much of the 1790s was gross and distorted, characterized by heated exaggeration and haunted by conspiratorial fantasy" (p. 150). Howe argues that this is because both partisan factions shared the dominant republican ideology of the time. However, while Federalists undeniably could and did engage in hyperbole and exaggeration during that decade (and certainly did on occasion in the Jay Treaty debate), the debate was mostly marked by *Republican* overstatement and vituperativeness, whereas Federalists in their writings and public appearances tended to practice what they preached to the nation; that is, the calm, careful, rational study of the treaty. In this debate, at least, the anti-treaty side's rhetoric more consistently displayed the "heat" and "exaggeration" which often marked the politics of the 1790s.

5 Some of the most fascinating and illuminating work now being done by scholars of early America, broadly defined, examines language, rhetoric, oral versus print culture, and the transitions between various linguistic landscapes. Although the list of such works is vast, leading examples which have particular implications for the public sphere, broadly conceived, include three by Robert A. Ferguson, *Law and Letters in American Culture* (Cambridge, 1984); *The American Enlightenment, 1750–1820* (Cambridge, 1997); and "'We Hold These Truths': Strategies of Control in the Literature of the Founders," in Sacvan Bercovitch (ed.), *Reconstructing American Literary History* (Cambridge, 1986), pp. 1–28; Michael Warner, *The Letters of the Republic: Publication and the Public Sphere in Eighteenth-Century America* (Cambridge, 1990); David S. Shields, *Civil Tongues and Polite Letters in British America* (Chapel Hill, 1997); Michael T. Gilmore, "The Literature of the Revolutionary and Early National Periods," in Sacvan Bercovitch (ed.), *The Cambridge History of American Literature, Volume One: 1590–1820* (Cambridge, UK, 1994), pp. 541–693; Thomas Gustafson, *Representative Words: Politics, Literature, and the American Language, 1776–1865* (Cambridge, 1992); Jay Fliegelman, *Declaring Independence: Jefferson, Natural Language, and the Culture of Performance* (Stanford, 1993); Jane Kamensky, *Governing the Tongue: The Politics of Speech in Early New England* (New York, 1997); Murray Edelman, *Constructing the Political Spectacle* (Chicago, 1988); Robert Hariman, *Political Style: The Artistry of Power* (Chicago, 1995); Kenneth

Cmiel, *Democratic Eloquence: The Fight Over Popular Speech in Nineteenth-Century America* (New York, 1990); Cynthia S. Jordan, "'Old Words' in 'New Circumstances': Language and Leadership in Post-Revolutionary America," *American Quarterly* 40 (1988), 491–513; and Sandra M. Gustafson, *Eloquence is Power: Oratory and Performance in Early America* (Chapel Hill, 2000). More broadly see Richard D. Brown, *Knowledge is Power: The Diffusion of Information in Early America, 1700–1865* (New York, 1989). Such concerns are also central to David Waldstreicher's *In the Midst of Perpetual Fetes: The Making of American Nationalism, 1776–1820* (Chapel Hill, 1997).

6 *Aurora,* August 14, 1795. "Notice is hereby given That in case the Treaty entered into by that d—n Arch Traitor J—n J-y with the British tyrant should be ratified—A petition will be presented to the next General Assembly of Virginia at their next session, praying that the said state may recede from the Union, and be left under the government and protection of ONE HUNDRED THOUSAND FREE AND INDEPENDENT VIRGINIANS."

7 For an excellent discussion—and further examples—of the often hyperbolic Republican press, see Donald H. Stewart, *The Opposition Press of the Federalist Period* (Albany, N.Y., 1969), chap. 6, esp. pp. 208–21; and Jeffrey L. Pasley, *"The Tyranny of Printers": Newspaper Politics in the Early American Republic* (Charlottesville, 2001), esp. pp. 91–97. See also the illuminating discussion of the New York newspaper wars in Alfred F. Young, *The Democratic-Republicans of New York: The Origins, 1763–1797* (Chapel Hill, 1967), chap. 21.

8 "Ca Ira," *Independent Chronicle,* July 20, 1795; *Aurora,* July 23, 1795, and July 30, 1795.

9 *Aurora,* July 30, 1795, and August 5, 1795. The latter issue went on to state plainly, "There is but one touchstone by which to try the treaty—JUSTICE. If it is incompatible with this, no collateral considerations ought to give a gloss to it—no influence distinct from its merits, ought to be a pretext for its acceptance—Can there be such a monopoly of wisdom as to incapacitate all but one man or a few to judge of the treaty?"

10 *Independent Chronicle,* August 10, 1795; *Aurora,* August 27, 1795.

11 *Aurora,* August 12, 1795; "Atticus," ibid., September 16, 1795; ibid., October 1, 1795.

12 *Aurora,* August 22, 1795. The editorial continued, "His conduct has impair'd their [the public's] obligations to him, and instead of being longer viewd as the father of his country, we behold in him a master. The new character he has disclosed ought to awaken us to our situation, and teach us to shake off the fetters that his name has hitherto imposed upon the minds of freemen." James Tagg sees Washington's decision to sign the treaty as a turning point for Bache and his position regarding the president. In July and August of 1795, Tagg argues, Bache tried mainly to fan public opposition in order to persuade Washington not to sign. Once he did sign, the *Aurora* kept up an unremitting attack which dealt not so much with specific parts of the treaty or with the consequences of ratification, but, instead, with general arguments and an appeal to reject the treaty on the grounds of nationalism. In this critique, Bache raised

four main points: Britain was a dishonorable ally; the talk of war by Federalists was a ruse to avoid addressing the substance of a bad treaty; the treaty would harm U.S. relations with France; and (in the most sustained theme) the democratic will of the people was opposed to the treaty. See Tagg, *Benjamin Franklin Bache,* chap. 9. Many opponents likewise argued that the treaty would be harmful to the French. For one expression of this viewpoint see "Gracchus," who argued that a "hostility to the cause of France" consistently underlay many of the administration's actions and policies, including the treaty. *Independent Chronicle,* October 1, 1795.

13 *Aurora,* August 22, 1795. For similar expressions of this theme see *Aurora,* August 27, 29, and 31, and September 11, 1795. The last disparaged Washington's polite and supportive reply to a "*few individuals*" and his pointed insult to the people of the larger community. See also Tagg, *Benjamin Franklin Bache,* p. 252.

14 "Hancock," *Aurora,* August 27, 1795. These points were developed at length in this essay. "His answer to the *merchants & traders* of this city is in a stile different from that addressed to *the people,* that we should be tempted to believe the merchants and traders were the only people who had any claim to *respect,* who possessed any *information* & who had any *rights* among us . . . the contrast between the President's answer to the merchants and traders and that to the great body of the people, exhibits a trait in the present visage of our politics, which is astonishing and alarming. Altho' the constitution recognizes the right to petition, yet that right & the people who exercised it have been treated with the grossest disrespect; while the flatterers of public measures have received the most courteous attention."

15 "Atticus," *Independent Chronicle,* September 3, 1795. This piece also appears in the *Aurora* for September 21, 1795. The possibility of impeachment was broached by the *Aurora* periodically in the fall of 1795. "Pittachus" wrote in November that "The Opinion that the President ought to be *impeached* is gaining proselytes daily, and will soon become general as the subject is more fully understood." See *Aurora,* November 18, 1795.

16 "Pittachus," *Aurora,* November 23, 1795, and November 2, 1795. He concluded in the November 23 essay, "Let the President of the United States lay his hand upon his heart and say whether he has not inflicted an incurable evil upon the United States—whether his pageantry, his plans and his favouritism have not poisoned the sources of our felicity, and promised curses to posterity."

17 *Independent Chronicle,* January 21, 1796.

18 "One Eye Shut" and "A Carolinian Not Convinced," *State-Gazette,* October 15, 1795; *Aurora,* November 12, 1795.

19 This is not to deny that Federalists could be as acid-tongued as some Republicans in the treaty debate. See the pamphlet of the always contentious and acerbic William Cobbett, writing as "Peter Porcupine" in the *Political Censor, or Monthly Review of the Most Interesting Political Occurrences of The United States of America* (Philadelphia, 1796).

20 *GUS,* July 8, 1795. In this lengthy piece, Fenno set forth a moderate, realistic

tone and argued that the terms of the treaty were as good as the United States could expect. He also attacked the critics of the measure as dangerous, irresponsible malcontents—another recurring theme of the Federalists' campaign—emphasized the realities of the negotiating situation, and praised what the treaty did accomplish. On the theme of Jay's dealings with the British, Fenno continued, "But in truth he had to deal neither with fools nor supplicants, but with a people wise and politic, tho' deluded; with statesmen deep and experienced, tho' dishonest and corrupted."

21 *GUS,* July 8, 1795, and August 1, 1795.

22 "Nestor," *Daily Advertiser,* August 13, 1795; "William Willcocks," *Independent Chronicle,* September 14, 1795; *American Minerva,* September 17, 1795. Webster wrote in the *Minerva,* "Thus popular disturbances, though they menace the public peace for a moment, yet they awaken investigation and rouse the dormant faculties of a nation; they strip hypocrit[e]s and deceivers of their disguise, unfold the real merits of deceiving characters, and of salutary measures, and in the end, winnow the chaff from the wheat, and render truth triumphant."

23 *American Minerva,* July 11, 1795, and October 1, 1795.

24 "Curtius," "Vindication of the Treaty" no. 12, in *American Minerva,* August 6, 1795.

25 *GUS,* July 23, 1795; July 29, 1795; August 8, 1795. The August piece argued that opponents had injected "their poisonous prejudices into their unwary fellow citizens, even while the treaty . . . was in embryo, and who, if we may form a judgment from their incorrigible implacability, would as readily have condemned a treaty formed by the Hierarchy of Heaven, if it came sanctioned by any branch of our Executive department."

26 "Nestor," *GUS,* November 20, 1795; "An American," *GUS,* February 10, 1796.

27 This point is nicely made by Stanley Elkins and Eric McKitrick, *The Age of Federalism: The Early American Republic, 1788–1800* (New York, 1993), pp. 432–33.

28 Robert Livingston wrote sixteen "Cato" essays which appeared beginning July 15, 1795, in the New York paper *Argus, or Greenleaf's New Daily Advertiser* and ran periodically until the end of September. Brockholst Livingston wrote eleven essays, five as "Decius" and six more as "Cinna," which also appeared in the *Argus,* July 10–16, 1795, and August 1–18, 1795. Dallas's lengthy piece appeared first in *Dunlap and Claypoole's* in July and August 1795. "Cato," "Decius," and "Cinna" were reprinted in Mathew Carey (ed.), *The American Remembrancer, or an Impartial Collection of Essays, Resolves, Speeches, &c. Relative, or Having Affinity, to the Treaty with Great Britain* (Philadelphia, 1795), published in three volumes. Despite the title and its protestations of impartiality, Carey—who was staunchly opposed to the treaty—constructed the *Remembrancer* as an argument stacked solidly against the measure. Just as he had done with an earlier collection of documents, *Treaty of Amity, Commerce and Navigation,* Carey "neatly edited the collection so as to produce an overwhelming indictment against the Treaty. . . . The over-all effect of the col-

lection was anti-Treaty." See Edward Carter, "Political Activities of Mathew Carey," pp. 221–26, quotation at p. 224. Dallas's "Features of Mr. Jay's Treaty" is reprinted in George M. Dallas, *Life and Writings of Alexander James Dallas* (Philadelphia, 1871).

29 Raymond Walters, Jr., *Alexander James Dallas: Lawyer, Politician, Financier, 1759–1817* (Philadelphia, 1943), p. 66.

30 Jefferson to Madison, September 21, 1795, in *Papers of Madison,* 16:88. Yet Jefferson remained hopeful that a proper attack written by the right pen might still reverse the situation. "A solid reply," he told Madison, "might yet completely demolish what was too feebly attacked, and has gathered strength from the weakness of the attack."

31 See Jeffrey L. Pasley, "'A Journeyman Either in Law or Politics': John Beckley and the Social Origins of Campaigning," *Journal of the Early Republic* 16 (1996), 550. Pasley argues that Beckley was useful to Jefferson and Madison because he gladly assumed the necessary role of political professional and operative and, by doing so, allowed the Virginia leaders to maintain only a distant involvement in party politics, thus preserving their claims to be above the fray. For elaboration see Pasley, "*The Tyranny of Printers.*"

32 "A Detestable Faction," *Independent Gazetteer,* August 1, 1795. The final point made it clear where the writer stood on the European situation: "10th. And principally because we revere the cause of France, and heartily and gratefully wish her success over the hosts of tyrants leagued against her, and particularly over the despot of Great Britain, who we consider as our greatest foe, we are, and I hope ever will continue, A detestable faction."

33 *Aurora,* August 29, 1795. See also "Hancock" in *Aurora,* August 27, 1795, for the same sarcastic point about Washington. Republican leaders were dismayed at the dismissive tone they read in Washington's replies to anti-treaty petitions. Thomas Jefferson observed to James Madison—in a letter that bitterly denounced Federalist efforts, saying, "A bolder party-stroke was never struck"—that the apparent calming of public sentiment was due in large part to "the President's chiding answer to Boston & Richmond." See Jefferson to Madison, September 21, 1795, in *Papers of Madison,* 16:88–89. Thomas Paine, writing from Paris to James Madison, noted that with the ratification and signing of the treaty "America is falling fast into disesteem," and denounced the Federalists' plans for government as being "too much on the plan of European Courts and Mr. Washington appears to be too fond of playing the old Courtier." Paine to Madison, September 24, 1795, ibid., 16:92–93.

34 "Mr. Jay's Treaty," *Jersey Chronicle,* September 12, 1795.

35 *Jersey Chronicle,* September 19, 1795.

36 *Aurora,* August 20, 1795.

37 "Oneirophilus," *Aurora,* January 23, 1796.

38 *Aurora,* March 5, 1796, and March 23, 1796.

39 *American Minerva,* July 27, 1795; *GUS,* July 29, 1795.

40 See "Mr. Frothup's Beer-House," *GUS,* August 20, 1795.

41 "Chronicles II, Chapter 37," *GUS,* September 1, 1795.

42 "Federal Ship News," *GUS*, November 24, 1795.

43 *American Minerva*, January 13, 1796.

44 See the discussion in Gustafson, *Eloquence is Power*, esp. pp. 140–70 and 267–70.

CHAPTER FIVE

1 See *Aurora*, September 28, 1795, for the description of the town meeting and the resolution. The representative from the western district of Vermont was Israel Smith, but the petition was sent to Daniel Buck as well, prompting his response. Born in 1753 in Connecticut and trained as a lawyer, Buck served in the Revolutionary War and lost an arm in the battle of Bennington. Although Buck initially opposed ratification of the Constitution, he eventually supported it and served as attorney general for Vermont and in the state assembly. At the time of the Jay Treaty debate he was serving his first term in Congress. For biographical data see *Dictionary of American Biography* and David Hackett Fischer, *The Revolution of American Conservatism: The Federalist Party in the Era of Jeffersonian Democracy* (New York, 1965), pp. 239–40.

2 Buck's reply is in *Claypoole's*, March 3, 1796, although his letter to Timothy Browson, chairman of the Bennington County convention, is dated January 5, 1796. See also *Rural Magazine, or Vermont Repository* (January 1796) for Buck's letter. For his more general response to constituents about petitioning see Buck's "To the freemen of the Eastern district of Vermont," *American Minerva*, December 26, 1795.

3 Address of Newberry County, South Carolina, to Robert Goodloe Harper, *State-Gazette*, May 6, 1796, reprinted in *American Minerva*, May 26, 1796.

4 For the notion of the public sphere and its applicability in a variety of contexts see Jurgen Habermas, *The Structural Transformation of the Public Sphere* (Cambridge, Mass., 1989); Craig Calhoun (ed.), *Habermas and the Public Sphere* (Cambridge, Mass., 1992); Arlette Farge, *Subversive Words: Public Opinion in Eighteenth-Century France* (University Park, Penn., 1995); and the discussion in chapter one above. For important discussions of the public sphere in the early United States see Simon P. Newman, *Parades and the Politics of the Streets: Festive Culture in the Early American Republic* (Philadelphia, 1997); and David Waldstreicher, *In the Midst of Perpetual Fetes: The Making of American Nationalism, 1776–1820* (Chapel Hill, 1997).

5 Edmund S. Morgan, *Inventing the People: The Rise of Popular Sovereignty in England and America* (New York, 1988), p. 230. For fuller discussions of petitioning see Morgan pp. 224–30; and especially Alison G. Olson, "Eighteenth-Century Colonial Legislatures and Their Constituents," *Journal of American History* 79 (1992), 543–67. Olson cites studies that discuss petitioning in particular colonies. For examples of petitioning in a wide range of causes see also Lori D. Ginzburg, *Women and the Work of Benevolence* (New Haven, 1990); Ruth Bogin, "Petitioning and the New Moral Economy of Post-Revolutionary America," *William and Mary Quarterly*, 3d. ser., 45 (1988), 391–425; Harry Watson, "'The Common Rights of Mankind': Subsistence, Shad, and Commerce in the Early Republican South," *Journal of American History* 83 (1996), 13–43;

and Richard John, "Taking Sabbatarianism Seriously: The Postal System, the Sabbath, and the Transformation of American Political Culture," *Journal of the Early Republic* 10 (1990), 517–67. For examples of Revolutionary era instructions to representatives see Pauline Maier, *American Scripture: Making the Declaration of Independence* (New York, 1997), pp. 225–34. For additional documentary examples see Philip B. Kurland and Ralph Lerner (eds.), *The Founders' Constitution,* 5 vols. (1987; Indianapolis, 2000), 5:186–208.

6 The preceding paragraphs and the quotations cited are drawn from the record of the House of Representatives debate over amendments to the Constitution on August 15, 1789, reprinted in Kurland and Lerner, *The Founders' Constitution,* 5:200–06. The original debate may be found in *Annals of Congress. The Debates and Proceedings in the Congress of the United States,* 42 vols. (Washington, D.C., 1834–56), 1:731–45.

7 Accounts of the Boston town meeting can be found in the *Independent Chronicle,* July 13 and 16, 1795, and in *Dunlap and Claypoole's,* July 18, 1795.

8 *Independent Chronicle,* July 13 and 16, 1795; *Dunlap and Claypoole's,* July 18, 1795.

9 "Atticus," *Aurora,* September 4, 1795.

10 Charge by Judge W. Stith, Jr., to grand jury of Chatham County, Georgia, in Savannah (August 4, 1795), in Mathew Carey (ed.), *The American Remembrancer, or an Impartial Collection of Essays, Resolves, Speeches, &c. Relative, or Having Affinity, to the Treaty with Great Britain,* 3 vols. (Philadelphia, 1795), 2:53; "The Petition and Remonstrance of the Subscribers, Citizens of the State of New-Jersey," *Dunlap and Claypoole's,* July 16, 1795.

11 *Dunlap and Claypoole's,* July 28, 1795, and August 22, 1795.

12 *Aurora,* August 13, 1795; *Dunlap and Claypoole's,* August 8, 1795.

13 *Aurora,* August 24, 1795; *Dunlap and Claypoole's,* July 25, 1795.

14 "Petition to the General Assembly of the Commonwealth of Virginia," in *Papers of Madison,* 16:95–104, quotations at 95. Jefferson to Madison, September 21, 1795, ibid., 16:88–89. For more on Madison's role see Jeffrey L. Pasley, "'A Journeyman, Either in Law or Politics': John Beckley and the Social Origins of Political Campaigning," *Journal of the Early Republic* 16 (1996), 531–69, and Lance Banning, *The Sacred Fire of Liberty: James Madison and the Founding of the Federal Republic* (Ithaca, 1995), pp. 380–84.

15 Madison, "Who Are the Best Keepers of the People's Liberties?" *National Gazette,* December 22, 1792, reprinted in *Papers of Madison,* 14:426–27. See, for elaboration, the excellent discussion of these essays in Banning, *Sacred Fire of Liberty,* pp. 361–65.

16 Madison, "Political Reflections," *Aurora,* February 23, 1799, reprinted in *Papers of Madison,* 17:238–39. Also see Banning, *Sacred Fire,* p. 379.

17 "To the Boston Selectmen," July 28, 1795, in *Writings of Washington,* 34:252–53. This statement and ones very similar to it were sent by Washington in response to the cascade of petitions he received from other groups condemning the treaty and urging him not to ratify. This reply was also reprinted in Mathew Carey's widely distributed *The American Remembrancer* along with many of

the most pertinent statements on the treaty; see 2:38–39. For fuller discussion of Washington's role in the debate, including the significance of the Boston selectmen letter, see Todd Estes, "The Art of Presidential Leadership: George Washington and the Jay Treaty," *Virginia Magazine of History and Biography* 109 (2001), 127–58.

18 See Newman, *Parades and the Politics of the Streets,* chap. 6. The standard works on Federalism are David Hackett Fischer, *The Revolution of American Conservatism: The Federalist Party in the Age of Jeffersonian Democracy* (New York, 1965); Linda Kerber, *Federalists in Dissent: Imagery and Ideology in Jeffersonian America* (Ithaca, N.Y., 1970); and James Banner, *To The Hartford Convention: Federalists and the Origins of Party Politics in Massachusetts, 1789–1815* (New York, 1970).

19 "Curtius" no. 11, *American Minerva,* August 4, 1795.

20 *GUS,* September 12, 1795. For the same theme see also "A Subscriber," ibid., September 18, 1795, on the matter of how people delegate sovereignty to their elected officials. Both of these pieces illustrate the older conception of public responsibility in public issues.

21 *GUS,* July 29, 1795.

22 *GUS,* September 5, 1795. The *Gazette* also printed a three-part article by "An American" which contained a strong defense of Washington's conduct. Far from dismissing or ignoring the sentiments of the people, as treaty critics charged, "he declares that he has weighed with attention every argument which has ever been brought into his view; but that the constitution was his guide, which he could never abandon." Ibid., September 8, 1795. Hammering away at the theme of Washington's actions in support of the treaty as being fully constitutional, another correspondent noted that when "the President ratifies a treaty with and by the consent of the Senate, he does no more than execute the *public will* of the sovereign people of Amer[i]ca, who have solemnly ceded to him and his successors, a portion of their sovereignty for that very purpose." Ibid., September 18, 1795.

23 Resolution of the Boston Chamber of Commerce, August 11, 1795, in *GUS,* August 21, 1795.

24 *Georgia Gazette,* March 10, 1796; *Pittsburgh Gazette,* March 12, 1796, and *Western Telegraphe,* March 15, 1796. These views were consistently reinforced in Federalist newspapers. "Either the Constituted Authorities of the Union, as established by the Constitution of THE PEOPLE, must be supported entire, or anarchy must ensue!" See "A Plain Case" in *Columbian Centinel,* April 6, 1796. For more on the Federalists' view of the proper delegation of authority see ibid., April 27, 1796.

25 *Western Telegraphe,* April 26, 1796.

26 For a description of the Allegheny County, Pennsylvania, petitioning procedures see *Pittsburgh Gazette,* March 12, 1796.

27 *Dunlap and Claypoole's,* August 21, 1795; ibid., August 22, 1795; *Independent Chronicle,* October 8, 1795. The petitioners from Portsmouth also noted that they "strongly feel the impropriety of interference, as our best interests

may be hazarded in our future engagements with foreign nations, from their supposing no confidence can be placed in the negociations of the constitutional powers of the country." See also the grand jury resolution of Rensselaer County, New York, which read in part: "The Grand Jury, being also deeply impressed with the necessity of due submission to the constituted authorities, feel great satisfaction in declaring their perfect conviction, that every thing which human wisdom could devise, for the interest of this country, has hitherto been done by their various rulers." See *Claypoole's,* January 13, 1796.

28 *GUS,* July 29, 1795.

29 Resolution of the New York Chamber of Commerce meeting at the Tontine Coffee House, July 21, 1795, in *Dunlap and Claypoole's,* July 28, 1795. For his part, Alexander Hamilton was willing to go door-to-door if necessary to gauge public opinion and support for the constituted authorities. He "proposed several methods in order to 'obtain the true sense of the people, which had not been done, although asserted to have been.' One of the proposals was, 'to go round in the several wards of the city to the people individually.' He adds, 'we will let the question respecting the treaty, rest in the constitutional authority, and put the question to the people, *are you for or against the constitutional authorities!*'" See "Address on the Jay Treaty," *Papers of Hamilton,* 18:526. This address, a report on Hamilton's speech of July 30, 1795, was printed in *Argus,* August 13, 1795.

30 See *GUS,* August 22 and 24, 1795; and *Dunlap and Claypoole's,* August 24, 1795.

31 *GUS,* August 8, 1795; *Dunlap and Claypoole's,* August 21, 1795; *GUS,* August 19, 1795; *Claypoole's,* January 13, 1796. How deeply these sentiments were ingrained in Federalist thinking is suggested by toasts drunk in February 1796 on the occasion of George Washington's birthday: "The Constituted Authorities of our Country; may they ever meet the approbation and the support of their constituents," and "The constituted authorities of the United States—may they be loved, respected and obeyed, as the organs of a free people." See *Claypoole's,* February 27 and March 1, 1796. For additional examples of Federalists expressing similar themes see *GUS,* September 12 and 18, 1795; Daniel Morgan, "To the Inhabitants of Frederick County," *GUS,* November 11, 1795; and *Claypoole's,* January 25, 1796.

32 *State-Gazette,* May 6, 1796. Also *American Minerva,* May 26, 1796.

33 *American Minerva,* May 27, 1796.

34 *GUS,* June 3, 1796. Page's letter is dated May 7, approximately one week after the House vote.

35 See the petitions to Smith dated April 18 (*Claypoole's,* April 27, 1796) and April 24 (*Baltimore Telegraphe,* May 2, 1796).

36 Smith's replies are found in the *Baltimore Telegraphe,* May 2, 1796, and *American Minerva,* May 4, 1796. Federalists, knowing Smith's easily bruised temperament, genuinely worried about the effect the instructions might have on his vote. Rufus King wrote to Hamilton that the Baltimore merchants had drawn up a petition "in which they request *and instruct* him" to promote the treaty. King thought Smith was inclined to support the measure already, "but

I am apprehensive his Pride will be so wounded by *this instruction,* that he may vote agt. his Judgement, to prove his independence." See King to Hamilton, April 20, 1796, in *Papers of Hamilton,* 20:125. For more on Smith see Frank A. Cassell, *Merchant Congressman in the Young Republic: Samuel Smith of Maryland, 1752–1839* (Madison, Wis., 1971).

37 See *Rutland Herald,* May 16 and 23, 1796; *American Minerva,* May 31, 1796; and *Herald,* June 1, 1796.

CHAPTER SIX

1 Dwight Foster Journal, April 20 and 23, 1796, vol. 3, Foster Family Papers, American Antiquarian Society.

2 Jesse Appleton to Ebenezer Adams, April 23, 1796, Jesse Appleton Letters, American Antiquarian Society.

3 Thomas Jefferson to Edward Rutledge, November 30, 1795, in Paul Leicester Ford (ed.), *Writings of Thomas Jefferson,* 10 vols. (New York, 1892–99), 7:40.

4 James Roger Sharp, *American Politics in the Early Republic: The New Nation in Crisis* (New Haven, 1993), p. 129, makes this point effectively.

5 The preceding paragraphs draw on Jerald A. Combs, *The Jay Treaty: Political Battleground of the Founding Fathers* (Berkeley, 1970), pp. 171–78; Stanley Elkins and Eric McKitrick, *The Age of Federalism: The Early American Republic, 1788–1800* (New York, 1993), pp. 441–45; James Roger Sharp, *American Politics in the Early Republic: The New Nation in Crisis* (New Haven, 1993), pp. 127–29; and John C. Miller, *The Federalist Era, 1789–1801* (New York, 1960), pp. 171–74. For Madison's reaction see James Madison to Thomas Jefferson, March 6, 1796, in *Papers of Madison,* 16:247. Washington's proclamation was printed in the *Philadelphia Gazette,* March 1, 1796.

6 For purposes of this discussion, the New England states are defined as Connecticut, Massachusetts, New Hampshire, Rhode Island, and Vermont. The middle states are Delaware, New Jersey, New York, and Pennsylvania. The southern states are Georgia, Kentucky, Maryland, North Carolina, South Carolina, Tennessee, and Virginia.

7 George Washington to Gourverneur Morris, March 4, 1796, in *Writings of Washington,* 34:483. For more on Washington's constitutional thought and actions see Glenn A. Phelps, *George Washington and American Constitutionalism* (Lawrence, Kans., 1993), esp. chap. 6.

8 "To the House of Representatives," March 30, 1796, in *Writings of Washington,* 35:2–5.

9 For a fuller discussion of Washington's role in the treaty debate see Todd Estes, "The Art of Presidential Leadership: George Washington and the Jay Treaty," *Virginia Magazine of History and Biography* 109 (2001), 127–58.

10 *Connecticut Gazette,* April 7, 1796; *GUS,* April 23, 1796; *Columbian Centinel,* April 20, 1796; Peter Van Schaak to Theodore Sedgwick, April 25, 1796, Sedgwick Papers I, Box B, Folder 2.14, Massachusetts Historical Society. Federalists had earlier noted expressions of public support on Washington's birth-

day, February 22, which they believed evinced strong support for the President generally. Samuel Henshaw held that Washington "stands much higher in the estimation of the People since the ratification of the Treaty than He did before." He wondered whether the "Universal rejoicings on the Anniversary birth Day of the Saviour of his Country" would open the eyes of political opponents. See Samuel Henshaw to Theodore Sedgwick, March 12, 1796, Sedgwick Papers I, Box C, Folder 3.2, Massachusetts Historical Society.

11 John Adams to Abigail Adams, January 20 and January 23, 1796, in Charles Francis Adams (ed.), *Letters of John Adams Addressed to His Wife,* 2 vols. (Boston, 1841), 2:190, 192.

12 "Codrus," *Aurora,* March 21, 1796; "Verity," *Independent Chronicle,* April 4, 1796.

13 *Aurora,* April 30, 1796; ibid., April 16, 1796. In the latter essay Bache wrote with typical hyperbole and acidity: "If the treaty is permitted to die for want of sustenance, the people are triumphant and free; if, on the contrary, this monster is gorged with the vital fluid of our rights, and by the aid of our representatives, the President will be as sovereign and omnipotent as the Demi God of a Turkish Seraglio, and the people will soon be in a condition little superior to the sable HERD at Mount Vernon." For another example of bringing strong pressure on the House, see *Aurora,* April 26, 1796.

14 *Aurora,* April 26, 1796. For more on the Republicans' efforts in New York see Alfred F. Young, *The Democratic Republicans of New York: The Origins, 1763–1797* (Chapel Hill, 1967), pp. 445–67.

15 *Independent Chronicle,* April 28, 1796, and also in *Federal Gazette,* April 28, 1796; *American Minerva,* May 9, 1796.

16 This paragraph draws on Lance Banning, *The Sacred Fire of Liberty: James Madison and the Founding of the Federal Republic* (Ithaca, 1997), pp. 380–84; see also the expansive endnotes which continue the discussion on pp. 530–32. For Jefferson's role and activities see Joseph J. Ellis, *American Sphinx: The Character of Thomas Jefferson* (New York, 1996), pp. 186–94; and James Morton Smith (ed.), *The Republic of Letters: The Correspondence between Thomas Jefferson and James Madison, 1776–1826,* 3 vols. (New York, 1995) 2:881–95. A recent student of the "founding friendship" between Madison and Washington argues that the Jay Treaty debate ruptured the friendship deeply. Madison still respected Washington, but the president was angered and felt betrayed by Madison's role in opposing the treaty. Washington never again consulted him or even invited him to family dinners, and Madison would never again visit Mount Vernon. See Stuart Leibiger, *Founding Friendship: George Washington, James Madison, and the Creation of the American Republic* (Charlottesville, Va., 1999), esp. pp. 197–209.

17 Fisher Ames to George Richards Minot, April 2, 1796, in *Works of Ames,* 2:1140; Ames to Christopher Gore, March 11, 1796, ibid., 2:1137–38; Henry Van Schaak to Theodore Sedgwick, March 23, 1796, Theodore Sedgwick Papers I, Box C, Folder 3.3, Massachusetts Historical Society. For his part, Ames thought little of Giles: "Giles has no scruples, and certainly less brains." *Works of Ames,* 2:1138.

18 Alexander Hamilton to Rufus King, April 15, 1796, in *Papers of Hamilton,* 20:112–15. Hamilton also rejected a suggestion made by some Federalists to link funding for the Jay Treaty to funding for the treaties with Spain and Algiers, hoping to force Republicans to take an unpopular treaty alongside more popular ones. Such a linkage, Hamilton thought, "will be altogether wrong & impolitic. The misconduct of the other party cannot justify in us an imitation of their principles. . . . Let us be *Right,* because to do right is instrinsically proper & I verily believe it is the best means of securing final success & let our adversaries have the whole glory of sacrificing the interest of the Nation." Not all Federalists believed that keeping the treaties separate was wise, as will be discussed later in this chapter.

19 *Western Telegraphe,* March 29, 1796.

20 *Potomak Guardian,* April 21 and 28, 1796; *GUS,* April 22, 1796. At this same time, Noah Webster's Federalist paper the *Columbian Centinel* published a pro-treaty, apparently Federalist piece echoing many of the themes the Federalists had stressed all along. But, problematically, the piece was signed "A Calm Observer," the Republican John Beckley's pseudonym. I can find no evidence suggesting that this piece was *not* Beckley's, but I also have found no evidence other than the signature to suggest that it was. What might account for this discrepancy? The internal evidence (reprinted below) suggests strongly that the author was a Federalist, perhaps one who mockingly assumed Beckley's pseudonym to taunt him. The piece praises the people for their "patience," "coolness and judgment," and emphasizes the importance of "reason," all themes of Federalist writings. The fact that it was published in Webster's paper and makes explicit reference to a pro-treaty Boston town meeting also suggests Federalist authorship. Furthermore, the tone and the points made do not sound like Beckley's views, nor do they square with charges he had made throughout the debate. It seems unlikely that Beckley would have written this piece, which essentially concedes defeat three days before the House voted on the Jay Treaty. Still, I cannot prove that it was written by a Federalist and not Beckley. Here is the piece:

> The result of the late town-meeting . . . respecting the treaty with *England,* is a clear proof, if any was wanting, that in all great and momentous concerns which may be brought before them; nothing but a fair and full discussion of the subject, is necessary, to induce them to act with wisdom.—It is only in cases where they are taken by surprise, that the transaction of the people do not do honor to their judgment and honesty. Never was a fairer opportunity for making the experiment that on the occasion referred to; and the candour and good sense of the inhabitants of *Boston,* was never more conspicuously evinced, than in the patience and decency with which they attended to the debates; or in the coolness and judgment, with which they made up their
> sentiments on the subject:—And I hope it will be an everlasting lesson to the friends of their country, not to despair of convincing their fellow-citizens, of what reason dictates to be their interest, when any great national question is to be agitated. ("A Calm Observer," *Columbian Centinel,* April 27, 1796.)

21 On this point I follow David Waldstreicher's suggestive study of the role of newspapers in spreading accounts of nationalist rites and practices. I see a similar development taking place with respect to the Jay Treaty debate. See *In the Midst of Perpetual Fetes: The Making of American Nationalism, 1776–1820* (Chapel Hill, 1997), esp. pp. 1–14. See also Simon P. Newman, *Parades and the Politics of the Street: Festive Culture in the Early American Republic* (Philadelphia, 1997), chaps. 5 and 6.

22 *American Minerva,* April 19, 1796; Young, *Democratic Republicans,* p. 464; Rufus King to Alexander Hamilton, April 20, 1796, in *Papers of Hamilton,* 20:124–25; Hamilton to King, April 24, 1796, ibid., 20:136. The full text of the merchants' petition is reproduced ibid., 20:127–28. Hamilton was informed of efforts elsewhere by his network of correspondents. In Albany, Federalists also appointed a committee to gather signatures, to great effect. See Philip Schuyler to Hamilton, April 25, 1796, ibid., 20:138–39; and Young, p. 465.

23 "To the Citizens Who Shall be Convened This Day in the Fields in the City of New York," *Papers of Hamilton,* 20:131–34.

24 *Massachusetts Mercury,* April 26, 1796.

25 "The Memorial of the Subscribers, Merchants, Traders Mechanics and Other, Citizens of Boston," Jeremy Belknap Papers, Reel 7, 161.C, Massachusetts Historical Society.

26 Ibid. This circular was reprinted in *GUS,* May 5, 1796, and *American Minerva,* May 7, 1796.

27 "The Petition of the Freemen of the Town of Hartford in the State of Connecticut," *American Mercury,* April 25, 1796; *American Minerva,* April 27, 1796; *GUS,* April 28, 1796.

28 For the Frederick-Town proceedings see *Federal Gazette,* April 28, 1796. For the Washington and Prince George's counties proceedings see *American Minerva,* May 2, 1796. Thomas Sprigg served two terms in the U.S. House beginning in 1793, the second—at the time of the debate—with his uncle Richard Sprigg. For more information on Sprigg see the *Biographical Directory of the American Congress, 1774–1927* (Washington, D.C., 1928). The Philadelphia merchants and traders petition to which Fitzsimons made reference is in *American Mercury* (Hartford), April 25, 1796.

29 *Columbian Centinel,* April 6, 1796; *Western Telegraphe,* March 15, 1796; *Columbian Centinel,* April 27, 1796.

30 For the memorials and petitions see *Claypoole's,* April 28, 1796; *Columbian Centinel,* April 27, 1796; *American Minerva,* May 2, 1796; *Columbian Centinel,* May 7, 1796.

31 *Albany Gazette,* April 25, 1796; *Columbian Centinel,* April 27, 1796.

32 "Brutus," *American Mercury,* April 25, 1796; *Massachusetts Spy,* April 27, 1796. For other petitions typical of those that mention the fear of war see the New Haven, Connecticut, memorial in *American Minerva,* May 5, 1796, and the East Hartford, Connecticut, memorial in *Columbian Centinel,* May 7, 1796; also see "A Friend to Peace," *Potomack Guardian,* April 21 and 28, 1796.

33 Actually, there were three other treaties lately negotiated and funded by con-

gress in that same session, all of which were considered beneficial and highly popular. The Pinckney Treaty with Spain, the treaty with Algiers, and the Greenville Treaty with the Northwest Indian tribes all either settled disputes, redressed grievances, or obtained concessions thought highly favorable to the United States. For more background on the diplomatic issues see Jerald A. Combs, *The History of American Foreign Policy,* 2nd ed. (New York, 1997), pp. 18–39. For important considerations of the place of the western territories in the new nation and their special concerns see the important body of work by Andrew R. L. Cayton, especially *The Frontier Republic: Ideology and Politics in the Ohio Country, 1780–1825* (Kent, Ohio, 1986); "Radicals in the Western World: The Federalist Conquest of Trans-Appalachian North America," in Barbara Oberg and Doron Ben-Atar (eds.), *Federalists Reconsidered* (Charlottesville, Va., 1998), pp. 77–96; "'When Shall We Cease to Have Judases?': The Blount Conspiracy and the Limits of the 'Extended Republic,'" in Ronald Hoffman (ed.), *Launching the "Extended Republic": The Federalist Era* (Charlottesville, Va., 1996), pp. 156–89; and "'Separate Interests' and the Nation-State: The Washington Administration and the Origins of Regionalism in the Trans-Appalachian West," *Journal of American History* 78 (1992), 39–67.

34 *Claypoole's,* March 26, 1796; *Western Telegraphe,* April 19, 1796. See also *Pittsburgh Gazette,* March 12, 1796. The petition of the New York merchants and traders also linked the two treaties. See *GUS,* April 21, 1796.

35 Christopher Gore to Theodore Sedgwick, February 18, 1796; David Sewall to Sedgwick, February 19, 1796; and Loring Andrews to Sedgwick, March 14, 1796, all in Theodore Sedgwick Papers I, Box C, Folder 3.2, Massachusetts Historical Society. Alexander Hamilton's letter to Rufus King of April 15, which discussed Federalist strategy for the weeks ahead, also speculates on the tactical maneuvering of the treaties through Congress. See *Papers of Hamilton,* 20:114–15.

36 *Boston Gazette,* April 25, 1796, and *Independent Chronicle,* April 25, 1796, both quoted in Donald H. Stewart, *The Opposition Press of the Federalist Period* (Albany, N.Y., 1969), pp. 225–26. See James Tagg, *Benjamin Franklin Bache and the Philadelphia Aurora* (Philadelphia, 1991), pp. 260–61; and the issues of the *Aurora* for April 1, 2, 4, and 11, 1796.

37 Quoted in Tagg, *Benjamin Franklin Bache,* p. 261. See Tagg, pp. 260–63, and Stewart, *Opposition Press,* pp. 224–35, for press coverage in this final phase of the treaty debate.

38 *Massachusetts Mercury,* May 10, 1796; *Columbian Centinel,* May 7, 1796. Both papers contain either the texts of memorials from various towns or lists of towns and the numbers of signatures affixed to the petitions. Additional petitions may be read in nearly any newspaper for April or May 1796, as they were widely reprinted.

39 For an insightful discussion of the means of "seeding" and "collecting" public opinion in the early republic see Joanne B. Freeman, "Slander, Poison, Whispers, and Fame: Jefferson's 'Anas' and Political Gossip in the Early Republic," *Journal of the Early Republic* 15 (1996), 25–57, as well as her *Affairs of Honor: National Politics in the New Republic* (New Haven, 2001), chap. 2.

40 *GUS,* April 2, 1796; "Epistolary," *Columbian Centinel,* April 16, 1796; *American Minerva,* April 18, 1796.

41 *GUS,* April 29 and April 30, 1796.

42 *GUS,* May 5 and May 6, 1796. The *Gazette* also editorialized on the significance of the large numbers of citizens signing petitions backing the treaty. "This is justly due the public. In our popular government it is of the greatest importance that an accurate idea should be formed of the predominant sentiments of the people, on the important subject of national faith, in fulfilling national contracts." Ibid., May 14, 1796. For more on Virginia's involvement in the debate see Richard R. Beeman, *The Old Dominion in the New Nation, 1788–1801* (Lexington, Ky., 1972), pp. 138–51.

43 Wm. Willcocks, *Connecticut Journal,* April 27, 1796. See also *Argus,* April 29, 1796; and Young, *Democratic Republicans,* p. 465. This piece is suggestive of class and racial divisions. For more on the Federalists and these issues and the related consideration of gender see Waldstreicher, *In The Midst of Perpetual Fetes,* chap. 6; Waldstreicher, "Federalism, the Styles of Politics, and the Politics of Style," in Oberg and Ben-Atar, *Federalists Reconsidered,* pp. 99–117; Rosemarie Zagarri, "Gender and the First Party System," ibid., pp. 118–34; Paul Finkelman, "The Problem of Slavery in the Age of Federalism," ibid., pp. 135–56; and Rosemarie Zagarri, "The Rights of Man and Woman in Post-Revolutionary America," *William and Mary Quarterly,* 3d Ser., 55 (1998), 203–30.

44 Henry Van Schaak to Theodore Sedgwick, April 16, 1796 (two letters), Sedgwick Papers I, Box C, Folder 3.4, Massachusetts Historical Society; Jesse Appleton to Ebenezer Adams, April 23, 1796, Jesse Appleton Letters, American Antiquarian Society; Dwight Foster Journal, entries for April 23–30, 1796, Foster Family Papers, vol. 3, American Antiquarian Society. Van Schaak, writing from Pittsfield, Massachusetts, seemed to be unaware of the heavy flow of petitions already arriving in Congress. He asked Sedgwick, "ought there not to be 'a counter current' to the Petitions, before Congress ag[ainst] the Treaty?" Van Schaak assured Sedgwick that, should such a measure be undertaken, it would "unquestionably support" the Federalists' view that the nation now backed the treaty.

45 *GUS,* April 20, 1796. See also the discussion of the stoppage of underwriting in *Massachusetts Spy,* April 27, 1796. The New York underwriters' meeting is also mentioned in Alexander Hamilton to Rufus King, April 18, 1796, in *Papers of Hamilton,* 20:123. See also Combs, *Jay Treaty,* pp. 179–80; Elkins and McKitrick, *Age of Federalism,* p. 446; and James Madison to Thomas Jefferson, April 23, 1796, in *Papers of Madison,* 16:335–36.

46 Dwight Foster Journal, April 25, 1796, and April 28, 1796, Foster Family Papers, vol. 3, American Antiquarian Society. Foster's extensive entries, especially from April 23 until the House vote on April 30, provide a rich and important first-hand perspective on the proceedings in the House. For other summaries of the congressional proceedings see Elkins and McKitrick, *Age of Federalism,* pp. 441–49; and Combs, *Jay Treaty,* pp. 171–88. For an in-depth analysis of the roll call votes on the Jay Treaty see Rudolph M. Bell, *Party and Faction in American Politics: The House of Representatives, 1789–1801* (Westport, Conn., 1973), pp. 54–58, 146–49.

47 Banning, *Sacred Fire of Liberty,* pp. 382–84, quotation at p. 382. For Madison's speeches on the treaty see *Papers of Madison,* 16:254–63 and 313–27.

48 John Adams to Abigail Adams, April 16, 1796, in Adams, *Letters of John Adams Addressed to His Wife,* 2:220–21. Adams warned, "If the voice of the nation should be finally and decidedly in favor of the treaty, there will be a mortified party, so bitter, rancorous and desperate, fomented by foreign influence, in opposition, that the government will be very much embarrassed, and the public service very uncomfortable."

49 John Beckley to James Monroe, April 2, 1796; Beckley to DeWitt Clinton, April 11, 1796, both in Gerard Gawalt (ed.), *Justifying Jefferson: The Political Writings of John James Beckley* (Washington, D.C., 1995), pp. 114–16.

50 Rufus King to Alexander Hamilton, April 17, 1796, in *Papers of Hamilton,* 20:121; Combs, *Jay Treaty,* pp. 184–85.

51 James Madison to James Monroe, April 18, 1796, in *Papers of Madison,* 16:333–34; Madison to Thomas Jefferson, April 23, 1796, ibid., 16:335; see Elkins and McKitrick, *Age of Federalism,* p. 446, for a discussion. Other Republicans were reaching the same conclusions about the ultimate fate of the vote at the same time. Pennsylvania official Andrew Ellicott wrote to William Irvine, a former Republican U.S. congressman from Pennsylvania, on April 23 that "The Treaty has been most ably opposed, but I suspect it will nevertheless be carried into effect." Andrew Ellicott to William Irvine, April 23, 1796, William Irvine Papers, vol. 13, Historical Society of Pennsylvania.

52 Fisher Ames to George Richards Minot, April 2, 1796, in *Works of Ames,* 2:1139–41.

53 John Langdon to James Madison, April 28, 1796, in *Papers of Madison,* 16:340–41; Edmund Randolph to Madison, April 25, 1796, ibid., 16:338; "The Constitution," *Aurora,* March 18, 1796. See also Combs, *Jay Treaty,* pp. 182–83, on the Republican view of Federalists' cries of war.

54 Elkins and McKitrick, pp. 447–48. The debates and statements in Congress during this time can be followed in *Annals of Congress,* 4th Cong., 1st sess. Also see the discussion in David P. Currie, *The Constitution in Congress: The Federalist Period, 1789–1801* (Chicago, 1997), pp. 209–17, which focuses on the constitutional arguments made by participants.

55 Elkins and McKitrick, *Age of Federalism,* p. 447; see also n. 230 on pp. 845–46 for a discussion of petitions from western Pennsylvania.

56 "Speech on the Jay Treaty," in *Works of Ames,* 2:1142–82.

57 John Adams to Abigail Adams, April 30, 1796, in Adams, *Letters of John Adams Addressed to His Wife,* 2:226–27; Priestley quoted in Samuel Eliot Morison, "Fisher Ames," in *Dictionary of American Biography*; Smith quoted in Winfred E. A. Bernhard, *Fisher Ames: Federalist and Statesman, 1758–1808* (Chapel Hill, 1965), p. 272.

58 *GUS,* May 16, 1796; *American Minerva,* May 25, 1796; *Columbian Centinel* May 7, 1796.

59 Elisha P. Douglass, "Fisher Ames, Spokesman for New England Federalism," *Proceedings of the American Philosophical Society* 103, no. 5 (October 1959), 708; Bernhard, *Fisher Ames,* p. 268. For other accounts of the address, all emphasizing the drama and emotion surrounding it, see Elkins and McKitrick, *Age of Federalism,* p. 448; and Miller, *The Federalist Era,* pp. 174–75.

60 In his biography, *Alexander Hamilton: The National Adventure, 1788–1804* (New York, 1962), Broadus Mitchell discusses the circumstances of the speech and then notes succinctly, "His speech was *Camillus* compressed, but with an added eloquence that none but he could have supplied" (p. 350), referring to the powerful defenses of the treaty penned by Hamilton and Rufus King. Bernhard in his biography of Ames also analyzes the speech (*Fisher Ames,* pp. 268–72). But neither they nor the other scholars who describe the speech place it in the context of the broader pro-treaty campaign.

61 For a reexamination of Ames's speech which locates it in the context of the Federalist campaign see Todd Estes, "'The Most Bewitching Piece of Parliamentary Oratory': Fisher Ames's Jay Treaty Speech Reconsidered," *Historical Journal of Massachusetts* 28 (2000), 1–22. Two insightful treatments of the speech from other perspectives are Sandra M. Gustafson, *Eloquence Is Power: Oratory and Performance in Early America* (Chapel Hill, 2000), pp. 235–46; and James M. Farrell, "Fisher Ames and Political Judgment: Reason, Passion, and Vehement Style in The Jay Treaty Speech," *Quarterly Journal of Speech* 76 (1990), 415–34.

62 See Stephen G. Kurtz, *The Presidency of John Adams: The Collapse of Federalism, 1795–1800* (Philadelphia, 1957), p. 66, for information on the petitions. For commentary on Federalist petitioning efforts see Sharp, *American Politics in the Early Republic,* p. 131. For Van Cortlandt's circular letter on his reasons for voting for the treaty see Elkins and McKitrick, *Age of Federalism,* p. 845 n. 224.

63 Combs, *Jay Treaty,* pp. 184–85; Elkins and McKitrick, *Age of Federalism,* pp. 446–49; Sharp, *American Politics in the Early Republic,* pp. 132–33; Miller, *The Federalist Era,* pp. 174–76; Kurtz, *Presidency of John Adams,* pp. 69–70.

64 On Grove see Bell, *Party and Faction,* p. 147, and David Hackett Fischer, *The Revolution of American Conservatism: The Federalist Party in the Era of Jeffersonian Democracy* (New York, 1965), p. 391. On Hancock see Bell, pp. 147–48; Beeman, *Old Dominion and the New Nation,* pp. 150–52; and Ralph Ketcham, *James Madison: A Biography* (Charlottesville, 1971), p. 364.

65 For Dent see Bell, *Party and Faction,* p. 149; and Fischer, *Revolution of American Conservatism,* p. 359. On Christie see Bell, p. 149; Ketcham, *James Madison,* p. 364; Elkins and McKitrick, *Age of Federalism,* p. 448; and *Annals of Congress,* 4th Cong., 1st sess., p. 1280. For Smith see Frank Cassell, *Merchant Congressman in the Young Republic: Samuel Smith of Maryland, 1752–1839* (Madison, Wis., 1971), pp. 61–72. For a briefer discussion see John Pancake, *Samuel Smith and the Politics of Business, 1752–1839* (Tuscaloosa, Ala., 1972), pp. 44–46.

66 See *Annals of Congress,* 4th Cong., 1st sess., pp. 1173–76, for Kitchell's speech. See also Bell, *Party and Faction,* p. 148.

67 See James M. Banner, Jr., "Philip Van Cortlandt," in John A. Garraty and Mark C. Carnes (eds.), *American National Biography,* 24 vols. (New York, 1999), 22:170–71; Bell, *Party and Faction,* p. 148; William Nisbet Chambers, *Political Parties in a New Nation: The American Experience* (New York, 1963), pp. 88–89.

68 Chambers, *Political Parties in a New Nation,* p. 89; Jurgen Heideking, "Frederick Muhlenberg," in *American National Biography,* 16:54–56; Todd Estes, "Andrew Gregg," in *American National Biography,* 9:557–58; and Bell, *Party and Faction,* pp. 148–49.

69 Elkins and McKitrick, *Age of Federalism,* p. 449; Combs, *Jay Treaty,* pp. 186–87; James Madison to Thomas Jefferson, May 1, 1796, in *Papers of Madison,* 16:343. For the story on Findley and an analysis of the voting in general see Kurtz, *Presidency of John Adams,* pp. 71–73.

CHAPTER SEVEN

1 *GUS,* May 24, 1796.

2 *Independent Chronicle,* May 12, 1796; "Sydney," ibid.; "A Friend to the Clergy," ibid., May 26, 1796. For a strong defense of the clergy's involvement in political matters see "A Disciple," in *GUS,* May 12, 1796. For the political activities of the clergy more generally in the 1790s see Gary B. Nash, "The American Clergy and the French Revolution," *William and Mary Quarterly,* 3d ser., 22 (1965), 392–412.

3 The most definitive study of Republican newspapers is Donald H. Stewart, *The Opposition Press of the Federalist Period* (Albany, 1969). For the post-vote coverage see pp. 230–35.

4 *Independent Chronicle,* May 12, 1796, and May 23, 1796.

5 *Aurora,* May 6, 1796, and May 26, 1796.

6 *Aurora,* July 4, 1796. See also James Tagg, *Benjamin Franklin Bache and the Philadelphia Aurora* (Philadelphia, 1991), pp. 262–63. See Stewart, *Opposition Press,* for more examples and citations of Republican newspaper commentary in the aftermath of the treaty's passage.

7 For Manning's work see Michael Merrill and Sean Wilentz (eds.), *The Key of Liberty: The Life and Democratic Writings of William Manning, "A Laborer," 1747–1814* (Cambridge, Mass., 1993), esp. pp. 148–52. See also Manning's essay, "On the British Treaty and the War with France," ibid., pp. 183–85.

8 John Beckley to William Irvine, October 17, 1796, in Gerald W. Gawalt (ed.), *Justifying Jefferson: The Political Writings of John James Beckley* (Washington, D.C., 1995), pp. 128–29.

9 "To the Inhabitants of the District of Brunswick," *Aurora,* May 27, 1796. Also in *Independent Chronicle,* June 6, 1796.

10 James Madison to Thomas Jefferson, May 1, 1796, in *Papers of Madison,* 16:343; Madison to James Monroe, May 14, 1796, ibid., 16:357. See also Madison to John Langdon, May 1, 1796, ibid., 16:344. In all three letters

Madison commented acerbically on the "casual" absence of Massachusetts Republican Joseph B. Varnum, who though opposed to the treaty was absent during one of the crucial votes.

11 Madison to Jefferson, May 1, 1796, in *Papers of Madison,* 16:343. Madison's uncle and political informant, Joseph Jones, wrote to the congressman from Williamsburg at approximately the same time and detailed the "great exertions . . . made every where to obtain petitions with numerous signers." He also told Madison that such activities showed "to what lengths some creatures of the government are disposed to go" to win the treaty debate. See Joseph Jones to Madison, ca. May 1, 1796, ibid., 16:345–46.

12 Madison to Jefferson, May 9, 1796, in *Papers of Madison,* 16:352. Referring to Madison's "Aristocracy, Anglicism & mercantilism" charge, Stanley Elkins and Eric McKitrick have sagely noted, "All of which was in a sense true, except that those same influences had been impotent to prevent the enormous wave of sentiment on the opposite side the year before." See *The Age of Federalism: The Early American Republic, 1788–1800* (New York, 1993), p. 446.

13 Madison to Hubbard Taylor, May 10, 1796, in *Papers of Madison,* 16:353; Madison to James Monroe, May 14, 1796, ibid., 16:356; Madison to Jefferson, May 22, 1796, ibid., 16:363.

14 Alexander Hamilton to Rufus King, May 4, 1796, in *Papers of Hamilton,* 20:158; Fisher Ames to Thomas Dwight, May 19, 1796, in *Works of Ames,* 2:1183.

15 *American Minerva,* May 26, 1796, and May 5, 1796. The latter piece also appears in *GUS,* May 7, 1796.

16 *GUS,* May 2, 1796; *Columbian Centinel,* May 25, 1796.

17 *Rutland Herald,* May 9, 1796, and May 23, 1796. Accounts of the Hanover celebration and addresses to and from Buck are also found in *American Minerva,* May 31, 1796, and *Herald,* June 1, 1796.

18 *American Minerva,* May 26, 1796; *Rutland Herald,* October 24, 1796.

19 *Columbian Centinel,* June 22, 1796. The address to Smith read in part, "When our peace, happiness, and prosperity were at hazard . . . when discord, anarchy, and war, with all their horrors, were entering upon the peaceful borders of America; your patriotic exertions were not wanting to rescue her from a situation so humiliating and distressing." Smith replied in kind: "If I have, in the smallest degree, contributed to promote the real interests of the people I represent, next to the consciousness of having endeavored to do my duty, I consider your approbation as the best reward."

20 *Herald,* July 13, 1796. For more on Cooper and the Jay Treaty debate see Alan Taylor, *William Cooper's Town: Power and Persuasion on the Frontier of the Early American Republic* (New York, 1995), pp. 196–98.

21 *Herald,* May 4, 1796. This editorial was also reprinted in *GUS,* May 7, 1796.

22 *Columbian Centinel,* May 21, 1796.

23 *Columbian Centinel,* May 21, 1796; *American Minerva,* May 27, 1796.

24 "To the People of the United States," *American Minerva,* April 25, 1796 (also

in *GUS*, April 26, 1796); *GUS*, May 19, 1796. The power and influence of "party" had run its course, this last essay concluded: "It has had its day, and objections are shadows which have shortened as the sun approached the Zenith, and will entirely disappear before his vertical rays. It is not in the power of party, however desireable to stop the sunshine."

25 George Cabot to Rufus King, July 24, 1796, in George King (ed.), *Life of King*, 2:66; Oliver Wolcott, Jr., to William Heth, June 19, 1796, in George Gibbs (ed.), *Memoirs of the Administrations of Washington and John Adams Edited from the Papers of Oliver Wolcott*, 2 vols. (1846), 1:361–62.

26 George Washington to Charles Carroll, May 1, 1796, and to Edward Carrington, May 1, 1796, in *Writings of Washington*, 35:29–31, 31–33, quotations at 29–30, 32. The notion that the real source of opposition to the treaty was hostility to Great Britain was also voiced, years later, by Pennsylvania Federalist Alexander Graydon, who, recalling the treaty debate in his memoirs, argued that the controversy was largely an attack on Washington and another in a long line of Republican efforts to discredit Great Britain. The treaty debate dragged on for weeks, Graydon observed, "upon every point but the one really in issue, namely, whether any treaty, whatever might be its stipulations or advantages, was admissable with Great Britain; and whether the anti-federal party, should it relinquish the vital nourishment it derived from a deadly, implacable and everlasting emnity to this accursed island, would be able to sustain itself, or have chance of ever rising again." Graydon, *Memoirs of His Own Time* (1846; New York, 1969), p. 377. Originally published as *Memoirs of a Life, Chiefly Passed in Pennsylvania, Within the Last Sixty Years* (Harrisburg, 1811).

27 Washington to John Jay, May 8, 1796, in *Writings of Washington*, 35:37. Washington also told Jay, "These things do, as you have supposed, fill my mind with much concern and with serious anxiety. Indeed, the trouble and perplexities which they occasion, added to the weight of years which have passed over me have worn away my mind more than my body; and renders ease and retirement indispensably necessary to both during the short time I have to stay here."

28 Loring Andrews to Theodore Sedgwick, May 5, 1796, Sedgwick Papers I, Box C, folder 3.4, Massachusetts Historical Society.

29 For treatments of Webster see Richard J. Moss, *Noah Webster* (Boston, 1984), and Richard M. Rollins, *The Long Journey of Noah Webster* (Philadelphia, 1980). While both works are useful, there is a need for a fuller examination of Webster's role in the emerging political culture of the new nation, particular his crucial and thoughtful involvement as essayist and partisan editor.

30 *American Minerva*, May 3, 1796. Elkins and McKitrick (*Age of Federalism*, p. 449) mistakenly attribute this editorial to Fenno, citing the *Gazette of the United States* for May 5, 1796, which reprinted the Webster piece. However, Webster's original ran May 3, and the *Gazette* printed the piece two days later under a heading, "By This Day's Mail," dated May 3 from New York. On May 6, the *Aurora*, citing the *Minerva* as the source, reprinted this editorial (interspersed with commentary) and made several attacks on "the editor of the Minerva" for his statements.

31 *American Minerva*, May 3, 1796.

32 "To the Public," *Herald,* May 4, 1796.

33 *Herald,* June 1, 1796.

34 Thomas Jefferson to James Monroe, June 12, 1796, in Paul Leicester Ford (ed.), *The Writings of Thomas Jefferson,* 10 vols. (New York, 1892–99), 7:80. Other prominent Republicans shared Jefferson's sense of Washington's influence over the public. Philadelphia physician Benjamin Rush, in letters written both during the treaty debate and fifteen years after the fact, reached the same conclusion. Rush told Samuel Bayard, "The treaty with Great Britain, once reprobated by 19/20 of our citizens, is now approved of, or peaceably aquiesced in, by the same proportion of the people. Two reasons are given . . . [secondly], it has been signed by the President of the United States, in whose *integrity* all confide and in whose *wisdom* a great majority of our citizens have still the most unlimited confidence." Years later he wrote to John Adams and recalled, "no sooner did General Washington ratify it than a majority of our citizens defended it, and I well recollect hearing a respectable merchant who was uncommonly clamorous against it when he first read it abuse the rabble who objected to it as soon as he heard General Washington had approved of it." See Benjamin Rush to Samuel Bayard, March 1, 1796, and Rush to John Adams, June 13, 1811, in L.H. Butterfield (ed.), *Letters of Benjamin Rush,* 2 vols. (Princeton, 1951), 2:768–69, 1084.

35 Jefferson to Monroe, July 10, 1796, in Ford, *Writings of Jefferson,* 7:89. For Jefferson's views on the treaty debate see Dumas Malone, *Jefferson and the Ordeal of Liberty* (Boston, 1962), pp. 266–69; Merrill D. Peterson, *Thomas Jefferson and the New Nation* (New York, 1970), pp. 550–52; and Joseph J. Ellis, *American Sphinx: The Character of Thomas Jefferson* (New York, 1996), pp. 186–94.

36 On this point see Elkins and McKitrick, *Age of Federalism,* pp. 451–88; and Ellis, *American Sphinx,* p. 194.

37 See, for example, Joseph Charles,*The Origins of the American Party System: Three Essays* (Williamsburg, Va.. 1956); Stephen G. Kurtz, *The Presidency of John Adams: The Collapse of Federalism, 1795–1800* (Philadelphia, 1957); Noble E. Cunningham, Jr., *The Jeffersonian Republicans: The Formation of Party Organization* (Chapel Hill, 1957); and Richard Buel, *Securing the Revolution: Ideology in American Politics, 1789–1815* (Ithaca, 1972). For an exploration of the political culture of the election contest see Joanne Freeman, "The Presidential Election of 1796," in Richard Alan Ryerson (ed.), *John Adams and the Founding of the Republic* (Boston, 2001), pp. 142–67.

38 Simon Newman, *Parades and the Politics of the Street: Festive Culture in the Early American Republic* (Philadelphia, 1997), p. 7.

Index

Todd Estes was born in Akron, Ohio, and educated at the University of Tennessee. He did his graduate work at the University of Kentucky, where he earned his Ph.D. in 1995 under the direction of Lance Banning. His published work includes articles in *Journal of the Early Republic, The Historian,* and *Virginia Magazine of History and Biography.* He is currently associate professor of history at Oakland University in Rochester, Michigan, where he has taught since 1995 and where he won the Teaching Excellence Award in 2001. He lives in Rochester Hills, Michigan, with his wife, Kathleen Pfeiffer, and his children, Elizabeth and Brian.